STUDIO-BASED INSTRUMENTAL LEARNING

SEMPRE Studies in
The Psychology of Music

Series Editors
Graham Welch, *Institute of Education, University of London, UK*
Adam Ockelford, *Roehampton University, UK*
Ian Cross, *University of Cambridge, UK*

The theme for the series is the psychology of music, broadly defined. Topics will include: (i) musical development at different ages, (ii) exceptional musical development in the context of special educational needs, (iii) musical cognition and context, (iv) culture, mind and music, (v) micro to macro perspectives on the impact of music on the individual (such as from neurological studies through to social psychology), (vi) the development of advanced performance skills and (vii) affective perspectives on musical learning. The series will present the implications of research findings for a wide readership, including user-groups (music teachers, policy makers, parents), as well as the international academic and research communities. The distinguishing features of the series will be this broad focus (drawing on basic and applied research from across the globe) under the umbrella of SEMPRE's distinctive mission, which is to promote and ensure coherent and symbiotic links between education, music and psychology research.

Other titles in the series

New Perspectives on Music and Gesture
Edited by Anthony Gritten and Elaine King

Advances in Social-Psychology and Music Education Research
Edited by Patrice Madura Ward-Steinman

The Musical Ear: Oral Tradition in the USA
Anne Dhu McLucas

Musical Creativity: Insights from Music Education Research
Edited by Oscar Odena

Studio-Based Instrumental Learning

KIM BURWELL
Canterbury Christ Church University, UK

ASHGATE

Published by
Ashgate Publishing Limited
Wey Court East
Union Road
Farnham
Surrey, GU9 7PT
England

Ashgate Publishing Company
Suite 420
101 Cherry Street
Burlington
VT 05401-4405
USA

www.ashgate.com

British Library Cataloguing in Publication Data
Burwell, Kim.
   Studio-based instrumental learning. – (SEMPRE studies in the psychology of music)
   1. Musical instruments – Instruction and study –
   Psychological aspects. 2. Music – Instruction and study –
   Psychological aspects. 3. Clarinet – Instruction and
   study – Case studies. 4. Music – Instruction and study –
   Case studies.
   I. Title II. Series
   784'.07-dc23

Educ.

MT
1
.B89
2012

Library of Congress Cataloging-in-Publication Data
Burwell, Kim.
   Studio-based instrumental learning / Kim Burwell.
      p. cm. – (SEMPRE studies in the psychology of music)
   Includes bibliographical references and index.
   ISBN 978-1-4094-4765-8 (hardcover) – ISBN 978-1-4094-4766-5 (ebook)
  1. Musical instruments – Instruction and study – Psychological aspects.
  2. Music – Instruction and study – Psychological aspects. 3. Clarinet –
Instruction and study – Case studies. 4. Music – Instruction and study – Case studies.
I. Title.
  MT1.B89 2012
  784.193071–dc23

2012009617

ISBN 9781409447658 (hbk)
ISBN 9781409447665 (ebk)

MIX
Paper from
responsible sources
FSC
www.fsc.org
FSC® C018575

Printed and bound in Great Britain by the
MPG Books Group, UK.

Contents

List of Figures

List of Tables

Series Editors' Preface

There has been an enormous growth over the past three decades of research into the psychology of music. SEMPRE (the Society for Education, Music and Psychology Research) is the only international society that embraces an interest in the psychology of music, research and education. SEMPRE was founded in 1972 and has published the journals *Psychology of Music* since 1973 and *Research Studies in Music* Education since 2008, both now in partnership with SAGE (see www.sempre.org.uk). Nevertheless, there is an ongoing need to promote the latest research to the widest possible audience if it is to have a distinctive impact on policy and practice. In collaboration with Ashgate since 2007, the 'SEMPRE Studies in The Psychology of Music' has been designed to address this need. The theme for the series is the psychology of music, broadly defined. Topics include (amongst others): musical development at different ages; musical cognition and context; culture, mind and music; micro to macro perspectives on the impact of music on the individual (such as from neurological studies through to social psychology); the development of advanced performance skills; musical behaviour and development in the context of special educational needs; and affective perspectives on musical learning. The series seeks to present the implications of research findings for a wide readership, including user-groups (music teachers, policy makers, parents), as well as the international academic and research communities. The distinguishing feature of the series is its broad focus that draws on basic and applied research from across the globe under the umbrella of SEMPRE's distinctive mission, which is to promote and ensure coherent and symbiotic links between education, music and psychology research.

Graham Welch
Institute of Education, University of London, UK
Adam Ockelford
Roehampton University, UK
Ian Cross
University of Cambridge, UK

Acknowledgements

The research presented in this book owes much to Graham Welch who as series editor, and mentor to me and to so many others, has done so much for music education. I would also like to thank, for their consistently generous encouragement and support, Grenville Hancox and Janet Mills; and my parents, first and best of teachers, in all things.

As a researcher I have enjoyed, and learned much from, team members David Pickup, Vanessa Young and Matthew Shipton. Our work together was supported by grants from the Performing Arts Learning and Teaching Innovation Network (PALATINE) in 2002 and 2009.

Parts of Chapter 2 are published as 'Apprenticeship in music: a contextual study for instrumental teaching and learning', in the *International Journal of Music Education* (Research).

Kim Burwell
February 2012

Chapter 1

Introduction

The broad intention in this book is to examine the interaction between teacher and student as they engage in studio-based instrumental teaching and learning. A case study based on a doctoral thesis, it undertakes a micro-analysis of the collaborative behaviour of teacher and student as they cultivate the complex skill of musical performance, and considers this behaviour in the light of the personal, social and cultural context.

It is assumed that the reader who is an instrumental teacher, an instrumentalist, a fellow researcher or any combination of these, will already know a good deal about these matters. The experience of engaging with instrumental teaching and learning offers all participants a personal and individual insight into the subject, that not only draws upon the technical and musical, but the emotional and social aspects of our selves. For many of us this has represented an ongoing and dynamic source of identity.

Instrumental teachers have been aptly described as reflective practitioners, developing their work and indeed identities through the process of reflection. Dewey explains that this involves 'not simply a sequence of ideas, but a *con-sequence* – a consecutive ordering in such a way that each determines the next as its proper outcome, while each outcome in turn leans back on, or refers to, its predecessors' (1933, p. 4). For reflective practitioners this can be a responsive and self-referential undertaking. It is also fluid: if it is a way of thinking, or a kind of knowledge in itself, it is not easily fixed or defined. Schön describes this in terms of on-the-spot experiments: 'We think up and try out new actions intended to explore the newly observed phenomena, test our tentative understandings of them, or affirm the moves we have invented to change things for the better' (1987, p. 28).

Viewed in this way, the business of instrumental teaching and learning involves the acquisition, development and application of reflective powers. All instrumental and vocal teachers will have met with the problem of supporting students who want answers, rules, certainties; who are bemused and frustrated to be told that 'it depends'. As they mature as practitioners, many students struggle to appreciate that the contingent nature of the subject is its very essence, and that what their lessons might offer is induction into a discipline that consists more in doing than in knowing: in cultivating dispositions to frame, work and solve problems that exhibit aspects of both art and craft.

These aspects of instrumental teaching and learning can be challenging and exciting, and yet they present teachers with particular problems. The teacher's work can be developed continually, experientially and reflectively, but the reference points available to teachers are typically narrow and in a sense, vertical:

each can respond to her ongoing experience as a teacher, and each can respond – positively or negatively – to her historical experience as a student, but few have the opportunity to share their reflections 'horizontally' – with contemporary practitioners. The aspects of the work that defy definition also set constraints on any discussion of that work outside the context of the activity itself. This problem is exacerbated by the professional circumstances of teachers, who are often engaged by institutions on a part-time basis or work privately; who are unlikely to share a background in formal teacher training; and who typically teach on a one-to-one basis. In this way the nature of the subject and the nature of the profession leave reflective practitioners working in relative isolation.

There is an obvious gap here, an opportunity to facilitate the reflective practice essential to instrumental and vocal teaching and learning, and this is where research comes in: in helping to develop frameworks for discussion that can support reflection.

Legend has it that reflective practitioners are likely to resist discussing their work outside the context of their own studios; Schön attempts to explain such an attitude by putting into their mouths remarks such as, 'While I do not accept [traditional academic views] of knowledge, I cannot describe my own', 'My kind of knowledge is indescribable' and 'I will not attempt to describe it lest I paralyze myself' (1983, p. viii). Such remarks are not without validity; in my own experience as a teacher I have sometimes wondered whether it is possible to explain too far – that the more concrete an explanation, the more likely it is to be simplified, artificial or misrepresentative; or the more temporary its value. It would seem that Howard is sympathetic to such notions, when he describes the teacher's choice of words as 'necessary to start things off and to make corrections' in a lesson, but quickly left behind, so that 'refinements in their usage seldom keep pace with the elaborate developments in the activities to which they refer'. In the context of practice this can result in a reliance on a shifting vocabulary, 'enlisted more or less ad hoc as the occasion demands' (1982, p. 74).

The practitioner's vocabulary-in-trade may make her remarks seem unhelpfully vague when taken out of context, and the 'vertical' and experiential traditions of learning mentioned above tend to limit the opportunities for finding common terms for discussion. These traditions can result in dynasties of teaching: thus Kingsbury, in describing conservatoire traditions, refers to pedagogical genealogies, to teachers as the nodal points of student cliques, and to highly individual approaches to teaching that members might wish to defend (1988, pp. 37–45). While individual approaches need not be regarded as incompatible or even as distinct schools of thought, the vocabularies and attitudes involved may represent obstacles in the development of professional discussion. It seems possible for example that teachers who have established sophisticated and successful practices through traditional approaches, might be cautious about embracing the 'training' opportunities that formal staff development might be taken to represent.

Similarly, there is probably a widespread attitude among practitioners of harbouring reservations toward research. Researchers are relative newcomers to the field: while studio-based instrumental teaching and learning represents centuries of tradition, much of the current body of research has been accumulated only over the last generation. Progress has been slow, too, not least because research knowledge is different in nature from practice knowledge. The researcher seeks to explain aspects of practice rather than to operationalize them, and must try to establish an objective distance between herself and the subject. Although personal insight and expertise may offer the researcher some clues about what questions to ask, and how to interpret findings, the intervening collection and analysis of data must be conducted as methodically and transparently as possible. Unlike the practitioner, the researcher must always explain how she knows what she knows, so that the reader is in a position to make reasoned judgments about its validity. If research has the capacity to enrich our understanding of a subject that otherwise relies on personal contact among practitioners for dissemination, such an aim can only be responsibly approached through painstaking procedure.

For the moment this has meant that for practitioners, research findings have often seemed either limited in relevance or too obvious to be interesting. In a relatively new field for research, the researchers are hardly in a position to offer conclusions or advice that might be of direct use to practitioners. It is not the role of research, however, to do so. Bowman argues, rather, that research has a more indirect relationship to practice, ideally serving to '[expand] the range of fruitful possibilities for future action and future decisions':

> The primary way research improves music education, [to the extent it does], is by helping us approach new problems more intelligently, more imaginatively, more creatively, more flexibly. It does this not by discovering and dispensing facts, but rather by helping us better understand problems and their significance for action. (Bowman 2005, p. 162)

If research findings cannot, and are not intended to, offer a prescription for action, they can help to identify issues, offer new perspectives, encourage and support ongoing reflection and assist practitioners in sharing their reflective processes. If researchers can convince practitioners that their observations represent authentic possibilities of practice, they might also be able to help them in developing a framework for discussion, and in identifying matter for discussion, that – perhaps unlike, for example, anecdotal evidence – can be shared among individual studios, specific instrumental traditions and even different musical styles.

A long-term engagement with research, and particularly in my own case, practitioner research, has allowed me to enjoy more opportunities than most to discuss instrumental teaching and learning with other practitioners, in formal and informal settings. In spite of what might be the inherent constraints on such discussion, I have always found my fellow practitioners to be equally fascinated by the subject, and enthusiastic about reflecting on, discussing and sharing their thoughts and feelings about it. Within the Music Department at South England University, and in visiting other institutions of music education, I have seen research findings provoke eager and insightful responses from teachers glad to have further food for thought, and glad to identify further common ground for shared reflection. With the research presented in this book, I would hope that I might be able to contribute more, and in other ways, to this conversation.

***

My interest in this subject stems from three related sources: my own student career, which in many ways has never ended; my professional work as both a performer and teacher of music; and more than ten years' involvement in research in a university music department, investigating the conduct of instrumental and vocal lessons.

Participating in and then observing many instrumental lessons over many years, I have been interested in the behaviour of teacher and student, not only in terms of what they say and what they play, but in terms of the roles that would seem to be laid out for them, as distinct from what each brings to that role. I have been interested too in how the behaviour of one is implicated in the behaviour of the other: how the participants act together in a collaboration which may be more or less smooth, more or less fruitful, constantly changing and often surprising. My conviction from experience as a teacher and a student is that neither can single-handedly determine the nature of the interaction.

To the extent that instrumental teaching and learning involves verbal behaviour, some preliminary efforts to contribute to the shared knowledge of the subject have been made previously at my own university, which will be known here as South England University (SEU), and these efforts provide a backdrop for the current study. Research into instrumental teaching and learning in the SEU Music Department was instigated in 1998, by a research team comprising David Pickup, Vanessa Young and myself. A large part of the team's research has been focused on the investigation of verbal dialogue between teacher and student in the setting of individual lessons. Salient issues have included the content of dialogue, as participants discuss the various areas of study within the subject (Young, Burwell and Pickup 2003; Burwell 2003a); the distribution of talk between teacher and student, and how that might vary according to the personal attributes of participants (Burwell, Young and Pickup 2003; 2004; Burwell 2005); and the vocabulary used to discuss a practice which is largely ineffable (Burwell 2003b; 2006).

Verbal behaviour of course represents only one aspect of instrumental teaching and learning that might be analyzed. The tools used in the early phases of our research were turned toward generalization over a sizeable number of lessons, particularly in quantifying the wordage devoted to various areas of study, and the distribution of lesson dialogue between teacher and student (Young, Burwell and Pickup 2003; Burwell 2003a; 2003b; Burwell, Young and Pickup 2003; 2004). Later a more qualitative approach was taken in the examination of lesson dialogue, with special reference to the teacher's use of questions and of metaphor, worth exploring in themselves (Burwell 2005; 2006). In this study I wanted to take an approach which was quite different: which would at once allow a deeper exploration of individual cases, and evoke a stronger sense of context for lesson behaviour.

In addition to reviewing verbal behaviour more closely, I had become interested in exploring another salient aspect of instrumental lessons: performance behaviour. To date, we had investigated how teachers and students talked, conscious however that it is somewhat artificial to consider that separately from what they were talking about (Folkestad 2005, p. 283). The nature of lesson talk is predicated by its subject to an extent that has only been recognized relatively recently, through developments in the epistemology of practice (Schön 1983; 1987; Howard 1982; 1992); to understand verbal behaviour in lessons it is necessary to examine its relationship with performance behaviour. This is all the more so because – as our research at SEU has suggested – the distribution of both kinds of behaviour between teacher and student is likely to be asymmetrical: whether in performing or in speaking, the roles of the two participants seemed to be quite different from each other, in quality and quantity. The notion that participant behaviour in instrumental lessons is likely to be distinct from what is found in other educational settings has also been endorsed, albeit indirectly, by a number of relatively early research studies in instrumental teaching and learning. In these, expectations of the teacher's verbal behaviour, based on classroom research, were disappointed (Kostka, 1984; Yarbrough and Price, 1989).

Finally, although verbal and performance behaviour seem to complement each other as interrelated aspects of instrumental teaching and learning, I had become interested in behaviours which fell into neither category. This interest evolved within the current study, as I moved repeatedly back and forth between the research problem and the analysis of data, and in the first instance it was driven by a felt response to the data: a feeling that the lesson interactions I observed were somehow variable in consonance. The feeling arguably stemmed from my experience and values as a practitioner, and in principle therefore I could position myself in the role of researcher as instrument, and make legitimate use of my tacit or intuitive knowledge (Lincoln and Guba 1985, pp. 39–40). This seemed reasonable enough, particularly if I were to be as self-conscious and explicit as possible about my position in the research; but although they might be seen as tools, or conscious influences on the research process, it would not be sufficient to present either myself or my tacit knowledge as research evidence. Instead, I sought first to substantiate my impressions, and second to understand the variation among individual cases.

The desire to substantiate my impressions led to a closer investigation of lesson behaviour. This included the addition of other functions of verbal and performance behaviours, including joking and apologizing, modelling and imitation. It also led to the investigation of nonverbal behaviours, such as the use of physical gesture, posture and space. Each of these added a little to the dimensions of the lesson that could be articulated and described. The desire to understand the variation among individual cases led to a consideration of how lesson behaviours could be connected or contextualized, through reference to the individual attributes and perceptions of participants; to the Performance Studies course of which instrumental lessons are part; and to the nature of the institution, which in turn draws upon traditions such as the university, the conservatoire and the broad musical culture.

As a performance student, a performance teacher, and – I would now wish to argue – performance researcher, what I have found most exciting about learning is that with each step forward its potential grows; each opportunity to learn more is another candle lit, revealing a little more of the expanse of the Aladdin's cave ahead. This personal aside is closely linked to the research aims of the current study. As suited to a subject that continues to prove, to me, ever-increasing in complexity and richness, my research aim is to understand more, to open the subject further by revealing more of its complexity, rather than attempting to define it. Wittgenstein helpfully questions whether it is always an advantage to replace an indistinct picture with a 'sharp' one; and although his *Philosophical Investigations* explore such thinking on too great a scale to be justly represented here, another of his remarks seems relevant:

> We feel as if we had to *penetrate* phenomena: our investigation, however, is directed not towards phenomena, but, as one might say, towards the '*possibilities*' of phenomena. (Wittgenstein 1953/1972, p. 42; italics original)

Through the micro-analysis and close description of a small-scale case study, this book seeks to give an interpretative account of lesson behaviour that might be recognized by practitioners as an authentic possibility within the practice of studio-based instrumental teaching and learning.

Research Aims

With a central interest in the processes involved in studio-based instrumental teaching and learning, this study explores a series of 'how' questions:

1. How is instrumental teaching and learning undertaken?
2. How does the conduct of instrumental teaching and learning vary with participants?
3. How is the interaction between teacher and student contextualized?

The focus of the inquiry is the instrumental lesson, and specifically, the example of clarinet lessons; but the procedure to be studied is not clarinet playing itself, but how it is taught and learned. Instrumental teaching and learning is regarded as a practice in itself, and the first research question asks how teacher and students engage in that practice through lesson interactions. The texture and dynamics of those interactions are explored through the micro-analysis of a small-scale case study, consisting in one teacher giving single lessons to two individual students. These lessons, captured on video tape, are examined in terms of specific collaborative behaviours, alongside the participants' own comments about their activity in the filmed lessons.

This will be case study research, and because its scope will therefore be bounded, the meaningful interpretation of the case may depend on the consideration of contextual issues. Thus the third question is focused on links that might be drawn between lesson behaviour and the sociocultural setting of the practice. This may include reference to the institution – the Performance Studies course at SEU along with its aims and assessment procedures – as well as the broader professional and indeed artistic aspects of musical performance. Further, it might be possible to draw other links among lesson behaviours and the individual characteristics, perceptions and biographies of participants.

The second question presupposes that lesson behaviour does vary with participants, though in a case study bounded by only two lessons, the scope to examine the potential variety of behaviour is necessarily narrow. Comparison however is not the chief object of this research, but a means of introducing a further dimension into the study of the subject, effectively an element of triangulation that might enrich the interpretation of lesson behaviour. Importantly, too, the study of two lessons rather than one highlights the significance of context, since it allows the investigation of the effect when even slight differences in context are present. This means that the second question may provide a significant link between the first and the third.

The nature and rationale for the choice of the case study is discussed further in Chapter 5.

Structure of the Book

The book is divided into nine chapters, including the Introduction. The conceptual framework is the underlying theme of first half of the book, comprising the next four chapters. This includes a discussion of epistemology, or the nature of the subject knowledge; it also gives an account of research literature specific to instrumental teaching and learning, and the theoretical perspective represented in the methodology.

In Chapter 2 the discussion of epistemology falls into two broad areas. Since teaching and learning cannot be meaningfully considered without reference to what is being taught and learned, the first area to be considered is the epistemology of skill, in general terms and with particular reference to instrumental teaching and learning as a regime of competence. Complementing the discussion of what is to be learned, the second issue for consideration is how it is to be learned. This is approached through an exploration of apprenticeship, often mentioned in music education literature, to see if it might offer ways of understanding the process and the nature of instrumental teaching and learning.

Chapters 3 and 4 consist of reviews of the research literature directly related to instrumental teaching and learning. Chapter 3 examines literature specific to lesson interactions, while Chapter 4 examines literature in which those lessons are framed by drawing links to a broader context. These literature reviews thus match the scope implied in the research questions, by focusing initially on activity located within the lesson, and then on ways of framing that activity.

In Chapter 5 the fieldwork design is discussed; this goes some way toward meeting the obligation of the researcher to explain the advent of her findings. While some readers may be tempted to skip ahead to the findings themselves, it is assumed that an explanation of the methodological approach will be of interest not only to other researchers, but to practitioners who might be starting to engage with research processes or enter into the kind of discussions they support. The chapter includes some remarks about the theoretical perspective specific to this case study, and its alignment with the research aims and questions, including consideration of the position of the researcher and of ethical issues. The detailed research methods adopted in the study are then outlined.

In Chapters 6 and 7 the findings from the empirical study are presented. The presentation is based essentially on description; an effort is made to keep these descriptions objective, so far as possible, in the hope that the reader might be able to imagine these situations as recognizable or lifelike, and even to draw some personal impressions from them. The analytical descriptions of video evidence are framed by the presentation of material drawn from interview data. Thus Chapter 6 is prefaced by a contextual sketch based on the teacher's views of instrumental teaching and learning, followed by a presentation of the findings from the observation and micro-analysis of a clarinet lesson. Chapter 7 begins with the presentation of parallel findings from a second lesson, and ends with some reflections on both lessons in the light of the participants' own views.

Chapter 8 offers a more freely interpretative discussion of the findings, drawing some comparisons between the accounts of the two lessons, proposing some ways of understanding lesson activity, and considering both in the light of the earlier literature reviews. Chapter 9 offers some concluding remarks and suggests implications for practice and for future discussion.

Chapter 2

The Epistemology of Instrumental Teaching and Learning

In this chapter the epistemology, or theory of knowledge related to instrumental teaching and learning, is explored, largely through an examination of the language that is used to discuss the subject. Essentially, the first part of the chapter examines the complex skill involved, while the second part examines its acquisition, in terms of apprenticeship.

Our use of words, in discussing music, musical skill and the acquisition of musical skill, encapsulates a good deal about our understanding of these concepts. Musical phenomena do not consist in words, and discussing them is notoriously difficult; and yet musicians do discuss them, and with some confidence, often in language particularly adapted to the purpose: 'special jargons in which recondite, mostly inarticulate procedures and traditional lore find verbal expression that is as fragmentary as it is pointed' (Howard 1982, p. 5). Our traditional lore, the 'folk psychology' in which the language is nested, itself represents 'the culturally shaped notions in terms of which people organize their views of themselves, of others, and of the world in which they live' (Bruner 1990, p. 137).

Much of Wittgenstein's *Philosophical Investigations* is devoted to demonstrating how language is naturally embedded in the active lives of its speakers, and by examining the common use of words clarifies 'the grammar of our concepts' (McGinn 1997, p. 14, p. 40). In the context of the current study, the tacit theories underlying our understanding of instrumental teaching and learning, as embedded in the language we use to discuss it, are examined in this chapter through two distinct lenses.

The first of these is focused on the conceptualization of the subject matter, 'variously labelled "artistry", "craft", "know-how", "technique", or "skill"' (Howard 1982, p. 5). An assumption here is that what is learned is inseparable from how it is learned (Folkestad 2005, p. 283), which implies that before examining the interaction between teacher and student in the music studio, it will be helpful to have some clear ideas about the nature of their subject matter. The section begins by considering the terms we commonly use to discuss the skills of musical performance, though many of those terms are found to be surprisingly unhelpful. In an effort to clarify matters, performance as a more general phenomenon is considered in the light of the broader literature on knowledge. Afterward, recent attempts to review and develop the epistemology of professional practice are discussed, with special reference to its potential application to instrumental teaching and learning. Finally, an attempt is made to characterize instrumental and vocal performance as a regime of competence.

In the second section of this chapter, the lens is focused on the acquisition of performance skill, looking in particular at apprenticeship as a way of understanding aspects of instrumental teaching and learning. The terms 'master' and 'apprentice' are often coined in the literature devoted to the subject, but they are rarely systematically defined, and the assumptions implied in their usage are rarely examined. The section begins with a brief overview of apprenticeship in history, before identifying features that continue to resonate with modern approaches to instrumental teaching and learning, and the language used to contextualize it.

The chapter concludes with a summary of the discussion of both skill and apprenticeship, and their relationship to the language commonly used to discuss instrumental teaching and learning.

Skill

Introduction: Talking about Musical Performance

Among musicians the artistry involved in instrumental and vocal performance is highly prized, and its prestige perhaps difficult to overstate. Kingsbury in his anthropological study of an American college of music reports that '[t]he value of playing (or singing) "musically" is a genuinely sacred value in the conservatory, quite possibly the ultimate value ...' (Kingsbury 1988, p. 51). Describing the resemblance of the institution to a seminary, he further asserts that '[t]he sense of commitment among conservatory students seems more personal, moral, and emotional than professional or economic' (p. 20). The pursuit of excellence in musical performance is the paradigmatic activity of the conservatoire, and superiority in outstanding professional performances is a matter of 'surprisingly general agreement' even among critics (Schön 1987, p. 13).

Standards of musical performance are widely agreed, and excellence admired, in the university music department as in the conservatoire; and yet, perhaps because ours is a non-verbal art, we are not particularly adept at explaining what we mean when we discuss our own skills. The language we use when we attempt to do so is often vague and self-contradictory, and in some ways even suggests that skill is inferior in kind to the mental operations that are more likely to be associated with the traditional values of the university.

The vocabulary we use to characterize musical performance must be common to almost any everyday discussion of skill, but it does not always stand up well to examination. A brief consideration of even a small number of examples quickly reveals ambiguities that make them inadequate for the task of defining what it is that performing musicians do.

'Talent' is perhaps the most obvious example of a word used to describe those who have a particular aptitude for performance. The term is widely accepted, with the National Academy for Gifted and Talented Youth (2002), for example, offering the straightforward explanation that talented learners are those 'who have practical skills in areas like sport, music, design or creative and performing arts' (DirectGov). Music education researchers however tend to view the term as being problematic and imprecise. Kingsbury suggests that it is 'frequently used to explain something that couldn't be explained otherwise' (1988, p. 81), while Schön describes talent, along with 'wisdom', 'intuition' and 'artistry' as being 'junk categories' that are substituted for genuine explanation, and indeed 'serve not to open up inquiry but to close it off' (1987, p. 13). Sloboda, in an effort to establish musicianship as an aptitude of the race rather than of lucky individuals, argues that 'talent' is a mythical inborn trait, and he relegates the term to folk psychology (Sloboda 2005, pp. 276–312). This 'myth' of talent, arising 'as if independent of teachers, tradition, or technique' (Howard 2008, p. 39), is challenged further in expertise theory, in which attention is drawn to the importance of deliberate practice (for example, Ericsson et al. 1993) rather than the notion that 'exceptional performance [might be] based in innate musical capacities' (Lehmann and Gruber 2006, p. 457).

'Sense' might be a more useful word to musicians than talent, in that it can evoke the indescribable way in which, for example, a performer might interpret a musical turn of phrase, or negotiate an idiomatic technical difficulty. Paradoxically perhaps, the same term that applies to these relatively ineffable procedures is also used to denote the five specific human senses, though of course ear, eye, and touch are all more or less implicated in musical performance. None of these however are regarded as intellectual procedures – we even use the term 'common sense' to distinguish the everyday from the scientific – and this might seem to put them in a lesser light. The meaning of 'sense' is further blurred too by the fact that it might be applied to an enormous range of skills: the potentially high level of achievement implied in interpreting a musical phrase or playing by ear might easily be categorized alongside the ability to 'see colours, feel a pinprick, or digest cabbage' (Howard 1982, p. 50).

'Feel' might be a still more useful term for practical musicianship, because it can imply a physical aptitude for playing an instrument or using the voice, or a grasp of rhythmic character, or the involvement of emotion in expressive performance. No matter how sophisticated they may become, however, technical skills belong to a category once again considered somehow inferior to the intellectual: Ryle observes that '[s]ince doing is often an overt muscular affair, it is written off as a merely physical process' (Ryle 1949, p. 32). Feeling is almost inevitably elided with 'emotion', too, which suffers from a 'strongly entrenched' comparison with thinking: thus Scheffler complains that '[this opposition of cognition and emotion] distorts everything it touches: mechanizing science, it sentimentalizes art, while portraying ethics and religion as twin swamps of feeling and unreasoned commitment' (Scheffler 1991, p. 3).

Skill in musical performance is sometimes discussed in terms of having a '"nose" for how things should go' (Jorgensen 2006, p. 11; Wittgenstein, in Howard 1992, p. 135). The same term is applicable to team sports, however, with Kingsbury for example referring to the concept of having 'a nose for the ball'.

The description hardly seems sufficient to describe the skills of a concert artist, and even when it is applied to the efforts of a novice in musical performance, it seems too ordinary to capture what should be regarded as a complex and intriguing phenomenon. Like Bruner's 'habit', the vocabulary we choose to discuss the nature of instrumental and vocal performance 'deserves to glow with mystery' (Bruner 1996, p. 152).

It seems that the 'folk' vocabulary used to discuss musical performance almost accidentally reveals an inability to characterize it clearly, and the words we use loosely cover a multitude of meanings that are not always distinguished from one another. Advanced levels of artistry and skill are often categorized with far more basic and common capacities, and by association they are thus regarded as inferior to purely intellectual procedures. The folk tradition however is not entirely responsible for confusion in such matters. The tendency to value intellectual more than skilful procedures has its parallel in the Rationalist tradition associated with Plato, Descartes and Leibniz, which privileges pure mathematics above the mere experience of applied science: this tradition 'supposes the source of genuine knowledge to be within', with the logical mind capable of producing 'the firmest of truths' (Scheffler 1965, p. 3). Schön describes the professional schools of the modern university in terms of technical rationality, with a clear division between the 'lower' technical school where professional arts are practised, and the 'hither' science held to be fundamental to those arts (1987, p. 8). In the tradition of aesthetics dating from the eighteenth century, too, practice is undervalued by implication: thus Elliot asserts that 'music education's official philosophy' is focused on music as an aesthetic object that the student, more a consumer than a practitioner, should learn to understand and appreciate. This philosophy neglects music-making as knowledge, regarding performance as a means to an end rather than an end in itself (Elliot 1991, pp. 22–3).

It is only relatively recently that inquiry into the epistemology of professional practice has been given widespread attention. Schön, in his influential work *The Reflective Practitioner* (1983), has complained that '[t]here is nothing here to guide practitioners who wish to gain a better understanding of the practical uses and limits of research-based knowledge, or to help scholars who wish to take a new view of professional action' (p. viii). Coining terms such as 'knowing-in-action' and 'reflection-in-action' to describe the skill of practitioners such as engineers, teachers, musicians, scientists, physicians and statisticians (p. 13), Schön goes on to examine the conduct of 'such deviant traditions of education for practice as studios of art and design, conservatories of music and dance, athletics coaching, and apprenticeship in the crafts, all of which emphasize coaching and learning by doing' (1987, p. vii).

Musical performance shares much with these arts and crafts, in being non-verbal in nature and in offering the scope for pursuit to a highly advanced level of accomplishment. Perhaps more than most, however, practical musicianship is a highly complex skill, consisting in a wide range of skills embedded within one another. According to Howard:

[M]usic education is education of an understanding that ranges from physical dexterity, to emotive discovery, to perceptual insight, to pattern recognition, to associative hunches, to logical argument – in no particular order and in every combination. Moreover, small acts of imagination mediate the many ways of understanding throughout, from running scales to public performances, from merely hearing to learned listening. If not alone in developing and continually calling upon these capacities, music is at the very least a vast and diverse arena for their highest exercise. (Howard 1992, p. 21)

Instrumental teaching and learning as a 'deviant' educational tradition has not, even now, been given comprehensive treatment by philosophers and researchers. Performance as a more general form of knowledge however has been given enough systematic attention to establish an epistemology of practice. A brief consideration of some of the points from this broader literature might therefore provide a useful context for inquiry into the nature of instrumental teaching and learning.

Knowing How and Knowing That

One of the most salient features in the philosophy of knowledge developed during the twentieth century is the customary division between thinking and doing, or 'know-how' and 'know-that'. This dualism was suggested by Dewey (1922) who as an adherent to the philosophy of pragmatism drew attention to the value of action by emphasizing the process of learning through experience (Scheffler 1965, p. 5). Dewey also cautioned against any 'extreme *Either-Or* philosophy' (1938, p. 21); such dualisms however may be particularly useful 'when they are used to highlight an aspect of a process that has not received enough attention' (Wenger 1998, p. 68). Thus the distinction has become widely accepted and influential, particularly through Ryle's much-cited work *The Concept of Mind* (1949) in which the implications of 'knowing how', as opposed to 'knowing that', are thoroughly explored. Parallel terms in Ryle's discussion are 'intelligent performances' versus 'intellectual operations', while in later work the terms 'procedural' and 'propositional' knowledge are often preferred (Scheffler 1965, p. 92).

The object of Ryle's discussion is to disprove the 'intellectualist legend' which attempts to reassimilate 'knowing how' to 'knowing that' by holding that performance consists in the application of theory. According to the legend, skill is often regarded as something subsequent to mental operations, which are more highly valued. Ryle argues however that performance is an intelligent capacity in itself:

'Intelligent' cannot be defined in terms of 'intellectual' or 'knowing *how*' in terms of 'knowing *that*'; 'thinking what I am doing' does not connote 'both thinking what to do and doing it'. When I do something intelligently, i.e. thinking what I am doing, I am doing one thing and not two. My performance has a special procedure or manner, not special antecedents. (Ryle 1949, p. 32; italics original)

Schön makes a similar argument with reference to the privileged position of the sciences in the positivist university tradition, in which the curriculum 'still embodies the idea that practical competence [only] becomes professional when its instrumental problem solving is grounded in systematic, preferably scientific knowledge' (1987, p. 8). He asserts that professional artistry should be recognized in its own right, and studied in its practical context:

> Once we put aside the model of Technical Rationality, which leads us to think of intelligent practice as an *application* of knowledge to instrumental decisions, there is nothing strange about the idea that a kind of knowing is inherent in intelligent action. Common sense admits the category of know-how, and it does not stretch common sense very much to say that the know-how is in the action – that a tight-rope walker's know-how, for example, lies in, and is revealed by, the way he takes his trip across the wire, or that a big-league pitcher's know-how is in his way of pitching to a batter's weakness, changing his pace, or distributing his energies over the course of a game. (Schön 1983, pp. 50–51; italics original)

It is easy to imagine a wide range of examples in music where the 'knowledge' of the player lies in her playing: in physically managing the instrument, projecting musical features, attending to other players or indeed, distributing her energies over the course of a performance.

Even where skill is allowed to be a kind of knowledge, however, there is a remaining tendency to consider skill to be a relatively primitive capacity. Bruner, in identifying 'four dominant models of learners' minds', gives 'the acquisition of know-how' as the first, being characteristic of traditional cultures 'that rely heavily upon an imitative folk psychology and folk pedagogy' (1996, p. 54). He refers to apprenticeship as a model of learning based on imitation and aimed at the transmission of skills, and points out that '[t]here is little distinction in such an exchange between procedural knowledge (knowing how) and prepositional knowledge (knowing that)' (p. 53).

Bruner does concede that similar processes might be involved in the acquisition of sophisticated as well as simple skills. However, he maintains that practice must be combined with conceptual explanation for the achievement of expertise, and turns to musical performance for an illustration: 'a really skilful pianist needs more than clever hands, but needs as well to know something about the theory of harmony, about solfège, about melodic structure' (p. 54). The illustration is not entirely apt, since although she does need more than clever hands, it is possible for a pianist or any performing musician to become 'really skilful' without knowing much at all about music theory. Perhaps the most famous documented example of this is the case of Louis Armstrong, whose expertise as a virtuoso jazz musician was achieved without the benefit of any formal instruction (Collier, in Sloboda 2005, p. 253).

Although practical expertise does not consist in the application of theory, we cannot sensibly assume that the expert performer has no theory about her own skill. Ryle allows that performance in certain domains of knowledge, ranging from swimming breast-stroke to medical surgery, relies on 'some propositional competence' (1949, p. 48), even if the propositional and procedural competences cannot be reconciled. Certainly, propositional knowledge is insufficient in itself to guarantee competent performance (p. 55). Polanyi takes up the example of medical diagnosis, which 'combines skilful testing with expert observation', and insists that 'knowing' always refers to both practical and theoretical knowledge (1983, p. 7). When theory does inform practice, however, it has been assimilated successfully enough to be transformed back into skill: Bruner's own words endorse this, even if they persist in the implication that knowledge is the superior capacity: '[k]nowledge helps only when it descends into habits' (1996, p. 152).

To clarify the relationship between theory and practice, it will be helpful to examine these interrelated concepts further.

Tacit and Explicit Knowledge

Polanyi reframes the dichotomy between know-how and know-that in terms of tacit and explicit knowledge. His premise is 'the well known fact that *the aim of a skilful performance is achieved by the observance of a set of rules which are not known as such to the person following them*' (Polanyi 1958, p. 49; italics original). An illustration offered for this is that of a cyclist, who according to Polanyi cannot be expected to explain the principle by which she keeps her balance on a curve:

> A simple analysis shows that for a given angle of unbalance the curvature of each winding is inversely proportional to the square of the speed at which the cyclist is proceeding.

> But does this tell us exactly how to ride a bicycle? No. You obviously cannot adjust the curvature of your bicycle's path in proportion to the ratio of your unbalance over the square of your speed; and if you could you would fall off the machine, for there are a number of other factors to be taken into account in practice which are left out in the formulation of this rule. (Polanyi 1958, p. 50)

It is worth examining this example in some detail. As it is explained here, it might seem that an incomplete rule lies at the root of the problem: if 'there are a number of other factors to be taken into account', then more – not less – information is needed for the cyclist to keep her seat. By providing a close description of the principles involved, Polanyi implies that the very length and verbosity of the required information would prevent it being of practical use to the cyclist who is actually undertaking the task of riding. It does not follow however that the cyclist is not thinking about what she is doing, nor that the nature of her thinking is not verbal. She may well be using some kind of self-talk to help in the negotiation of each curve, and inner speech is typically far more compact than Polanyi's explanation suggests. Vygotsky distinguishes between inner and outward speech by observing that 'in a speaker's mind the whole thought is present at once, but in [outward] speech it has to be developed successively' (Cazden 1996, p. 167). Even given this power of abbreviation, however, she is presumably not mentally rehearsing mathematical principles while riding: her inner speech is far more likely to be concerned with observation, self-command and coaching. This would be related more to her 'sense' of the task than to any explanatory analysis of riding, and indeed Vygotsky's account of language use reflects 'the relatively greater importance of sense as compared to meaning in inner speech' (Wertsch 1985, p. 127).

At the same time, it is unlikely that a capable rider will be incapable of offering some kind of explanation of her skills, even if the riding and the explaining are regarded as mutually exclusive capacities. Wenger describes this as a 'boundary' issue, and argues that 'asking someone which way they turn to keep their balance on a bicycle … is changing the regime of competence' (Wenger 1998, p. 140). Explanatory language may be regarded as a reification of subject matter, which is thus turned into something metaphorically concrete, distinct from the activity of performance itself. Wenger identifies reification as a traditional feature of educational design, citing grammatical categories and word problems as examples (p. 264). Examples of reified subject matter in instrumental teaching and learning might include the harmonic theory, solfège and concepts of melodic structure which Bruner supposed to be essential to the performance of the skilful pianist (1996, p. 54). The various forms of music notation perhaps provide a still more obvious example.

Such examples of reification are effectively a codification of knowledge, through which the classical repertoire is archived; it also facilitates communication between teacher and student, and provides a valuable tool for reflection. At the same time, however, it might also represent an obstacle to understanding: Vygotsky, who advocated theoretical instruction using precise verbal definitions, also recognized that 'the difficulty with scientific concepts lies in their *verbalism*' (Karpov 2003, p. 66; italics original). Symbolic or verbal knowledge is inert until it is transformed into understanding (p. 70) and in the context of instrumental performance, theory remains inert until it can be transformed back into practical skill. Wenger explains:

> This kind of educational reification creates an intermediary stage between practices and learners. … Because of this additional step, making sense of the reification becomes an additional problem that may not exist in practice. Reification is therefore potentially a hurdle as well as a help to learning. In other words, there is a pedagogical cost to reifying in that it requires additional work – even, possibly, a new practice – to make sense of the reification. (Wenger 1998, p. 264)

In music education research, problems of this nature have been investigated in terms of interpretation, where the printed score acts as a mediator of musical meaning (Hultberg 2000; 2002).

One further point about the relationship between skilful and verbal behaviours should be made here. This is that whether practitioners are able to explain their skills or not, the language of instrumental instruction is often highly developed and distinct. Howard remarks on 'the seemingly endless stream of talk that accompanies the learning of such a complex skill as singing' (1982, p. 50), but this draws upon the 'language of the ear' rather than of physiology, and is often closely intertwined with demonstration (p. 73). Like the self-coaching inner speech that might be used by the cyclist, it has a commanding rather than a theoretical function (p. 35). Schön makes a similar point with reference to professional practitioners in general:

> Our descriptions are of different kinds, depending on our purposes and the languages of description available to us. We may refer, for example, to the sequences of operations and procedures we execute; the clues we observe and the rules we follow; or the values, strategies, and assumptions that make up our 'theories' of action. (Schön 1987, p. 25)

The language of instruction is of considerable importance in instrumental teaching and learning, and a recurring theme in the research literature to be discussed at length in Chapter 3.

Levels of Skill

Practical skill, then, is distinct from propositional knowledge, though it can be explained to some degree in a theoretical sense, and coached to some degree through the language of craftsmanship. Practical skill may be informed by propositional knowledge insofar as that knowledge can be assimilated successfully and put back into practice. It does not follow however that what results will amount to an inarticulate or routine state of affairs. The constituent skills of instrumental performance may be made habitual, and aspects of musicianship may typically operate at an intuitive level; but the complex of interrelated skills implies a varying level and focus of attention. Howard points out that '[t]he extent to which a critical skill actually becomes routine will vary with times, persons, and situations: one man's hard-pressed decision is another's routine choice', and adds that:

> Grandmasters at chess and master musicians alike are conspicuous not only for their virtuosity but for the perspicacity of their play, an economy of means aided by the routinizing of vast areas of judgment and strategy. In short, it is not that critical skills as such resist routinization but rather that such activities as chess and music allow for indefinite further development of critical skills as others become routinary. To that extent, neither chess nor music is routinizable; but such critical skills of chess or music as can be are no less judgmental for becoming second nature. (Howard 1982, pp. 181–2)

Ryle and Vygotsky both address varying levels of skill by distinguishing between habits acquired through drill, and intelligent capacities acquired through training (Ryle 1949, p. 42; Vygotsky, in Wertsch 1985, p. 71). Although Ryle surely exaggerates in his claim that 'drill dispenses with intelligence', the distinction is helpful in outlining the idea of musicianship as a complex skill, with components of varying levels of sophistication and acquired through varying methods of practice, embedded within one another.

Polanyi's assertion that the skilful performer in action is observing rules that are unknown to her may also seem to be an exaggeration, but he refines his claim by examining the point at which abilities become unconscious, or move from focal to subsidiary awareness. He even suggests a musical example, attributing a form of 'stage fright' to the self-consciousness that leads the performer to attend to isolated notes or gestures – matters that should be routine – instead of the broader sense of context necessary for fluent execution (Polanyi 1958, p. 56). Polanyi does seem to assume however that routine habits were once points of focus, explaining for example that 'in practical terms, as we learn to handle a hammer, a tennis racket or a motor car in terms of the situation which we are striving to master, we become unconscious of the actions by which we achieve this result' (p. 61), and this recalls Ryle's complaint that theory is often taken to precede practice. Certainly many of the lower-level skills that an accomplished performer takes for granted will have been inculcated piecemeal through a good deal of explicit instruction and practice during childhood. It should also be noted however that music students often acquire their component skills intuitively, some through apparently instantaneous leaps of the imagination, and others through a more gradual accumulation with repeated practice. The experienced musician may have forgotten that she originally acquired some of her skills through conscious thought-processes, but this is not to deny that many of them will never have been articulated in that way.

The ability to manage skills that may be more or less unconscious is in itself a high-order skill. Schön uses the term 'reflection-in-action' to denote the skill of 'practitioners [who] themselves often reveal a capacity for reflection on their intuitive knowing in the midst of action and sometimes use this capacity to cope with the unique, uncertain, and conflicted situations of practice' (1983, pp. viii–ix). This concept of 'thinking what they are doing while they are doing it' (1987, p. xi) is helpful in capturing the essential fact that musical performance is always an experience in time.

Distinct from the capacity to reflect in action is the ability to verbally articulate aspects of performance skill. Howard labels this 'accountable know-how' and observes that it is demanded of teachers in particular (1982, p. 68); indeed, this may be a useful way to distinguish the essential skills of performers from the essential skills of teaching performance. Ryle's description of know-how as a disposition may be helpful in the same way (1949, p. 46).

If performance skills can be simple or complex, focal or subsidiary, articulate or intuitive, they can also be intelligent or unintelligent. Scheffler takes issue with Ryle's term 'intelligent performance' because it fails to distinguish between facilities or routinizable competence, and what he calls 'critical skills' (Scheffler 1965, p. 98). He asserts that the difference is to be found in the acquisition: 'knowing how to do something is one thing, knowing how to do it well is, in general, another, and doing it brilliantly is still a third, which lies beyond the scope of *know how* altogether, tied as the latter notion is to the concept of training' (p. 96). The implication here is that a critical or reflective disposition is associated with the most advanced levels of skill, and indeed artistry; and this makes it keenly relevant to the practice of instrumental teaching and learning.

Reflection in Action

One of the most influential recent contributors to the epistemology of practice has been Donald Schön, whose books *The Reflective Practitioner* (1983) and *Educating the Reflective Practitioner* (1987) call for a review of the epistemology dominant in the modern research-based university.

Schön emphasizes his personal experience as 'an industrial consultant, technology manager, urban planner, policy analyst, and teacher in a professional school' as the motivating background to his review of the epistemology of practice (1983, p. vii). He argues that the discourse of professional schools within the modern university has been much affected by the positivist tradition of technical rationality, which privileges pure science over practice. So long as practice is discussed as if it were an application of theory, its essential nature cannot be genuinely appreciated and explored; the resulting research is likely to suffer 'a dilemma of rigor or relevance':

> The question of the relationship between practice competence and professional knowledge needs to be turned upside down. We should start not by asking how to make better use of research-based knowledge but by asking what we can learn from a careful examination of artistry, that is, the competence by which practitioners actually handle indeterminate zones of practice – however that competence may relate to technical rationality. (Schön 1987, p. 13)

The musical conservatory is cited by Schön as one of the 'deviant traditions of education for practice' that should be studied (1987, p. 16), and indeed even his use of the word 'deviant' implies that instrumental teaching and learning has deviated from the prior, university tradition. Although musical performance is a fruitful area for investigation, however, there are some issues within Schön's argument that call for examination.

Schön focuses very much on professional artistry, strongly featured in all three of the basic premises for his 1987 book: that professional skill has a core of artistry, that artistry is itself a form of knowledge, and that although science and technique may be incorporated in practice, these are bounded by artistry (p. 13). However, it is a characteristic weakness of his argument that he tends to offer relatively simple skills to illustrate his points. On one hand, with reference to coaching in artistic endeavours, he describes 'a powerful sense of mystery and magic in the atmosphere – the magic of great performers, the mystery of talent' (p. 21). On the other hand, when he makes a general point, he seems to find that the everyday is more fit for purpose:

> [K]nowing-in-action is dynamic, [whereas] 'facts', 'procedures', 'rules' and theories' are static. When we know how to catch a ball, for example, we anticipate the ball's coming by the way we extend and cup our hands and by the on-line adjustments we make as the ball approaches. Catching a ball is a continuous activity in which awareness, appreciation, and adjustment play their parts. Similarly, sawing along a pencilled line requires a more or less continuous process of detecting and correcting deviations from the line. (Schön 1987, pp. 25–6)

Since musical performance can incorporate a tremendous range of psychomotor skills as well as professional artistry, it would seem to be an example that could provide Schön with all of the illustrations he needs. Had he described some of the principles of violin bowing here, instead of catching a ball, he could have illustrated a sophisticated point without resort to a skill that many children can muster without any coaching at all. At the same time, it is worth keeping in mind the disjuncture in Schön's discussion between the physical and the artistic: more than catching a ball, playing a violin can illustrate both technique and the 'mystery and magic' of interpretation. Physical and artistic skills may belong in the same broad category, but they are very different, and we cannot expect the relationship between them to be a direct one.

Schön himself allows for different 'types of knowing' that result in 'different conceptions of a practicum' (1987, pp. 38–9). In one of these, that includes the musical conservatory, he explains that '[r]eflecting-in-action has a critical function, questioning the assumptional structure of knowing-in-action' (p. 28). A musical illustration is offered for this:

> When good jazz musicians improvise together, they also manifest a 'feel for' their material and they make on-the-spot adjustments to the sounds they hear. Listening to one another and to themselves, they feel where the music is going and adjust their playing accordingly. ... They are reflecting-in-action on the music they are collectively making and on their individual contributions to it, thinking what they are doing and, in the process, evolving their way of doing it. (Schön 1983, pp. 55–6)

Two points might be made about this illustration. One is that although the jazz setting might make it a more obvious example to general readers, the procedures described here could arguably be applied to ensemble performance in any style of music. Schön's claim would be equally valid if it simply referred to 'when good musicians play together'. The second point stems from the first, however: these are advanced and complex skills, and we cannot expect that every performer, once again regardless of the style of music, will be able to display them. The apparent assumption that reflection-in-action is a normal characteristic of performance, rather than an aspiration – a work in progress for all practitioners – recalls Scheffler's quibble with Ryle's 'intelligent operations': not all skills are best described as intelligent, and not all performances demonstrate the full gamut of skills available in any domain of expertise.

Schön's attempt to identify a 'type of knowing' that can encompass both rudimentary procedures and artistry 'in unique, uncertain, and conflicted situations of practice' might seem to founder when we try to include all practitioners: novice through to expert, as well as perhaps poor through to excellent. It might be helpful here, however, to refer to Dewey's description of originality. Although he writes in general terms rather than making specific reference to musical performance, Dewey elides thinking, inquiring and questioning, and suggests that questioning in particular cultivates originality in the pupil, 'even in dealing with things already well known by others' (1933, p. 266). This would imply that performers need not be at the cutting edge of their practice, to be engaged with artistry as characterized by Schön. Dewey further explains the notion of originality at even an elementary level of accomplishment:

> *[A]ll* thinking is original in a projection of considerations which have not been previously apprehended. ... The charm which the spontaneity of little children has for sympathetic observers is due to perception of this intellectual originality. The joy which children themselves experience is the joy of intellectual constructiveness – of creativeness, if the word may be used without misunderstanding. (Dewey 1916, p. 159; italics original)

Elsewhere, Schön's inquiry incorporates some further questionable assumptions about music education, an area that apparently lies outside his personal experience. His thumbnail description of conditions in the conservatoire is a case in point: it offers students

> ... freedom to learn by doing in a setting relatively low in risk, with access to coaches who initiate students into the 'traditions of the calling' and help them, by 'the right kind of telling', to see on their own behalf and in their own way what they need most to see. (Schön 1987, p. 21)

The instrumental lesson may seem a low-risk setting to the casual observer, compared for example to a public recital in London's Wigmore Hall; but any performance situation, including individual lessons, can represent high pressure to the student. Thus Sosniak, in a study of the student careers of concert pianists in America, describes masterclasses as 'anxiety-provoking situations' (1985a, p. 64) and lessons with a master-teacher in terms of terror, tears and awe: the 'slave-driver and slave' (1985b, p. 421). One pianist's description of her teacher is offered as an example of a common experience among ambitious students:

> He was an impossible taskmaster. It was incredible. He would just intimidate you out of your mind. He would sit there … You played a concert, you didn't play a lesson. You walked in prepared to play a performance … You would get torn apart for an hour. (Sosniak 1985b, p. 421)

Schön makes up for his own lack of specific expertise in music education by examining a previously published account of a high-level music lesson, which he rather loosely labels a masterclass, as an example of professional practice. This is the narrative given by cellist Bernard Greenhouse of his study with Casals (Delbanco 1985; also in Schön 1987, Chapter 8). Schön's discussion of this narrative, however, is not entirely convincing. As he is described in action by Greenhouse, Casals is highly directive, insisting on a close copy of every detail of his own performance, at least at first:

> [A]fter several weeks of working on that one suite of Bach's, finally, the two of us could sit down and perform and play all the same fingerings and bowings and all of the phrasings alike. And I really had become a copy of the Master. It was as if that room had stereophonic sound – two cellos producing at once. And at that point, when I had been able to accomplish this, he said to me, 'Fine. Now just sit. Put your cello down and listen to the D Minor Suite.' And he played through the piece and changed every bowing and every fingering and every phrasing and all the emphasis within the phrase. I sat there, absolutely with my mouth open, listening to a performance which was heavenly, absolutely beautiful. And when he finished he turned to me with a broad grin on his face, and he said, 'Now you've learned how to improvise in Bach. From now on you study Bach this way.' (Delbanco, 1985, pp. 50–51)

To a musician it is curious that Schön accepts Casals' own conclusion at face value: that through this procedure his pupil has somehow learned to 'improvise' in Bach. It is not at all clear what this means, and neither is the command that Greenhouse should carry on in 'this way'. The point intended by Casals, and the point taken by Greenhouse, which may or may not have been the same, remain unquestioned and unexplained.

Perhaps more curiously, the account of this lesson is offered as an example of what Schön has described as coaching, something quite distinct, in his proposed epistemology, from deliberate teaching. Casals' behaviour provides a surprisingly clear contrast to the other professionals whose practices provide the focus for other chapters in *Educating the Reflective Practitioner*: the architect and the psychoanalyst provide far clearer cases of the coaching Schön describes. Indeed, the student himself, in a part of his account not repeated by Schön, goes on to insist that Casals was 'assuredly' a teacher rather than a coach (Delbanco

1985, p. 51). Greenhouse's description of a coach as a respected colleague who offers opinions and advice (p. 46) might provide some support for Schön's notion of the reflective practitioner, but his description of Casals' lesson does not.

These reservations about the specific application of Schön's ideas to instrumental teaching and learning do not deny the value of many of those ideas in discussing professional practice in more general terms. His description of the practicum, in which the student becomes a member of a community of practice (1987, p. 36), has helped to broaden the notion of how and where learning takes place, as well as the nature of what is learned. In addition, although Schön's choice of the conservatoire as a model needs to be qualified, his account of what occurs in a practicum places some emphasis on its relatively decentralized structure, and this draws attention to the fact that the 'coach' may not be the sole source of knowledge for the novice:

> The work of the practicum is accomplished through some combination of the student's learning by doing, her interactions with coaches and fellow students, and a more diffuse process of 'background learning'. (Schön 1987, p. 38)

Schön's description of professional practice also helps to emphasize the effect of interpersonal relations among participants, and this in turn highlights the affective aspects of learning, not always sufficiently acknowledged in theories of education. Schön's explanation of the vulnerability and loss of confidence felt by some learners, and the significance of communication or miscommunication between expert and novice (p. 166) would seem to be particularly relevant in the examination of the one-to-one setting that characterizes instrumental teaching and learning.

Situated Learning

Several points in Schön's argument draw attention to aspects of learning that are sometimes overlooked. It would oversimplify matters to imply that there has been a coherent body of received wisdom that ignores these aspects, and yet it seems that the 'cognitive revolution' which exerted considerable influence on theories of education from the late 1950s onward, tends to characterize intelligent operations as if they were matters of computation rather than of experience. Bruner asserts that this view is insufficient to explain the 'process of knowing':

> [The] computational view is concerned with information processing: how finite, coded, unambiguous information about the world is inscribed, sorted, stored, collated, retrieved, and generally managed by a computational device. It takes information as its given, as something already settled in relation to some preexisting, rule-bound code that maps onto states of the world. This so-called 'well-formedness' is both its strength and its shortcoming ... For the process of knowing is often messier, more fraught with ambiguity than such a view allows. (Bruner 1996, pp. 1–2)

The ambiguities of learning are often exemplified in features of the reflective practice described by Schön. These features include subject matter that might be unique or uncertain in nature; learning through a dynamic combination of instruction and practice, which results in procedural more than propositional knowledge; and interpersonal relations which draw attention to the affective aspects of learning. All of these are more easily highlighted by looking at learning in the context of social practice, than by focusing on the mind as an internal computer.

To this end, a number of education theorists have embraced aspects of social and cultural theories, providing a view of learning that is broader than the common conception of education as a deliberate, discrete and formal procedure. Wenger explains some relevant aspects of social theory, in general terms:

> Theories of *situated experience* give primacy to the dynamics of everyday existence, improvisation, coordination, and interactional choreography. They emphasize agency and intentions. They mostly address the interactive relations of people with their environment. They focus on the experience and the local construction of individual or interpersonal events such as activities and conversations. The most extreme of them ignore structure writ large altogether. (Wenger 1998, p. 13; italics original)

Wenger's own contribution has been a careful characterization of 'communities of practice' among which formal education is only an example, since they might also include settings in the workplace and a range of other social institutions. This view emphasizes the interactional nature of learning through everyday interpersonal exchanges that may occur between student and teacher, but also with other significant participants. Meaning is not objectively fixed, but negotiated; the learner, far from being an information processor, brings her own subjective intentions and perceptions to the table. The history of the practice – its cultural connotations – is also taken into account as a matter of context; the conduct of the practice is a matter of collaboration among participants; and what is learned represents a dynamic combination of the sociocultural context and the agency of the learner.

Lave and Wenger (1991) characterize learning as 'legitimate peripheral participation', and all three parts of this rather unwieldy term can be helpful in describing the learning of performance as a practice. The aspect of participation is helpful in highlighting the active engagement of the student, and the collaborative nature of the learning as teacher and student interact through a continually evolving stream of discussion and performance. The notion of peripherality can reflect the fact that the student is effectively a junior member of the practice, with the potential to develop her seniority and to influence the practice itself. Legitimacy refers to the fact that, even within an institution designed for education, the student's participation is a genuine part of the broader practice of musical performance: in principle she may engage at whatever level with the same complex of musical procedures employed by the most senior practitioners in the field.

In broadest terms, the concept of 'situated learning' allows for almost any eventuality in the teaching and learning of performance. The implications are explained by Lave:

> Knowledgeability is routinely in a state of change rather than stasis, in the medium of socially, culturally, and historically ongoing systems of activity, involving people who are related in multiple and heterogeneous ways, whose social locations, interests, reasons, and subjective possibilities are different, and who improvise struggles in situated ways with each other over the value of particular definitions of the situation, in both immediate and comprehensive terms, and for whom the production of failure is as much a part of routine collective activity as the production of average, ordinary knowledgeability. (Lave 1993, p. 17)

Scaffolding Theory

The complexity of the concept of situated learning has the virtue of being well suited to the complexity of the subject it seeks to explain. Conversely, however, it may seem to represent the subject as being so ill-formed that it can hardly be subjected to analysis. Among social learning theories, the notion of scaffolding would seem to offer a more specific focus in the analysis of teaching and learning.

'Scaffolding' first appears in education literature with reference to learning in early childhood, with mothers observed leading their children through certain sequences of behaviour (Wood, Bruner and Ross, 1976). These sequences are likened by researchers to providing a scaffold that assists learners through their 'zones of proximal development' (ZPD). The concept of the ZPD first appears in the work of Vygotsky (1896–1934) and it should be noted that this too refers chiefly to the learning development of young children. The wide range of interpretations subsequently made of the ZPD has been usefully summarized by Lave and Wenger (1991, pp. 48–9). One of these directly informs scaffolding theory: this is the view that the ZPD represents 'the distance between problem-solving abilities exhibited by a learner working alone and that learner's problem-solving abilities when assisted by or collaborating with more-experienced people' (p. 48). The assistance provided by a more expert other can help to address the learning paradox that underlies the problem of performance: if one learns to talk by talking, to ride a bicycle by cycling, or to play the clarinet by playing it, how is one to begin – to enter into this circle of practice?

Schön describes this as a virtuous learning circle, identifying an example in the learning of architectural design: '[t]he student must be able to take part in the dialogue if she is to learn the substantive practice, and she must design to some degree in order to participate in the dialogue' (1987, p. 165). He goes on to explain the role of the coach in helping the student to overcome the paradox:

[T]he coach assumes that an initial instruction or demonstration will be sufficient to get the student to do *something*. This initiative, rooted in what the student already knows, begins the learning circle. Its function is to get the dialogue started. It provides a first occasion for feedback, which given the qualities of a designlike practice, the student is very likely to find confusing or ambiguous. So the stage is set for a continuing dialogue of actions and words, of reciprocal reflection in and on action. Through this process, the student may increase her grasp of designing by participating in the dialogue and enhance her ability to learn from the dialogue through her increased capacity for designing. (Schön 1987, p. 166; italics original)

In the context of instrumental teaching and learning, several researchers have gone further, to identify sequences of scaffolding behaviours in individual lessons. The most direct reference to the scaffolding sequences identified by Bruner is made by Kennell (1997) who filmed seven lessons given to an American university student, apparently on a wind instrument. These lessons were analyzed in units of 'teacher interventions' or 'teacher–student interactions', brief exchanges occurring at the average rate of 190 in each 30-minute lesson. Among these, occurrences of six 'scaffolding strategies' that were originally described by Wood et al. (1976) were identified and counted.

Given that the context of the original study – of mother and child interactions – is so far removed from the university studio setting, it is perhaps unsurprising that the fit between the scaffolding strategies and the features that Kennell found salient is not always good. Kennell's examples represent each phrase of speech or performance as being an occurrence of a strategy, and reports that most interventions consist of only one (65 per cent) or two (21 per cent) strategies. This offers little support to the notion that the strategies might constitute regularly ordered sequences of behaviour. The distribution among strategies also raises questions about the usefulness of the method. Kennell finds it necessary to include two additional categories, labelled 'off task' (17 per cent) and 'unknown' (4 per cent) leaving only 79 per cent that can be classed among the original strategies. One of these – 'marking critical features' – dominates by occurring in 46 per cent of the interventions, while the others – 'demonstration', 'reduction of degrees of freedom', 'recruitment', 'direction maintenance', and 'frustration control' — range from 1 to 12 per cent. Frustration control occurs in only 1 per cent of interventions, and this perhaps implies that it has little relevance in a university music lesson. Demonstration, on the other hand, accounts for 9 per cent of the identified strategies, and – given its widespread use that would presumably be expected in any setting where professional practice is cultivated – this suggests that comparing it to verbal strategies simply by counting the number of occurrences of each will give a misleading impression of their relative importance.

Gholson (1998) criticizes Kennell's study for being deductive in nature, attempting to apply a pre-existing theory to practice, rather than using an inductive approach to generate theory by studying practice. Her own study of lessons given by a highly successful violin teacher proposes a 'theory of proximal positioning' which clearly draws upon Vygotsky's concept of the zone of proximal development. The unit for analysis here is once again teacher interventions, characterized by Gholson as 'turns taken between teacher and student during instructional interaction' (p. 538). There seems to be no attempt to quantify the occurrence of strategies, for comparison; but two broad categories are identified 'as global patterns of practice'. These are preparatory strategies, through which the teacher can 'probe student frames of reference, organize instructional interventions, and establish contextual goals' (p. 539), and facilitative strategies, which include 'going for the obvious area of weakness, establishing a comfortable lesson atmosphere, cognitively magnifying critical features of details of lesson content, and the use of metaphor' (p. 540).

Several of these strategies have a clear resemblance to those originally identified in scaffolding theory, and it seems obvious that marking critical features is a significant element in all of the interactions observed by Wood et al., Kennell and Gholson. It is interesting that demonstration is not reported to be a significant element in the lessons observed by Gholson, and that the interactions reported are highly instructive in nature: it appears that among the variously interpreted features of the ZPD model, assistance from a more expert other is given more emphasis than the collaborative nature of problem solving through participation.

In a more recent study Kennell offers a further possible approach to scaffolding theory by returning to the notion that the strategies involved should fall into regular sequences of behaviour. His 'Teacher attribution scaffolding theory' (2002) refers specifically to music in Higher Education, and proposes that the strategy employed by the teacher will depend on her diagnosis of the student's current understanding or ability. Where conceptual problems are involved she might, in order of increasing challenge, demonstrate, offer information, or question the student in order to mark a critical feature; where a skill is involved she might manipulate the task to make it more accessible, offer information, or ask for a demonstration from the student (p. 246). As in Kennell's previous study, the focus is very much on the teacher as the more active agent – the teacher's request for a demonstration is labelled a command – and there seems little room for the negotiation of understanding emphasized elsewhere in social learning theory.

While scaffolding seems a useful way to conceptualize what takes place in teaching and learning, the application of scaffolding theory to instrumental teaching and learning has perhaps had limited success. Even so, the efforts made by Kennell and Gholson have taken significant steps toward viewing the instrumental lesson in terms of social practice, examining not only what is taught and learned but how transactions between teacher and student are structured by the participants.

Summary: Instrumental Teaching and Learning as a Regime of Competence

The preceding section has examined the subject matter of instrumental teaching and learning as a regime of competence or skill, on the assumption that the nature of the subject matter must affect the way it is to be learned. This in turn will presumably affect the nature of lesson interactions between teacher and student. Skill is a kind of knowledge, and is not necessarily consequent or inferior to the 'mental' operations traditionally privileged by the university sector or in Rationalist philosophy.

Skills can be simple or complex, focal or subsidiary, articulate or intuitive, intelligent or unintelligent, practical or artistic. Musical performance is a complex skill, with components at varying levels of sophistication embedded within one another. These components are inevitably acquired and developed in a variety of ways, and this is something that researchers observing lesson interactions should keep in mind: presumably the behaviour involved in the cultivation of routine skills or techniques, for example, will be distinct in some ways from the behaviour involved in the cultivation of critical or interpretative skills.

The nonverbal nature of musical performance means that descriptions of it tend to be vague and ambiguous, and terms like talent, sense, feel and nose have been found surprisingly unhelpful in characterising the musician's skill. These weaknesses in the 'folk' epistemology of practice are associated with the (false) impression that skill is itself vague and ambiguous. Verbal behaviour is associated with skill, both through self-talk, which has its own peculiar nature, and through the 'language of craftsmanship' which serves to elicit and coach rather than to explain. A misapprehension of such language may, again, give observers the (false) impression that its function is vague and ambiguous.

Explanation too has its place in the acquisition of performance skill, but when know-how is reified to become verbal instruction, it must be translated back into action to become meaningful to the student performer. The two-way translation may itself pose an obstacle to understanding, and this presumably means that nonverbal behaviours – particularly those involved in demonstration – have a position of central importance in instrumental teaching and learning. Nonverbal aspects of musical performance also include issues of expression and emotion, and these touch on the affective aspects of learning.

Because so many aspects of instrumental teaching and learning are nonverbal in nature, it will presumably be difficult for empirical researchers to observe, articulate or quantify what takes place in lesson interactions, difficult to obtain precise verbal data from participants about what they are doing in instrumental lessons, and challenging to interpret what they say, within and about their practice.

What happens as the learner acquires her skill has been observed through a broader, sociocultural lens in theories of situated learning. If learning is situated, the student is not merely learning to internalize her own construction of the subject matter: she is learning to participate in a community of practice. In addition to learning the professional language of musical craftsmanship, she is learning to talk like a musician. This is a skill in itself, and like all others is to be learned by doing. The broader conceptualization of learning through participation is particularly apt for a skill-based subject area, and helps to draw in the social, cultural and historical aspects of learning.

These in turn can provide a contextual framework for what happens in instrumental lessons. Specific applications of such frameworks to instrumental teaching and learning have been proposed by Schön in terms of professional artistry, and by Kennell and Gholson in terms of scaffolding theory. These examine the acquisition of skill in the setting of individual instrumental lessons, with Schön asking how experts practice and reflect on – or in – their own skills, and all three asking how expert practitioners induct learners into their discipline through the adaptive use of instruction and modelling. These issues are contextualized in the following section, focused on apprenticeship in music.

Apprenticeship

Introduction

Having explored musical performance as a complex skill, and emphasizing once again the close relationship necessary between subject matter and the way it is learned, the focus of discussion is now shifted to an exploration of apprenticeship, to see if it might provide a way of understanding how that skill is acquired.

The range of possible meanings and implications of 'apprenticeship' is intriguingly broad and rich. The terms 'master' and 'apprentice' are often coined in the literature on instrumental teaching and learning, but they are rarely systematically defined, and the assumptions implied in their usage are rarely examined. This section begins with a sketch of apprenticeship in history, proceeding to identify features that continue to resonate with modern approaches to instrumental teaching and learning, and the language used to contextualize it. The exploration of these features should shed some significant light on the nature of instrumental teaching and learning, and indeed of learning generally.

Apprenticeships in History

The notion of apprenticeship seems to be at least as old as the notion of education. Egan and Gajdamaschko name it as 'the first, and most ancient, conception of the educator's task', being 'the most common in human cultures across the world and … almost the exclusive mode of instruction in hunter-gatherer societies' (2003, p. 83). In medieval Europe formal apprenticeships were established by the fourteenth century in a range of occupations, and normally involved indenture to a master, who provided bed and board as well as workplace training. The social structure of the apprenticeship system was typically formalized in guilds, which were granted by charter and associated with civic privileges and duties (Baillie 1956, p. 6).

Although apprenticeships were chiefly characteristic of manual pursuits, it is significant to their modern descendents in professional and technical training that they were also characteristic of professions such as medicine and law (Aldrich 1999, p. 15). In addition, the arts in medieval Europe were not normally distinguished from crafts. Perhaps similarly, Polanyi, in discussing apprenticeship, uses the terms 'art' and 'craftsmanship' interchangeably, referring to both skill and connoisseurship (1958, pp. 49–55). An outstanding example of this rather undifferentiated view of practice is the experience of Leonardo da Vinci who spent ten years from the age of 14 as pupil, apprentice and assistant to Verrocchio, before setting up his own studio. His apprenticeship 'was certainly an education, though it took place in a workshop rather than an ancient university, it taught skills rather than intellectual accomplishments, and it was conducted in Italian rather than Latin' (Nicholl 2004, p. 54). Even so – and particularly in the Italian renaissance – the division between manual skills and liberal arts was not rigid. Hence Lorenzo Ghiberti in 1450:

> 'It is fitting that the sculptor and painter have a solid knowledge of the following liberal arts – grammar, geometry, philosophy, medicine, astronomy, perspective, history, anatomy, theory, design and arithmetic'. (Nicholl 2004, pp. 54–5)

In addition to the incorporation of a broad range of skills and knowledge, guilds often retained a mixed social and trade character in their membership. In medieval England for example the Guild of Parish Clerks was granted its full charter in 1444, but had previously existed as a social and religious fraternity – the Company of Parish Clerks – since 1240. Its mixed membership included men and women, musicians and non-musicians, and even interested members of the nobility: in short, the patrons of church music as well as the craftsmen producing it (Baillie 1956, pp. 6–7).

Trade guilds declined very gradually from the mid-sixteenth century onward (Aldrich 1999, p. 14) and equally gradually, art and craft, trade and profession became distinct from one another. Sociologists Frederickson and Rooney assert that until the seventeenth century, music was participation-oriented, with patrons among the nobility frequently taking part in early ballets and music dramas. From this point on however it became increasingly performance-oriented, with performers separated from an audience whose role was now to listen attentively. As 'aesthetic standards of listening' were established, the practice of eighteenth-century opera audiences meeting socially, chatting and even dining during performances died out. In spite of these general trends, Frederickson and Rooney argue that the distinction between professional and amateur has never become entirely clear, and that this is one of the features demonstrating that music never became a 'profession' in the modern sense (1990, pp. 192–3).

The rise of the conservatories in the nineteenth century was associated with the further specialization of musicians' skills, and balanced the decline of musical apprenticeship as a formal institution (Weber 2008). The decline of apprenticeship generally was similarly balanced by the rise of schools of technical education, as 'it became apparent that some elements, for example basic scientific and technical knowledge necessary for [various] forms of apprenticeship, could be supplied more efficiently in the classroom than in the workplace' (Aldrich 1999, p. 19).

In modern educational institutions the role of the traditional master has been '[dispersed] into a combination of college-based modules, institutional training and workplace experience' (Gamble 2001, p. 185). Although the conservatory may in some ways be seen as an example of this general trend, musical training retains features of traditional apprenticeship which make it unique. An obvious example is the continuing emphasis on the master-apprentice dyad, found in both conservatories and university music departments. A similar dyad is arguably to be found in the architect's 'practicum' and other settings for professional training, as described by Schön (1987). However, although music and other professions share an orientation toward doing, rather than knowing, musical performance retains a craft orientation in being evaluated by its product, whereas the professions, having become more standardized in their approach to training, are evaluated by their methodology (Frederickson and Rooney 1990, pp. 10–11).

This very brief sketch of apprenticeship in history shows that the picture of apprenticeship is by no means cohesive. The traditional roots of instrumental teaching and learning clearly lie within the apprenticeship approach, and this is likely to have implications for many of the concepts involved in the practice. These include the master-apprentice dyad; the nature of the subject matter, viewed in terms of either art or craft, or both; the nature of the skills involved, and whether these are acquired in a single setting or separated among several; and social aspects of both the practice and the performance of music.

Apprenticeship in Music Research Literature

In the literature on instrumental teaching and learning, the terms 'master', 'apprentice', or the two combined are widely accepted. Jørgensen for example reports that the 'master-apprentice relationship' is historically predominant in instrumental instruction (2000, p. 68), Callaghan describes traditional vocal instruction as 'an oral, master/apprentice process' (1998, p. 25), while Persson applies the term 'master-apprenticeship relationship' generally to lessons 'in, but not limited to, a conservatory setting' (2000, p. 25).

The wide use of the term however does not reflect close agreement on its meaning, and none of these authors offers a clear definition of it. Indeed, 'master-apprentice' is not always clearly distinguished from other terms that might describe the relationships found in music and music education settings. For Persson, 'master' is elided with 'maestro', and his paper, subtitled 'Deconstructing the myth of the musical maestro', blurs the distinction among 'master performers', teachers and conductors (p. 26). For Schön, discussing what he describes as a 'master class in musical performance', the terms 'master teacher', 'master', 'coach' and 'teacher' are interchangeable (1987, pp. 175–6).

It may seem that a term so loosely used can have little meaning in this context. However, while music researchers and theorists have not often given their direct attention to the term itself, the fact that it is so often used suggests that there must be assumptions – perhaps common assumptions – made about its relevance. It must therefore be important to examine the ways in which apprenticeship is characterized in the context of instrumental teaching and learning, in order to identify any generally accepted features. In the following sections, salient features are extracted from references to apprenticeship in the literature on instrumental teaching and learning, and briefly contextualized in terms of the broader literature.

Apprenticeship and the Development of Experiential Knowledge

One assumption common among writers on instrumental teaching and learning seems to be that experiential knowledge is an essential feature of apprenticeships, in which skills rather than propositional knowledge are to be cultivated. This assumption is clear for example in Callaghan's discussion of the nature of teaching and learning within the *bel canto* tradition of vocal training, influential since the early seventeenth century:

> That tradition was an oral, master/apprentice process based on shared knowledge of musical form and vocal style. Because many components of the vocal mechanism could not be seen, teaching relied on expert practitioners *conveying experiential knowledge* to students through demonstration and description of the results to be achieved and of the accompanying sensations. (Callaghan 1998, p. 25; italics added)

Historically, as noted above, formal systems of apprenticeship have covered a wide range of occupations, chiefly based on crafts and professions, with music arguably representative in some ways of both. The clear emphasis on experiential knowledge tends to lie on physical skill in crafts and trades, while the professions are associated with what Polanyi describes as 'connoisseurship', also to be regarded as a skill, since for example 'the medical diagnostician's skill is as much an art of doing as it is an art of knowing' (1958, p. 54). Polanyi insists that such an art can only be passed on by master to apprentice: by example, not by precept (pp. 53–4).

The etymology of 'apprenticeship' casts some light on the acquisition of skill that it is taken to involve. From the Latin root *apprehendere* – to seize, or lay hold of – come two distinct verbs, apprehend and appraise. Webb explains the implications of each:

> In apprehending something, properly, we learn not only to do something (as we might through instruction, mimed copying, repetition, practice), but [through appraisal] we learn also to understand the principles of operation together with that shaped knowledge which informs what we are doing. (Webb 1999, p. 101)

Essentially, then, the skill acquired through apprenticeship involves both doing and knowing.

Apprenticeship through Demonstration and Imitation

Both Polanyi in his general discussion of skill acquisition, and Callaghan in her discussion of *bel canto* training, touch on another commonly assumed feature of musical apprenticeships: the use of demonstration and imitation. This is also clear in Jørgensen's description of the master-apprenticeship relationship as one 'where the dominant mode of student learning is imitation' (2000, p. 68). In the more general literature, Polanyi describes the apprentice 'watching the master and emulating his efforts in the presence of his example' (1958, p. 53), and Bruner explains that know-how is acquired by imitative learners, through a modelling process that is 'the basis of apprenticeship' (1996, p. 53).

Accordingly, the master in instrumental teaching is expected to demonstrate a high level of expertise: thus Persson's maestro 'gains prominence by virtue of outstanding musical skills' (2000, p. 25). Nerland and Hanken, describing the 'apprenticeship-like' education in a Norwegian higher music academy, elaborate on this point:

> Students are linked directly to a teacher of a principal instrument who is, or in some cases has been, a professional musician at the highest level. Interaction with their teacher gives students the opportunity to *observe and participate* in profession-related practices under the supervision of an experienced 'master' of the discipline, thus providing them with access to crucial knowledge and standards of the discipline. (Nerland and Hanken 2002, pp. 168–9; italics added)

'Observe and participate' have been highlighted here because of their significance to the issue of imitation. The nature of imitation has been much discussed, in terms of instrumental teaching and learning and in learning theory generally; it seems that imitation might be represented as a continuum between a relatively passive process of direct copying, and a highly active conception of participation in a community of practice. Imitation has further implications in performance as a re-creative art, in which individuality is highly valued, and it is likely to give rise to mixed feelings among practitioners. For these reasons, some further consideration of imitation will be made parenthetically, here.

Learning through Imitation

It might be assumed that imitation would be indispensable in the teaching and learning of an aural art and a nonverbal skill. Hallam, investigating the practice strategies employed by young instrumentalists, asserts that 'knowledge of appropriate strategies and their implementation is not useful in increasing the effectiveness of practice unless appropriate aural schemata have been developed to enable the monitoring of errors' (Hallam 2001, p. 20). Although an internal aural model may be developed in part when 'the sounds are simply absorbed' by the pupil, it is the teacher's responsibility to ensure that such a model is acquired.

In spite of this obvious and basic use of modelling and imitation, musicians sometimes betray anxiety about the idea of copying. Nielsen, interviewing students at a Danish conservatoire, reports:

> From the interviews it was possible to trace ambivalence due to some of the students who, on the one hand, saw imitation as part of the learning process, while on the other hand, there was some resistance or reservations about imitation as a core mode of learning. In the students' community of practice it is seen as embarrassing to copy one's teacher. Several of the students stress that one ought not to copy one's teacher. This gives the concept of imitation another status as something that the students negotiate among themselves, and from which, in general, they distance themselves. (Nielsen 2006, p. 9, n. 6)

This apparent ambivalence in student attitudes toward imitation might perhaps be clarified by specifying what is to be imitated. Accuracy in rhythm and notation, tonal quality and certain aspects of technique, can be quite specific in nature and it seems possible that they can be learned in no more effective way than by imitating a model. Even aspects of interpretation, such as the use of expressive gestures, can be usefully acquired, initially, in this way, though they will eventually be incorporated into the individual learner's own expressive vocabulary. But in broad terms, individuality of interpretation is highly valued in musical performance, particularly by the time students have reached the level of Higher Education (Mills and Smith 2003, p. 9; Nerland 2007, p. 409). Although expert performers are able to incorporate aspects of masterly interpretations into their own performances, more or less consciously (Lisboa et al. 2005), it seems possible that undergraduates, still in the process of adopting professional values, might feel self-conscious about doing so.

In addition to broadening the possible applications of imitation, the understanding of the process of imitation might also be broadened. Vygotsky sought to distinguish imitation from copying, to reflect his theoretical position that '[i]mitation is possible only to the extent and in those forms in which it is accompanied by understanding' (Chaiklin 2003, pp. 51–2). Thus conceptualized, imitation is part of a collaborative process with the more expert other. Later theorists have taken Vygotsky's ideas further, and have variously characterized the learning process in terms of internalization and participation (Matusov, in Daniels 2001, p. 40), apprenticeship, guided participation, and participatory appropriation (Rogoff 1995, p. 141) and legitimate peripheral participation (Lave and Wenger 1991). Any of these could arguably be situated within a musical apprenticeship.

The Master as Representative of the Community of Practice

However the learning process is characterized in the apprenticeship situation, some features of the role taken by the master would seem to remain relatively consistent. While the master's personal expertise is given considerable emphasis by Nerland and Hanken (2002), it also seems important that the master may be regarded as a representative of, and link to, the professional community. Complementing this, too, Persson asserts that the maestro 'legitimizes his or her instructional behaviour based on historical tradition' (2000, p. 25). By entering the 'practice' of the master, the apprentice is thus given access to both the state and the history of the art. This two-dimensional effect is explained by Howard, who takes care to distinguish between 'practice', by which he means the art itself, and 'practise', which refers to the active engagement of practitioners:

> The rituals of art, science, technology, and education have a similar function. Practising their rituals simultaneously exemplifies *the* practices of those fields and becomes a way for others to learn them – and to surpass them.
>
> Accordingly, we may distinguish the cross-sectional, 'synchronic' instructional pay off of practising particular facilities from the longitudinal, 'diachronic' pay off of traditional practices. The latter teach across historical time, as it were, from one generation to the next. The former is more a matter of identifying *with* the practices of a given field or discipline, of taking them into oneself, of mastering them for the sake of competency. That is very like a process of initiation into a tradition by aspiration, demonstration, and precept. (Howard 1992, p. 103; italics original)

In the broader literature on learning as a social practice, such issues are discussed in terms of the learner's access to a community of practice. This access might be viewed from the perspective of either the master or the apprentice: the apprentice gains access to the practice, through the master's (present) skill and (past) experience, while the master's sponsorship confers legitimacy on the apprentice as a newcomer to the practice. Wenger notes the parallel between this aspect of the master-apprentice relationship, and that between university tutors and their doctoral students, seeking entry to academic communities (Wenger 1998, p. 101).

The Apprenticeship as a Source of Identity

Clearly related to the notion of entering a practice is the development of the learner's personal identity, which is often assumed in discussions of musical apprenticeships. One of the fullest accounts of this comes from Manturzewska (1990), who uses the term '"master-student" relationship' to characterize a particular stage in the lifespan development of professional musicians, reaching a peak at 18–20 years of age and typically ending with graduation from a higher music academy. Manturzewska's research makes a study of 165 professional musicians in Poland, aged 21 to 89, and her findings are no doubt specific, to some extent, to their own cultural traditions. Even so, the stage of development she describes clearly has some resonance with Sosniak's study of 24 American concert pianists, for whom '[t]he most critical step in the transition from being a talented teenage pianist to becoming a professional performing soloist seems to be that of moving to a master teacher' (1985a, p. 59). The 'master-teacher' is given central importance in Manturzewska's description of this stage:

> An important factor in the optimal artistic and professional development of musicians ... is the personality, musical competence, and personal culture of the teacher. The future musician's personality now develops within the 'master-student' relationship. This relationship is paramount for the entire future career. In this stage of life the musician usually forms deep friendships, lasting the rest of his or her life. The teacher-master (if the musician was lucky enough to find one) does not only concentrate on the technical side of the student's performance, but steers the development of the entire personality. The master helps choose books, not only on music; passes on his or her professional and non-professional experience, and together with the student studies the musical literature and discovers the beauty of the world of music. He or she accompanies the student to concerts and auditions, lets the student sit in at lessons with other students, steers the student's initiation in the world of musical values and conventions, introduces the student into professional circles, and helps him or her enter the professional market and international arena. He or she often helps the student to make personal decisions. Within this ever-deepening 'master-student' relationship the personality, aesthetic attitudes, life philosophy, professional standards and attitudes toward his or her own artistic and professional activity and the role of musician in contemporary society are developed in the future musician. (Manturzewska 1990, pp. 134–5)

It is interesting that this description of the master's role moves so far beyond purely musical issues, and it seems that the master's considerable authority and influence extend to the development of the student's career and cultural sense, as well as – perhaps most importantly – identity. Of course, the students in Manturzewska's study had become professional performers, and we might wonder whether the amount and nature of attention they had received from their masters could be enjoyed by all instrumental and vocal students, regardless of their apparent potential in the profession. Manturzewska herself allows that even these highly successful students had to be 'lucky enough to find' the kind of master she describes. In principle however the notion of identifying with the master seems common enough, with Jørgensen in his brief characterization of apprenticeship remarking that the master is 'usually looked at as a role model and a source of identification for the student' (Jørgensen 2000, p. 68).

The Master-Apprentice Relationship

The personal and even emotional nature of the relationship between master and apprentice is often emphasized. Nerland and Hanken discuss the 'apprentice-like organisation' of teaching in terms of 'close ties and intimacy', with a 'mentor or even parental role that many principal instrument teachers tend to acquire for their students'. This is associated with the nature of the subject matter: 'Working with the music implies that both student and teacher must expose themselves emotionally, and therefore they grow closer to each other on a personal level' (2002, p. 180).

The emotional attachment to music recalls Kingsbury's comparison of an American college of music to a seminary, inspiring a sense of commitment that 'seems more personal, moral, and emotional than professional or economic' (1988, pp. 19–20).

There is little or no reference to emotional commitment in historical studies of apprenticeship, no doubt because the affective aspect of learning is very much a modern concern: but there is an interesting parallel to be found in a recent study of apprenticeship among Kyrgiz nomads in Central Asia, who explain the mastery of traditional crafts in terms of 'birth talent', and for whom skill might not necessarily be connected with economic activities:

> Many essential features of nomadic high culture [such as the making of special felt wedding carpets known as *shyrdak*, are] not connected with trade. The motivation for making such work and for becoming skilful is uncomplicated by profit motives. This shows an important dimension to being skilful and to apprenticeship that is often overlooked – the love of being skilful and of making – the love of the job and the desire to give. (Bunn 1999, p. 82)

The intrinsic motivation in students of music, along with the notion of talent, are fundamental assumptions in the practice of instrumental performance. Thus Jørgensen, in an overview of research into the motivation of student music teachers in America, reports the 'love of music' as a strong influence for 'nearly all' of the students (2009, p. 70). The person of the master however may also be described as a source of motivation for the student. Uszler, referring to piano lessons in particular, characterizes the master in this way, and depicts a dominating figure:

> The master is the model who demonstrates, directs, comments, and inspires. The apprentice is the disciple who watches, listens, imitates, and seeks approval. Although the authoritarian position assumed by the master is open to question and criticism, notably by those who advocate learner-oriented teaching and by proponents of adult education, the presence of a master model is a powerful, universal motivating force. (Uszler 1992, p. 584)

The Authority of the Master

The master's authority is clearly related to the issue of power relations which according to Lave and Wenger characterizes 'every concrete case' of apprenticeship (1991, p. 64). According to Nerland and Hanken, authority is 'a crucial and productive resource in the teacher–student interaction' (2002, p. 168), and 'such dominant authority … is not only accepted, but also desired and even sought after among the students' (p. 172).

The dominance of the master in an apprenticeship situation is however not always assumed. Nielsen, preparing a background to his discussion of teaching and learning in a Danish academy of music, points out that the characteristics of apprenticeship vary in the traditions of different countries:

> Apprenticeship is translated differently in Scandinavia and Anglo-Saxon countries. In Anglo-Saxon countries, focus is placed on how apprentices learn from being a part of a community of practice. However, in Scandinavia apprenticeship can be translated as 'master learning' (mesterlæ) and focus is placed on how the apprentice learns from working with the master. (Nielsen 2006, p. 3)

The Anglo-Saxon interpretation of the term is shared by Schön, who distinguishes between an apprenticeship, in which the novice enters a genuine practice that is not designed for her education, and a practicum, 'designed for the task of learning a practice' (Schön 1987, p. 37). In the practicum, the student is engaged with an approximation of 'real-world projects', in 'simulated, partial or protected form'. Guidance is provided by the 'studio master', whose role is not necessarily a dominant one; Schön envisages instead an environment in which learning may be stimulated through group participation.

> From time to time, these [studio masters] may teach in the conventional sense, communicating information, advocating theories, describing examples of practice. Mainly, however, they function as coaches whose main activities are demonstrating, advising, questioning, and criticizing.

> Most practicums involve groups of students who are often as important to one another as the coach. Sometimes they play the coach's role. And it is through the medium of the group that a student can immerse himself in the world of the practicum – the all-encompassing worlds of a design studio, a musical conservatory, or psychoanalytic supervision, for example – learning new habits of thought and action. Learning by exposure and immersion, background learning often proceeds without conscious awareness, although a student may become aware of it later on, as he moves into a different setting. (Schön 1987, p. 38)

Although Schön considers the musical conservatory, here, as an example of a general type of educational setting, his description has some resonance with Sosniak's study of American pianists, which emphasizes the role played by other student-members of the master-teacher's class:

[I]t wasn't until they began working with a master teacher that they shared the company of others with aspirations and abilities similar to theirs day after day. ... The 'group' of young pianists provided exciting comradeship and frightening competition. The pianists used the group to compare notes about what they were being asked to do and how they were going about learning to do it, and occasionally to commiserate with each other about the abuse they were taking from their teachers. They shared gossip and tidbits of knowledge about competitions, performances, and other such experiences. They went to hear important performances together, and they went to movies or played cards together. (Sosniak 1985a, p. 64)

The communal learning found – if not often noted – among students of classical music may be far more significant in non-classical genres. In a detailed questionnaire study of 244 adult musicians, Creech et al. (2008) found that the developmental profiles of students varied with the genre involved:

Classical musicians tended to have begun to engage with music at an earlier age and were influenced musically by parents, instrumental or vocal teachers and formal groups. Conversely, non-classical musicians tended to be slightly older in their formative musical encounters and report that they typically were most influenced by well-known performers and informal groups. (Creech et al. 2008, p. 230)

This impression is supported by Lebler (2007) who offers some reflections on the teaching and learning of popular music in Higher Education, and reports that students' previous experience is often based on learning 'through informal means and peer-based experiences rather than under the tuition of a personal expert mentor' (p. 208). Drawing a contrast to the traditional approach to the principal study area in conservatoire training, he describes a conception of popular music studies in terms of a 'masterless studio' rather than individual lessons (p. 207).

There is apparently a range of possibilities, then, regarding the level of authority that might be represented by the master, which presumably varies with the characteristics of individual participants as well as musical genres. The variety might also be explained by distinguishing between group and individual settings. Whereas participation in group activity as described by Schön would seem to imply a relatively decentralized organization, Nerland and Hanken assert that 'great authority' in masters is associated not only with their professional status but with the one-to-one relationship developed in individual instrumental lessons (2004, p. 4). Sosniak, interestingly, describes students in groups of a supportive social character, but also adds that masterclasses, where individual students are taught with an audience of peers, were '[p]erhaps the most anxiety-provoking situations' (1985a, p. 64). It seems that in such situations, the presence of fellow apprentices might actually reinforce the master's authority.

The Role of the Apprentice

Broadly, it seems that instrumental lessons can be considered at once representative of 'real-world' practice, through the figure of the master, and separate from it, in being designed for learning. The extent to which the apprentice is regarded as participating in genuine practice, therefore, is variable. Kingsbury, in his study of a 'conservatory cultural system', emphasizes the relatively advanced standing of many of its students:

> [P]rofessions such as law, medicine and nursing are regulated by governmental licensing agencies, and students in law schools, for instance, are precluded from practising law until after finishing school and obtaining the appropriate license. By contrast, many students come to the conservatory as already developed performing musicians, and conservatory students are frequently engaged at least part-time as wage-earning performers, and have a certain self-image as 'professional' musicians. (Kingsbury 1988, p. 19)

Nerland, studying 'cultural practice' in a Norwegian academy of music, also identifies specific connections between educational practice within the institution and professional practice beyond it. The education of professional musicians is described generally as 'apprenticeship-like' (2001, p. 1), but beneath that general title some subtle distinctions are made among the approaches taken by teachers, through a careful consideration of individual case studies. The practice of one teacher is described as being framed by concert performance, with the lesson to some extent a simulation of one. Thus, within the lesson, the student takes a position 'as on a stage', while the teacher positions himself as 'critical audience', five metres away; instruction is driven by the performance product rather than by the process of preparation represented by the student's individual practice (p. 5). A second teacher explicitly prepares his students for an orchestral career, with instruction focused more on their individual practice:

> The teacher sees it as important not to organise his teaching as a 'blind institution' … but rather to open up the boundaries between the practice in his teaching studio and the other activities in which the students participate. As an effect of this style of reasoning, the students are encouraged to bring in repertoire and problems they are working on in other situations into the teaching situation. (Nerland 2001, p. 9)

It seems that although the practice of instrumental performance in Higher Education brings with it some of the older traditions of apprenticeship, particularly in the distinction between expert and novice, there is also some scope for softening that distinction and for viewing participants as members with varying degrees of expertise, in a more or less decentralized community of practice.

The Apprenticeship Setting

Although the instrumental tutorial may be designed for learning, it is also expected to exhibit features of 'real-world practice', or close simulations of it.

Folkestad (2005; 2006) argues that in considering learning, there need not be a clear-cut dichotomy between informal settings and settings designed specifically for education. He suggests, as an alternative, a continuum based on five sub-concepts of music education proposed by Jorgensen (1997). The continuum begins with 'schooling', in which 'the idea is that the student develops from novice to expert as a result of a sequenced exposure to teaching' (Folkestad 2006, p. 139). At the opposite end of the continuum are 'socialisation' and then 'enculturation', in which the learning is 'socially contextualized ... within a specific domain or practice' and ultimately within 'isolated traditions or considerable blocs of custom' (p. 139). Folkestad concludes that the distinction between formal and informal learning need not be dependent on whether it takes place within an institutional setting (p. 142).

The institutional setting of course cannot be expected to exhibit a single cohesive practice, particularly given the hybrid nature of traditions contributing to it. Apprenticeship has been examined here chiefly in the light of the western classical tradition, but other musical styles such as jazz, folk and popular music are often characterized in terms of apprenticeship, and these are well represented particularly in modern university music departments. Alongside the variety of attitudes among musicians of classical and non-classical traditions, identified by Creech et al. (2006), research focused on individual lessons in the university setting has revealed distinct patterns of behaviour associated with the traditions of 'conservatoire' and 'non-conservatoire' instruments, and in instrumental as distinct from vocal tuition (Burwell 2006).

If the institution itself is taken to be a community of practice, then, it should also be acknowledged that it will draw upon and overlap with many others. Wenger discusses this in terms of boundary processes – asserting that learning communities must push their own boundaries to interact with others – and multimembership, through which various traditions of practice should be reconciled within the institution (1998, p. 274).

Theorizing Apprenticeship

The description of the features of apprenticeship offered in this paper is intentionally indefinite. Paraphrasing Wittgenstein, *defining* apprenticeship could only succeed with reference to a circumscribed region of it, and not for the whole of what we are attempting to *describe* (Wittgenstein 1953, p. 3; italics added). The very multiplicity of meanings attached to apprenticeship is what persuaded Lave and Wenger to avoid the term, rather than 'rescue' it (1991, p. 29), and their theory of situated learning, broadly focused on learning as an everyday aspect of communities of practice, is instead described as legitimate peripheral participation. Because of the 'long and varied train of historically and culturally specific realizations' associated with apprenticeship (p. 31), Lave and Wenger argue that the use of the term with reference to learning theory would be metaphorical.

Apprenticeship as metaphor is found in the work of Rogoff (1995) who names it as one of three inseparable layers in sociocultural activity: in this theoretical model, apprenticeship, guided participation and participatory appropriation are planes of focus accounting for the institutional, the interpersonal and the personal, respectively (p. 141). In keeping with the notion of situated learning, the idea of apprenticeship is broadened so that it may be applied to everyday practice rather than limited to educational settings:

> This metaphor extends the idea of craft apprenticeship to include participation in any other culturally organized activity, such as other kinds of work, schooling, and family relations. The idea of apprenticeship necessarily focuses attention on the specific nature of the activity involved, as well as on its relation to practices and institutions of the community in which it occurs – economic, political, spiritual, and material. (Rogoff 1995, p. 142)

The consideration of apprenticeship-like situations in terms of everyday social practices is by no means irrelevant to instrumental teaching and learning, and indeed Nielsen, in a study set in a Danish academy of music, adopts the terms of situated learning in order to investigate circumscribed regions of the practice: specifically, 'how apprentices learn with little being taught' (1999, p. 2). Nielsen describes apprenticeship as a 'frame of inspiration' which need not be considered 'mediaeval, concrete and context-bound' (p. 232), and he uses the frame to draw attention to transparency, imitation and scaffolding as theoretical features of apprenticeship.

Of course, no study or theory can account for every aspect of instrumental teaching and learning, given the flexibility, complexity and dynamism in the practice. The same description might be made, however, of apprenticeship, and this is what makes it so apt a way of understanding instrumental teaching and learning. The features described in this paper are often variable and ambiguous, amounting to family resemblances that are likely but not guaranteed to be present in any specific case. So long as we keep the variety and ambiguity in mind, apprenticeship may provide us with valuable and meaningful access to the dimensions of music education.

Summary: Apprenticeship and Instrumental Teaching and Learning

It would seem that, given the complex nature of skills involved in the subject matter of instrumental teaching and learning, apprenticeship may offer a suitably complex way of understanding how that teaching and learning takes place. Apprenticeship has been historically associated with the fostering of musical performance skills, preceding the development of the conservatoire model.

Historical apprenticeships traditionally embraced a wide range of skills, from art to craft, and from skill to connoisseurship. A background of mixed social and trade character coincides with the notion that in music, professional and amateur have never been sharply divided; and the master-apprentice dyad remains characteristic of most instrumental teaching and learning today, whether it takes place within institutions or in other settings.

An examination of references to apprenticeship in literature focused on instrumental teaching and learning reveals some common assumptions about what it entails: these include the acquisition of experiential knowledge or skill; the use of demonstration and imitation; the master positioned as representative of the practice, with a high level of expertise; the apprenticeship as a source of identity for the learner; and the important and rather particular nature of the master-apprentice relationship.

These historical features and assumptions will presumably vary in each concrete case, and would seem to comprise a loosely related set of possibilities rather than a well-formed and specific social institution. Elements such as the affective aspects of learning and the roles that might be taken by the apprentice will vary with individuals as well as settings, though there is some evidence to remind us that the 'love of the job' is a motivation shared by 'almost all' students of music. In addition, the place of the educational institution in each individual case may overlap with and influence the traditional frameworks of apprenticeship. In spite of the variety exhibited among specific instances, apprenticeship would seem to offer researchers a set of related issues that might help to contextualize interactions with the instrumental lesson.

Epistemology: Conclusion

The epistemology of practice and the exploration of apprenticeship have been considered at some length in this chapter because they form distinct and important backdrops to our understanding of instrumental teaching and learning. In many ways the discussion has consisted in an investigation of theories of knowledge that are already implicit in the language commonly used to discuss the subject. A range of distinct vocabularies have been involved in this: musical skills and artistry are typically discussed in everyday terms like talent, sense and feeling; performance skills are taught and learned through a language of craftsmanship that is adapted to the purpose of eliciting and cultivating practical responses rather than serving an explanatory function; traditional modes of studio behaviour have been labelled in terms of the master and apprentice who characterize historical instances of apprenticeship, in music among other arts, crafts and trades.

The discussion has identified a number of assumptions lying behind these vocabularies, and in some cases challenged them. The 'folk' vocabulary used to characterize musical skill seems, under close scrutiny, to be ambiguous and vague, and its applications often seem too wide and loose to be helpful: it will be recalled that Schön refers to wisdom, talent, intuition and artistry as 'junk categories' that effectively close inquiry rather than opening it (1987, p. 13). On the other hand, the professional vocabulary employed by practitioners, whether coaching themselves through inner speech or coaching others in educational settings, might be highly specific in having a commanding rather than a theoretical function (Howard 1982, p. 35). Such language is highly sensitive to context, and cannot be fully understood without reference to its purpose, and its close relationship with demonstration (p. 73).

Finally, the assumptions behind terms associated with apprenticeship, which tend to be coined rather than explained in the literature specific to instrumental teaching and learning, have been examined in terms of historical precedents and general usage, as well as applications in music education research. Many of the features of apprenticeship have resonance with modern practice, and it seems well worth reviewing them in order to appreciate their multidimensional nature. Imitation is an important example, in that it can refer to copying, something that music students are likely to see as embarrassing and to be resisted (Nielsen 2006, p. 9, n. 6). In the context of learning the complex skills of musical performance, however, imitation, demonstration and experiential knowledge are closely entwined, and the usefulness and perhaps indispensability of imitation depends on what is being imitated. Conceiving of the learning situation as a social practice, too, supports the interpretation of imitation as a far broader activity, that depends on the learner's current and potential understanding, and may involve participation in collaborative behaviour.

Similarly, the presence of power relations in the apprenticeship setting is a feature exhibiting several dimensions. It is often associated with a highly commanding position occupied by the master. Thus the master-teacher described by Manturzewska (1990) seems to take command of almost every aspect of the student's life – 'personality, aesthetic attitudes, life philosophy, professional standards and attitudes' (p. 135) – while in the lesson behaviour described by Uszler the master 'demonstrates, directs, comments, and inspires' (1992, p. 584). Not all of these characteristics sit comfortably with the aims and learning outcomes espoused by the modern university. Even less palatable is the power abuse implied in Sosniak's account of an American master-teacher, whose student found him an impossible and intimidating taskmaster (1985b, p. 421). In contrast, however, it has been argued that the master's authority can be an invaluable resource for teaching and there is evidence suggesting that students actively seek and maintain it (Nerland and Hanken 2002, p. 172).

Authority as sought by students must be related to the position of the master as representative of the professional discipline; it touches on the affective aspects of learning, given that an emotional investment is likely to be made by the musical apprentice, and it serves to emphasize the perceived importance of a high level of expertise, and the ability to demonstrate it. The issue is complex, but in spite of a rich and ambiguous texture, or perhaps because of it, authority, like apprenticeship itself, would seem to provide a meaningful sense of context for instrumental teaching and learning as a rich and complex practice.

The epistemology discussed in this chapter has represented the skills of musical performance as a regime of competence, complemented by apprenticeship as a way of understanding how that regime may be entered. The construction of the conceptual framework for this study continues in the next two chapters, which are focused more specifically on the research literature related to instrumental teaching and learning.

Chapter 3
The Instrumental Lesson

Chapters 3 and 4 offer a sketch of research focused on studio-based instrumental teaching and learning, with particular reference first to what actually happens in individual lessons, and second to how lesson interactions are framed. A broad summary of both chapters will appear at the end of Chapter 4.

The research focused on instrumental teaching and learning has been accumulated essentially over the last generation, giving it a brief history compared with its subject. It has been remarked that instrumental teaching and learning is not always well connected to research (Rostvall and West 2003, p. 224), nor to scientific knowledge (Callaghan 1998, p. 37), theory (Lindström et al. 2003, p. 39) or philosophy (Bowman 2005). It might also be remarked that instrumental teaching is an unregulated profession compared with those larger areas of education that are characterized by formal teacher training. Practitioners – musicians who have had substantive experience with instrumental teaching at an advanced level, and many who may have engaged at a more modest level – know however that what happens in an individual lesson can be uniquely complex, rich, sophisticated and exciting, the source of inspiration, identity and practical support at the centre of many musical lives.

The variety among teachers' approaches to instrumental lessons appears to be enormous, depending not just on the differences among individual participants but on the historical traditions and current practices associated with their specialist instruments. In addition, as remarked in Chapter 1, studio-based instrumental lessons typically take place on a one-to-one basis, while tutors are typically engaged on a part-time basis, rarely sharing a background in formal teacher training. Instrumental teaching and learning therefore is not only unique in its subject matter and conduct: it is normally undertaken by individual teachers and students in a setting that is largely isolated both from other practitioners and from researchers.

The problem of characterizing instrumental teaching and learning is correspondingly large, and compounded by the nonverbal nature of the artistry and skills involved. Researchers who seek to explore what happens in instrumental lessons have been incrementally piecing together information, insights and sidelights, and tentatively developing a representation of the subject. There is a tendency for some studies to investigate isolated components of instrumental teaching and learning in what Jørgensen (2009) has called 'microstudies': these, he argues, have often led to interesting results in the description of particular situations or states of affairs, but in the context of institutional policy he asserts that relational studies, drawing connections among settings and issues, are likely to be more illuminating (p. 190). Even within microstudies, undertaken perhaps with the aim of developing deeper understanding rather than informing policy-making, subjects considered out of their natural context need to be contextualized again to become meaningful. Welch encourages researchers to '[take] account of a multifaceted reality, even if the research's prime focus may be on one particular aspect of that reality' (Welch 2007, p. 23). He explains further:

> In an educational setting, the 'reality' is likely to embrace, for example, the individual biographies and neuropsychobiological dispositions of the participants …, the nature of the pedagogical process, the actual/intended musical behaviours, as well as the contexts for learning, including various historical and socio-cultural perspectives. Reality will also encompass the interrelationships between the constituent elements. (Welch 2007, p. 23)

In the sketch that follows, an effort is made to respect the complexity of the subject and the tentative nature of knowledge about it. Research studies and their findings are characterized as inseparable from their aims and methods, along with their underlying assumptions and connections, drawn from or connected to other fields of education or other related disciplines. Far from accumulating established facts to build a consolidated model of the subject, research into instrumental teaching and learning is gradually revealing its rich, fluid, exciting possibilities.

***

In 2005 Triatafyllaki called for more research into instrumental teaching, citing various authors who have claimed that there is too little investigation and understanding of what takes place in and around individual lessons in musical performance. In our own research into the conduct of instrumental and vocal lessons at South England University we described the individual lesson as something of a 'secret garden' compared with the scrutiny given to classroom behaviour in schools (Young et al. 2003, p. 144; Burwell 2005, p. 200), while Mills in her book, *Instrumental Teaching*, described work by the same team as one of the 'rare examples of research that has been carried out directly by performer-teachers' (Mills 2007, p. 76).

There is a good deal of research work related to instrumental teaching and learning, however, flourishing particularly in recent years, even if the development of a coherent core of knowledge remains a work in progress. In very broad terms the history of research into instrumental teaching runs parallel to the evolution of research paradigms as characterized, for example, by Denzin and Lincoln (2005): the approaches taken in early studies tend to rely on quantitative methods and on evaluation, and although these have been by no means discarded, there has been a gradually increasing tendency to employ qualitative approaches emphasizing description, interpretation and contextualization, resulting perhaps in more richly textured accounts of the areas studied.

This discussion of the literature extends across the same broad spectrum of approaches. The research contributions considered here are divided among three broad categories, according to their focal points of interest: studies focused on the distinction between modelling and verbal behaviour; studies focused on verbal behaviour, including teaching strategies and vocabulary; and studies focused on the personal, interpersonal and social attributes of participants.

In the first of these sections research studies are further divided according to the methodological approach taken: experimental, observational and questionnaire studies. The emphasis on methodology in this section is made because it is argued that, particularly in early work, the theoretical assumptions and associated research tools in some of these studies has a tangible effect on the findings and their potential application. Although methodology is no less significant in later sections, recurring issues are noted without being laboured further. The theme of methodologies and their relationship with the subjects studied is nevertheless carried through the literature reviews, and is discussed at greater length elsewhere (Burwell 2012).

Studies Distinguishing Modelling from Verbal Behaviour

Experimental Studies

An early landmark in research into instrumental teaching and learning is the study represented in Rosenthal's paper, 'The relative effects of guided model, model only, guide only, and practice only treatments on the accuracy of advanced instrumentalists' musical performance' (1984). The paper is cited in literature reviews by Dickey (1992), Hallam (1997) and Kennell (1992; 2002), and citations recur in papers by various other researchers close to the subject (Woody 1999; 2000; 2003; 2006b; Young et al. 2003; Highben and Palmer 2004; Henniger, Flowers and Councill 2006; Gaunt 2008; 2009; Duke et al. 2009; Triantafyllaki 2010). It is worth exploring this study in some detail, for several reasons: its frequent citation suggests that it has been an influential paper; it can usefully be regarded as a good representative of early, quantitative approaches to the subject; and it raises several issues that recur in the literature focused on modelling behaviour in instrumental lessons.

Because Rosenthal's aim in the 1984 paper was to evaluate the potential roles of modelling in student learning, this component was extracted from the natural setting of instrumental lessons, and studied in isolation. The subjects for the study were 44 'graduate and upper level undergraduate' students enrolled in music or music education programmes at an American college. The method involved asking each participant to prepare a performance of a set piece in a ten minute period, and each was randomly assigned one of four possible conditions for the preparation. Some participants were left to practise the piece unassisted, for ten minutes; the others were given an audio recording for guidance, and then allowed just three minutes to practise. The audio recordings might contain the piece performed three times; or a verbal guide to mastering the piece, illustrated by performance; or the verbal guide, without any performance at all. The salient finding was that those who were assisted by the recording of the piece without any verbal guidance were most accurate in their own subsequent performances, in terms of rhythm, tempo, notation, dynamics, articulation and phrasing. Those who had verbal guidance without any performance model were the least accurate in performance.

These rather striking findings suggest that modelling alone may be the most effective tool for helping instrumental students to achieve accuracy, while talk alone may be the least effective. It is clear that the experiment has been undertaken with scientific precision and care, and the results would seem to have potency in any debate about the relative merits of verbal and performance behaviour in instrumental teaching and learning. The results however should be considered with some caution, before either teachers or researchers attempt to apply them in other contexts. Fortunately, the clarity and integrity of the paper make it possible and worthwhile for readers to examine it closely and critically.

It may be noted, for example, that at this early stage in the development of research literature focused on instrumental teaching and learning, the premises of the study are drawn largely from research focused on classroom teaching. The research studies that most resemble Rosenthal's own are investigations into teacher training undertaken during the 1970s, which suggest that student teachers benefit from being able to observe real or simulated classroom behaviour (Rosenthal 1984, p. 266). Transplanting the broad ideas of this research into the context of instrumental teaching is not unreasonable, but doing so has some significant implications for the nature of the study. One significant difference lies in the characteristics of participants: in both settings these are students in Higher Education, but unlike trainee school teachers, the participants in Rosenthal's study have already achieved an advanced level of expertise in the skill being assessed; and that skill – of learning to perform instrumental music accurately – is fundamentally different in nature to managing a classroom.

In addition, too, the nature of the modelling employed is distinct in each context, with Rosenthal taking a more limited view of what modelling might entail. In the studies addressing classroom management, the experimental groups were invited to observe real or simulated instances of the skills they were to acquire. Their attention might be directed toward certain attributes of those models (p. 266), but implicit in such an exercise would be the opportunity for students to notice various other attributes as well, and to interpret the models for themselves. In Rosenthal's study, the exercise required of participants is more narrowly conceived, as they are effectively asked to replicate a performance of a piece of music. It might be argued that phrasing – alone among the attributes assessed – allows participants some scope for interpretation, particularly as the piece is marked *Adagio espressivo* (p. 268); but phrasing is assessed, here, in terms of accuracy alone, and this shows how limited that scope is taken to be.

The decision to assess musical performance in terms of accuracy alone makes this a slightly artificial exercise, and indeed other issues of authenticity in the experiment might usefully be explored. Presumably the participants must have found this a novel experience in several ways. All of them were woodwind or brass players, for example, but to ensure that all were examined under similar conditions – that no particular student had any personal advantage in the exercise – the performance illustrations were recorded on solo violin. Aside from this, it seems unlikely that many of the students will have been in the habit of preparing an unseen piece for performance assessment, in just ten minutes, with or without the assistance of an audio recording. The modelling experience for students of the classical tradition, too, would not normally be limited to listening and thinking. The procedure for students in the experimental groups was to listen to the whole of the audio tape, which might incorporate appropriate pauses for reflection or mental rehearsal, before beginning to practice the piece. In contrast, a teacher's model in an 'authentic' lesson could allow the student the opportunity to respond and participate during the modelling process; it would also offer the student the opportunity to see another performer engaging with the piece, thus adding another dimension to the model. Finally, it seems likely that verbal guidance in a real lesson, with or without performed illustrations, would be responsive in nature as the teacher coached an individual rather than delivering preconceived instruction.

Many of these little compromises in authenticity have been made because of the priority given to establishing scientific rigour. The date of publication places Rosenthal's study early in the 'quiet methodological revolution' that according to Denzin and Lincoln has occurred over the last generation (2005, p. ix). Prior to this, the prestige of the natural sciences was such that its methodology was applied in the humanities, conceiving of 'the social sciences as natural sciences, to be based on objective quantifiable data' (Kvale 1996, p. 11). Rosenthal is clearly aware that modelling is potentially a rich and complex activity, when she characterizes its benefits in helping to 'illustrate various stylistic features, the flow of phrases, tempo, and interpretation of rhythms'. With the exception of tempo, however, these benefits are ineffable features of music, difficult to define or articulate, and harder to measure in a reliable way. Implicitly committed to measurement and evaluation, Rosenthal therefore limits the exercise to the assessment of variables that can be reliably quantified, with a creditable level of agreement between two assessors of 0.87 (p. 269).

The methodological difficulties with authenticity in experimental research are effectively summarized by Bronfenbrenner:

> The emphasis on rigor has led to experiments that are elegantly designed but often limited in scope. This limitation derives from the fact that many of these experiments involve situations that are unfamiliar, artificial, and short-lived and that call for unusual settings that are difficult to generalize to other settings. From this perspective, it can be said that much of contemporary developmental psychology [for example] is *the science of the strange behavior of children in*

strange situations with strange adults for the briefest possible periods of time.
(Bronfenbrenner 1979, pp. 18–19; italics original)

One further feature of Rosenthal's study is worth noting here, though it may not be directly related to methodological issues. This is the nature of the verbal instruction made available to two of the experimental groups. The language employed is almost entirely technical in nature, and it would be difficult to argue that it employs an expressive vocabulary. This is perhaps in keeping with the emphasis on measurable features of the piece; the most direct reference to ineffable features comes at the outset, with the following remark:

> One of the first things to keep in mind while playing this selection is the marking *dolce*, which means 'sweetly and softly'. This is also marked *adagio expressivo* [sic] and should be played expressively ... (Rosenthal 1984, p. 270)

Aside from this very limited foray into expressive language, the verbal instruction employs no imagery, no emotional vocabulary and few adjectives. Rosenthal is clearly more interested, here, in exploring modelling than in verbal behaviour, but the teacher's vocabulary is itself an important and recurring issue in music education research and will surface again in this review of the literature.

Of course, the methodological revolution reported by Denzin and Lincoln has not been a tidy one, and there has been no neat switch from quantitative to qualitative approaches in music education research. Since the publication of Rosenthal's 1984 paper, several authors have made similar experiments comparing the effectiveness of modelling and verbal instruction, with a commitment to quantifying the data and evaluating the results (Kendall 1988; Dickey 1991; Woody 1999; 2006a). Other experimental studies have evaluated the use of modelling without necessarily comparing that to verbal instruction. Henley (2001) and Hewitt (2001) both found that high school wind band players performed more accurately if they were assisted by an aural model. Hewitt (2002) however found that junior high school band players were not significantly assisted by modelling, in developing their self-evaluation skills; while May (2003) found that the ability to imitate an aural recording was less significant than the ability to self-evaluate, in determining the success of undergraduate players' improvisation skills.

All of these studies attempt to evaluate modelling as an independent variable, and like the Rosenthal study, all entail some compromises in authenticity by asking participants to undertake tasks that must lie outside their normal experience in some ways. This must also be true for two further studies, which have attempted to evaluate the more ineffable ability to perform expressively, assisted by aural models. Woody (2003) gave a sample of 25 university students the interesting task of imitating performances of two pieces of music using six different recordings that were more or less idiomatic, in an effort to identify underlying 'rules of expressivity' (p. 60). The students were also asked to make line drawings of the phrase contours that they were attempting to produce in their imitations. The authenticity of his study is limited by the fact that the pieces of music were only two bars long, and performances were undertaken on an electric keyboard so that their features could be accurately measured. With that reservation, several of the findings are interesting: the recording that proved most difficult to imitate was also the most unidiomatic, in that it included a 'confounding tempo-dynamics conflict' (p. 56); a 'high-achievement group' within the sample showed superior imitative skills (p. 59); and there was a clear relationship between successful performances and the students' line drawings, suggesting that they had explicit goals in mind (p. 60).

In a more elaborate experiment, Lisboa et al. (2005) asked five conservatoire students and one professional musician to prepare a 'perceptually indistinguishable copy' of a recording made by Heifetz, of a piece of unaccompanied Bach (p. 82). The authors admit that the use of imitation in this rather strange exercise was 'somewhat exaggerated' (p. 104), but it should also be admitted that the procedure of making an exact copy of a master's performance very much resembles aspects of the cello lessons given by Casals to Greenhouse, as discussed in Chapter 2 (Schön 1987; Delbanco 1985). In the Heifetz experiment none of the participants succeeded entirely, but all were able to imitate certain features of the model performance and to adopt influences of the model into their personal interpretations of the set piece (Lisboa et al. 2005, p. 95, p. 97).

Among the studies discussed above, the later experiments show some tendency to use more refined and complex methods, perhaps incorporating a more refined and complex conception of the subject matter being researched. All necessarily focus on a limited number of components of instrumental teaching and learning, and this in turn limits their potential to capture the 'multifaceted reality' of the subject as a whole. There is however a complementary stream of research studies which attempt to characterize broader issues related to modelling, and which increasingly employ aspects of qualitative methodologies to do so.

Observational Studies

The discussion above addresses experimental studies in instrumental teaching and learning, undertaken since the publication of Rosenthal's paper in 1984. Lesson observations have also been used to collect data for study, throughout the same period, with Kostka's observational account of piano lessons published in the same year as Rosenthal's experimental study. Perhaps the most important difference between experimental and observational studies lies in the return to the natural setting of the instrumental lesson, and this has implications for the methods used. The method employed is not synonymous with the methodology behind it, however, and the use of observation does not imply that the approach is necessarily anti-quantitative (Lincoln and Guba 1985, p. 198): the observational studies to be discussed here make more or less use of quantification, according to the aims and nature of each project. Even so, the use of observation makes a potentially richer range of data available to the researcher, particularly when it is triangulated by the use of multiple methods typical of qualitative research design (Denzin and Lincoln 2005, p. 5).

The avowed aim of Kostka's study is to ascertain the 'natural rates' of various lesson behaviours, including student and teacher performance and talk (Kostka 1984, p. 114). She characterizes the project as descriptive in nature (p. 115), but also employs a 15-point coding schedule for live observations, supported by audio recordings through which reliability can be tested. As with Rosenthal's paper, this early study draws on classroom research for its premises, asserting that there has been, to date, 'virtually no' research into the conduct of private piano lessons (p. 114). Kostka offers some useful findings, noting that lesson behaviour in her sample is dominated, in terms of time spent, by student performance (56.57 per cent) followed by teacher talk (42.24 per cent). In contrast to the expectations associated with research into classroom behaviour, it seems that individual lessons are characterized by a remarkably high level of student attentiveness, even though the rate of verbal approvals offered by the teacher, compared to disapprovals, is far lower than the rate recommended for classrooms (p. 120). Taking her cue nevertheless from classroom research, Kostka suggests that teachers should consider reducing the time spent on verbal instruction, in favour of more performance modelling, during which there is 'surprisingly little' student inattentiveness (p. 61).

The time spent on various lesson behaviours is measured again by Colprit (2000), in observations of Suzuki violin lessons given to groups of children aged 5–17. The proportions here are slightly different, with 45 per cent spent on teacher talk, 41 per cent on student performance, and 20 per cent on teacher performance; the higher proportion of teacher demonstration is presumably due to the emphasis on modelling in the Suzuki method (Gardner 1983, p. 377). Colprit also describes the behavioural episodes as being 'frequent and brief' (p. 215), with more than twice as many teacher approvals as disapprovals. This exceeds the rate of approvals noted by Kostka, whose study however included adults, and who found that adult students were less likely than children to be given teacher approvals (Kostka 1984, p. 115).

The background of classroom research seems to have left some observers with concerns about the rate of teacher approvals and disapprovals, and studies of group tuition (Yarbrough and Price 1989) and private piano lessons (Speer 1994) have suggested that the rate of teacher disapprovals actually increases with the teacher's experience. Siebenaler's 1997 study of individual piano lessons begins to explore the issue in the light of other teacher and student behaviours, finding complex interrelationships among these and lesson effectiveness. Even in 1997, Siebenaler remarks that there is little previous research in his chosen area of study, and his literature review depends very much on generic research into education and psychology, as well as studies of rehearsals and group tuition in music.

The complexity of Siebenaler's study is impressive, and although he employs a rigorous coding system to quantify the behaviour found in the lesson segments observed, this method is triangulated by asking experts to evaluate the teaching effectiveness of each, independently. The student participants were divided into two groups aged 7–13 and over 24, so that the behaviour for child and adult lessons could be compared (p. 7), and this suggests that the findings will be of particular relevance to the consideration of instrumental teaching and learning in Higher Education, though the level of expertise seems to be significantly lower among Siebenaler's participants, who had been learning the piano for an average of less than five years (p. 17).

Siebenaler analyzed lesson segments of 8–12 minutes from a total of 78 lessons, given by 13 different piano teachers. The decision to analyze segments rather than whole lessons was no doubt driven by the need to manage the large volume of data generated: the number of lessons observed could have been reduced, of course, but this would have undermined the reliability of the statistics, and there is a clear commitment here to a quantification of data sufficient to support generalization. For the same reason, lesson behaviours were coded to identify the frequency, duration and sequence of various activities. The teacher behaviours include clap/sing, play and play/talk; general or specific directives, questions and 'music talk'; and feedback, divided between approvals and disapprovals, which might be general or specific, correct or mistaken. In contrast to previous studies, student behaviour was also coded, to identify a selection of the same behaviours (pp. 8–9).

It was found that in the lessons of adults there was more talk from both teacher and student, than in the lessons of children. Compared with children, adult students asked more questions, though their teachers asked fewer, with more play/talk, and less clap/sing behaviour. On average over all of the observed segments, '[t]eachers talked about the music more frequently when the playing was going well' (p. 17).

While such details are certainly interesting, more thought-provoking results were found when the independent evaluation of teaching effectiveness was brought into play. The desire to evaluate teaching success is consistent with many of the research studies previously discussed, but Siebenaler found that without being given his coded criteria for assessing the lesson segments, five expert judges varied considerably in their conclusions. There was a good level of agreement among them in identifying the teaching that was least effective, but not about which was most effective. Setting that problem aside, it was found that high levels of teaching effectiveness tended to coincide with more incidents of teacher performance, verbal instruction and feedback, while teacher-student interactions, as in the Suzuki classes observed by Colprit (2000), were frequent and brief.

Two little reservations about the study might be suggested. In explaining his method Siebenaler specifies that the independent judges were asked to evaluate *teacher* effectiveness (p. 10), and although this is later elided with *lesson* effectiveness, in the discussion of the findings (p. 14, p. 16), this seems to have led to a focus on teacher behaviour – on what the teacher is doing in each excerpt – rather than what the student might be doing or learning. The most effective teaching appeared to coincide with excerpts in which the teacher is highly active and the student largely 'inactive', but this might be an accident due to the expert evaluators having their attention directed toward the teacher rather than the student. This suggestion would seem to be supported by Duke and Prickett (1987) who asked 143 non-music education majors to evaluate a filmed excerpt of a violin lesson, and who found statistically significant differences among evaluations when the observers were asked to focus on the teacher, the student or both (p. 27).

The second reservation is that in coding lesson behaviours, Siebenaler marks as 'inactive' any point where the participant is not engaged in one of the coded behaviours sought: it is not acknowledged, for example, that the 'inactive' participant might be listening, thinking, reading or learning. It is not acknowledged, either, that the effectiveness of the lesson, or part of it, might be developed or felt beyond each 8–12 minute segment that was observed. The study is limited in what it can reliably measure, but in teaching and learning there must be a good deal that escapes any measuring tool.

In a study by Rostvall and West (2003) quantitative methods are largely eschewed in a descriptive account of individual instrumental lessons in four Swedish municipal schools. Once again lamenting the lack of shared knowledge about the interaction of teacher and student, the authors describe instrumental lessons as 'a hidden and almost secret activity' (p. 214); the processes involved might be difficult to articulate, and might involve personality, talent or tacit knowledge, but this difficulty has been used to stall the development of the profession (pp. 215–16). Rostvall and West's study involves a relatively small number of lessons (n = 11), and although they have been videotaped and coded according to lesson behaviour, description and interpretation are more salient in the published paper than statistical analysis (p. 216). The findings are critical of a music-school system ill supported by professional language, and the authors report little use of teacher demonstration, expressive vocabulary and interpersonal skills.

A more freely interpretative approach is adopted by Davidson (1989) in a fascinating account of a single lesson on the yang ch'in, an instrument akin to the dulcimer, in China in 1986. A musician and psychologist, Davidson attempts to measure nothing, but he does articulate different attitudes to modelling and verbal instruction found in America and in China, and offers a close description and interpretation of the 'live' lesson he observed. According to Davidson, American musicians 'prefer to discuss music in terms of its primitives, its basic elements: pitches, rhythmic shapes, timbres, and motives. Above all, we prefer to speak about its formal structures and physical properties in a context of hierarchical structures and organizational schemes' (Davidson 1989, p. 96). This remark would seem to be supported by the nature of verbal instruction offered to American students by Rosenthal (1984), as previously discussed. Because these features are evidently part of his own experience, Davidson is surprised by the degree to which the Chinese lesson is conducted from memory rather than using music notation, by the amount of performance modelling, and by the expressive and metaphorical nature of the vocabulary used. Davidson uses description to convey a vicarious experience to the reader, of a lesson focused on the ineffable:

Turning his attention to the middle of the piece, [the teacher] played: He started slowly, in the mood of the opening, then began speeding up the tempo little by little in that mysterious way I am convinced only the Chinese know, the way I have heard only the Chinese play – an imperceptible, carefully paced accelerando. He made slight ornamental slides, creating the illusion of connecting the lower notes to the upper notes, suggesting a greater tonal space than the individual notes and intervals would suggest.

He asked his student to play that section. She started, and while she played, he spoke of storms, of winds and storms in the trees. 'Through it all, the tree stands strong,' he said. The performance took on new dimensions as the student used her teacher's metaphors to shape the musical energy and flow. He approved. (Davidson 1989, p. 88)

The modelling described by Davidson is prepared and accompanied by teacher talk, and even if this is so far removed from his own experience that he concludes that 'the entire lesson was carried out in performance' (p. 92) the procedure bears a clear resemblance to the pointed demonstrations discussed by his compatriot Howard, who explains the function of teacher talk in 'cueing a salience' (Howard 1982, p. 99). Howard also explores the relationships among talk, demonstration and gesture (p. 59) which Davidson, in describing the yang ch'in lesson, labels an 'inspired nonverbal metaphor' (p. 93). Davidson's descriptive method would seem to be appropriate to the phenomena he wished to study: the teaching and learning of '[a] wide variety of types of knowledge' through modelling, and which 'ultimately cannot take place in any other way' (p. 97).

A study by Benson and Fung (2005) complements Davidson's research in some ways, reviewing the issues he raises by employing some quantitative tools in their observations. Their study compares the use of verbal instruction and modelling, in recorded segments of piano lessons given to Chinese and American children. In their sample of 16 lessons given by eight teachers, the Chinese teachers use modelling and metaphor more, while the American lessons include more discussion and teacher questions. The use of various media to convey musical information – singing, gestures or playing along – is described as 'multiple modelling' (p. 69), which occurs more in the Chinese than in the American lessons observed.

Questionnaire Studies

Parallel to the experimental and observational research into modelling in instrumental teaching and learning is a small number of studies employing questionnaires, aimed at exploring the views of teachers and students. Once again these studies typically report a lack of previous work of the kind, in this area of study (Woody 2000, p. 16; Lindström et al. 2003, pp. 22–3, p. 26; Laukka 2004, p. 46). Hultberg warmly recommends the consideration of participants' views in a kind of collaboration between researchers and practitioners, arguing that practitioners 'collect data in the naturalistic context of their own lessons' and that they in turn 'might certainly benefit from independent researchers' systematic exploration and analysis in applied research, directly aimed at developing the area studied' (Hultberg 2005, p. 212).

Participants' views have been particularly relevant to researchers attempting to characterize the teaching and learning of the more ineffable features of music, such as musical expression. In previous research at South England University 21 undergraduate students completed a loosely structured questionnaire, asking them to explain a range of terms relevant to their studies in instrumental and vocal performance (Burwell 2003b). The findings suggested that although students are able to discuss technical areas of study with confidence and clarity, there is some confusion in attempting to characterize interpretation. In accounting for this aspect of musicianship there is a tendency to emphasize personal differences among performers, and an apparent lack of confidence that interpretation can be taught and learned, or even improved. The difficulty in articulating ideas about interpretation is reflected in quotes from professional artists as wide-ranging as Casals, Liszt, Furtwängler, Galway and Heifetz (pp. 7–9).

Lindström et al. (2003) administered a far more extensive questionnaire, among 135 conservatory students in England, Italy and Sweden, in order to explore their understanding of a range of issues related to musical expression. There was a strong agreement that 'expressivity' is important, but – as with the SEU study – a tendency to define it in rather vague terms such as 'playing with feeling' (p. 38). In terms of teaching and learning, the use of metaphor was the preferred tool, followed by 'felt emotion' and then 'aural modelling' (p. 36); among students who had experienced all three in their lessons, this ranking was even more distinct. On average the students estimated that 50 per cent of their lesson time was devoted to expressivity, though the researchers remark that this high proportion rather contradicts 'previously claimed views' (p. 38); they also suggest that the difficulty in discussing expressivity reflects a lack of theoretical instruction which could bring about a 'vast improvement [in] commonsense teaching' (p. 39). It should be recalled however that there is no very substantial body of research-based knowledge in this specialist area, to support the 'previously claimed views', nor to support the notion that 'commonsense teaching' is either common, or commonly understood.

In a similar study, Woody asked 46 American college students to complete an interview questionnaire about their experience as students, and their intentions as teachers, when it comes to addressing musical expression. Almost half reported that they had not become concerned with this issue 'until they were well into high school or even their first year of college' (Woody 2000, p. 17). Consistent with the study by Lindström et al. discussed above, a majority of 61 per cent reported that their individual teachers used verbal instruction more than modelling, to teach expressivity (p. 18). However, 54 per cent of the students envisaged using modelling when they themselves taught. In the light of Davidson's assertion that American musicians prefer to employ technical language in their lessons, discussed above, it is interesting that only a few recommended 'concrete musically based instruction' with 'technical terms rather than adjectives': most were accustomed to 'feeling-oriented terminology' (p. 21).

It is interesting too that Laukka (2004), exploring the views of teachers rather than students, found that their preferred tool for teaching expressivity is modelling, followed by language emphasizing felt emotion, and the use of metaphor. Laukka's questionnaire was adapted from Lindström et al. (2003) and administered to 51 teachers in five conservatoires, in Sweden and England. Like many of the students mentioned above, teachers tended to define expressivity in terms of emotion (59 per cent), though 31 per cent defined it in terms of 'the music itself' and 10 per cent emphasized its personal, unique aspects (p. 48). They distinguished between expression and interpretation (p. 49) and although there was no strong agreement on the subject, felt that the ability to express emotion through music is both innate and learned (p. 50). In contrast to the student experience reported by Woody, these teachers thought that expressive abilities should be taught at an early stage of studying an instrument, though they felt that students tend to underestimate its importance (p. 51). Their estimate of the time spent teaching expressivity in lessons was 46 per cent, rather closely matching the proportion reported in the student questionnaire administered by Lindström et al.

Summary and Reflections

Research focused on studio-based instrumental learning has only recently begun to flourish. It has been much supported by premises taken from research focused more generally on education (Rosenthal 1984; Kostka 1984; Yarbrough and Price 1989; Speer 1994; Siebenaler 1997) or, within the subject of music, research into group tuition and ensemble behaviour (Siebenaler 1997; Colprit 2000; Henley 2001; Hewitt 2001; 2002), but the development of its own character has at least partly been a process of recognizing and testing the assumptions carried over from those group settings.

There is evidence to suggest that modelling can be useful in instrumental lessons, though the assumption that this is needed to secure student attentiveness may not be imperative in the setting of individual lessons, where levels of attentiveness are already high (Kostka 1984). The optimum proportion of time taken by teacher talk, and the rates of teacher approvals and disapprovals expected in a classroom, may also need to be reconsidered in the context of instrumental lessons (Kostka 1984; Colprit 2000; Siebenaler 1997). Indeed, the expectations regarding what constitutes effective teaching may need to be reviewed in this context, since this is an issue on which expert judges cannot always agree (Siebenaler 1997).

There is evidence to suggest that instrumental students are able to respond effectively to modelled performances, and that these can help them to achieve accuracy (Henley 2001; Hewitt 2001), though perhaps not in developing self-evaluation or improvising skills (Hewitt 2002; May 2003). It has been found that in some cases, high-achieving students have good imitative skills, though they are likely to have explicit goals in mind, and have more difficulty in copying unidiomatic performances (Woody 2003). Some advanced musicians have proved able to incorporate expressive features of a model performance, deliberately, into their own interpretations (Lisboa et al. 2005).

Clearly, the use of modelling in instrumental lessons has been found to be important, to be related to the effectiveness of the teaching and learning process, and to vary with characteristics of the participants, including their age and culture. Researchers have already provided some information about whether modelling is used, to what extent, and to what end, and participants' views on its use have been ascertained in some settings.

While all of these issues remain to be explored more fully, there are gaps in the literature where research has barely begun. These include the interactive aspects of instrumental lessons. Studies to date have identified features of participant behaviour, but there is a range of behaviours that cannot be easily observed and which have therefore hardly been addressed by researchers. What either teacher or student is doing while the other is performing, for example, has been little explored. In addition, there has been no substantial exploration of the role played by teacher performance in lessons: how modelling functions, and how both teacher and student are implicated in the process.

Although these and no doubt other gaps remain, a growing body of careful research work is gradually leading to an increasingly coherent picture of the roles taken by modelling in instrumental lessons. Consistent with the evolution of the qualitative research paradigm, and of confidence in its use, this process is leading not toward an elegantly simple scientific theory, but toward a more richly textured understanding of the subject.

Studies Focused on Verbal Behaviour

Some of the recurring issues evident in research focused on modelling in instrumental teaching and learning have their equivalent in the research to be discussed here, though the focus now lies largely on verbal behaviour in lessons. Particularly from the early days, there is a body of research literature which draws its premises from classroom research, applying and testing some of the assumptions taken from the generic field of education. Efforts have also been made to discover what lesson participants say to each other, to analyze that and to quantify or characterize it. Studies focused on verbal behaviour have often highlighted the difficult issue of articulating and expressing the ineffable aspects of music and of instrumental teaching and learning. In all, a picture of increasing refinement and complexity begins to emerge, and in some studies connections are made with contemporary theories of social psychology, adding a further dimension to the shared understanding of instrumental teaching and learning.

Verbal Strategies: Systematic Observations

An early example of music education research focused on verbal behaviour is that by Marchand (1975) who attempts to evaluate the use of 'discovery' and 'expository' teaching approaches in instrumental lessons. Although the author does not explain the advent of these terms of inquiry, they have been traced in generic education research to Bruner in 1960 (Entwistle 1988, p. 228). Marchand's own explanation of them is as follows:

> Discovery treatment strategies were distinguished by attempts to produce intrinsic learning motivation in subjects, self-initiated problem solving, and subject assessment of achievement. Expository treatment strategies were distinguished by authoritarian teacher behaviours in which subjects were told of the task, provided the content, drilled on the task, and subsequently assessed by the teacher. (Marchand 1975, p. 16)

After an experiment involving 89 non-music majors in an American college, however, Marchand reports no discernable difference in the success of either type of strategy; he reports that students with more expertise responded best to 'straightforward, lecture-type instruction', as represented by the expository approach, though he suggests that all students in his sample seemed to enjoy the discovery approach more (p. 22).

A contemporary study by Verrastro (1975) addresses music teacher training in terms of the construct of verbal behaviour analysis, which dominated classroom research in America in the 1970s (Delamont and Hamilton 1986, p. 27). This involves systematically coding verbal behaviour as being either teacher- or learner-centred, which Verrastro explains:

> A learner-oriented climate is one in which the predominance of verbal behaviour is supportive, acceptant, and problem-structuring. A self-oriented climate is one in which the major portion of teacher statements are directive, reproving, or teacher self-supportive. (Verrastro 1975, p. 173)

The learner-oriented climate is held to be more conducive to learning; Verrastro finds that student teachers are not predisposed to use the verbal strategies required for this, though they can be taught to do so.

Although he does not name his sources, Petters (1976) seems to have the same construct in mind when he investigates the effects of participating in decision-making, on the ability of high school orchestra students to perceive aspects of musical expression and to perform expressively; in this case, decision-making proves to be of no statistically significant benefit, with some participants expressing a reluctance to discuss the music they were performing (p. 186). Yarbrough and Price, similarly, code and analyze behaviour in rehearsal situations, led by teachers and student teachers. They espouse the use of 'complete and correct teaching cycles' (Yarbrough and Price 1989, p. 185) in which the teacher presents a task, the student responds, and the teacher provides reinforcement; they seek these sequences in 64 rehearsals, and calculate the proportion of time spent on them. The authors regretfully find that there is more time spent on 'incorrect' cycles (p. 183); they also note a large proportion of rehearsal time devoted to student performance, a high number of interruptions of those performances, and a high number of disapprovals from more experienced teachers, which Yarbrough and Price find 'particularly disturbing' (p. 184). In a similar use of systematic observation, Speer confirms these findings in the context of individual piano lessons, which however feature a higher number of teacher approvals (Speer 1994, p. 23).

Even if the authors of these studies are surprised and sometimes disappointed at their own findings, the conscientious conduct and presentation of their work means that those findings can begin to distinguish features peculiar to instrumental teaching and learning, providing signposts that might eventually find their place in a coherent map of this specialist area of education. Whatever the nature of classroom teaching and learning, it seems that instrumental lessons are likely to exhibit their own patterns concerning the amount and nature of verbal instruction, the roles taken by teacher and student, and – as previously discussed with reference to studies focused on modelling – the use of disapprovals.

In considering these studies based on systematic observation, however, it should also be noted that the coding of preconceived verbal behaviours means that other features are missed. This is hardly a problem in itself, since any method of observation and analysis must focus on certain features and miss others. The features missed, however, are potentially more relevant to the peculiar nature of musical performance. According to McIntyre and MacLeod, '[t]he issue is not one of whether information is neglected, but rather one of how it is determined what information will be neglected' (1986, p. 12). Kennell (1992) argues that the tendency for researchers to rely on experimental tools familiar from classroom research means that 'we have framed our research questions to fit our evaluation tools' rather than attempting to theorize instrumental teaching as 'a multidimensional acoustic phenomenon involving complex and invisible human cognitive processing' (p. 5). His own response, mentioned in Chapter 2, is to review and adapt aspects of scaffolding theory to account for aspects of lesson interactions (1992; 1997; 2002).

Verbal Strategies: Observations at SEU

Previous research in the Music Department of SEU has largely been focused on the verbal strategies employed by a range of instrumental teachers, which have been explored in various ways. In an early study, Young, Burwell and Pickup (2003) investigated the verbal dialogue of 27 lessons given by nine instrumental and vocal teachers. The verbal strategies were identified and characterized prior to the collection and analysis of data, and were ultimately derived from school-based research, since the document on which they were based had in turn been derived from literature on physical education (MANA 1995; Mosston and Ashworth 1972). These strategies were spread along a continuum from teacher-led ('command') through to student-led ('flexible') with, for example, 'guided discovery' falling between (Young et al. 2003, p. 143). 'Command' was regarded as the most commonly employed strategy, but rather than attempt to quantify its frequency we characterized examples of its use, finding that 'simple instruction' could in fact be complex and subtle in nature (p. 148). Commands were rarely given without some sort of explanation from the teacher, and it was suggested that in some cases a demonstration might constitute an explanation of a sort. Teachers might also soften the form of an instruction by expressing it as a question, or by introducing an element of implied subjectivity. It was argued that 'by presenting [his view] as a matter of opinion, [the teacher] perhaps leaves it open to the student to develop or to voice one of his own' (p. 149).

A later study in the same Music Department investigated episodes of lesson dialogue that were characterized by teacher questions, and that emerged from transcribed data rather than fulfilling a preconceived sequence of verbal behaviours (Burwell 2005). The implications of this approach may be illustrated by examining an example from the study, of a verbal exchange between teacher and student. Student speech is given in italics, and performance behaviour shown in square brackets.

1	Are you happy with that?
2	*Yeah.*
3	Are you happy with the beginning?
4	*No.*
5	[STUDENT PLAYS]
6	How do you feel about that?
7	*Okay.*
8	Yeah, it's nice. Let's put it into context.
9	[STUDENT PLAYS]
10	That's it. Still a slight tendency to push on the down beats. Once again. If you put too much effort to it, it sounds laboured. Don't work, just stand back from it.
11	[STUDENT PLAYS]
12	*I don't like some of that. The crotchets, I keep chopping off.*
13	Okay, what are you going to do about it?
14	*Do I need to make it more strong or will it go out of tune?*
15	Not if you adjust the fingering. Tell me where you've got to in terms of the music at that point.
16	*It's got through two different themes, ideas and it seems to be developing from that. Then there's a new harmonic idea …*

(Burwell 2005, pp. 207–8)

If this extract were coded according to the classic sequence, Teacher presents – Student responds – Teacher reinforces, there would be only one 'correct' sequence to be found, in events 8–9–10. But focusing on this would reduce much of the complexity and substance of the exchange, and although such an approach would no doubt have a certain usefulness, particularly if applied over a large number of samples, this study shows a preference for description and interpretation, in order to characterize the particular case. Thus the exchange is described as being collaborative and inductive in nature; the teacher 'offers information as necessary [but] the onus is on the student to do the work, and the teacher is clearly not prepared to do her thinking for her' (p. 208). Much of the teacher talk is highly instructive in nature with disapprovals perhaps more salient than approvals, and in the light of the studies discussed above, influenced as they are by classroom research, this might seem problematic or even 'disturbing'; but the process here seems a highly constructive one, depending on a degree of confidence and trust between the participants. These findings are triangulated to some extent by interviews with teacher and student, undertaken shortly after their lesson was filmed. In these, the teacher shows that his approach is deliberately and carefully gauged to match the student's stage of development (p. 212) while the student characterizes her teacher's approach in terms that are articulate and positive (p. 208). Perhaps, in this context, 'disapprovals' would be better described as 'critical support' (Howard 1992, p. 18).

The distribution of verbal behaviour between teacher and student has also been investigated through research at SEU, with the unsurprising finding that teachers tend to dominate lesson dialogue (Burwell 2003a; Burwell, Young and Pickup 2004). The student's verbal contribution in a sample of 67 instrumental and vocal lessons grows gently, however, with the student's age and year in the degree programme (Burwell 2003a, p. 9) and there seem to be links between the amount of student talk, measured in wordage, and the student's instrumental ability, ascertained by her next examination mark (p. 8). The culture associated with various instruments also seems to be reflected in the distribution of teacher-student dialogue: in lessons in the 'conservatoire tradition', represented by clarinet, flute, trumpet and piano, the student contribution is smaller, and more consistently on-task, than lessons outside that tradition, represented by guitar, electric guitar, recorder, saxophone and drum kit (Burwell 2006, p. 338).

The influence of student characteristics, and of cultural traditions extending beyond the individual lesson, are a reminder that the distribution of lesson dialogue is not determined solely by the teacher. Indeed, interviews with teachers and students at SEU revealed that either could feel frustrated with the patterns of dialogue in their lessons. The following extracts come from an interview with a vocal teacher, undertaken shortly after some of her lessons had been filmed for research purposes. The interviewer's speech is shown in italics.

> I felt there wasn't – we hadn't got time now to, for me to say, 'Oh, what do you think about this? – the mood, or the composer – Why don't you go away and have a think about it and come back next week?' At this stage, they should've already done that, and if they haven't, then basically I feel that I've got to say, 'Okay, this is my interpretation of it, this is how you're going to practise it'. [When I am teaching stronger students], I'm actually much more flexible, and it's to do

with – I think – a greater level of trust, that what they're doing is – that they've actually taken part; [that] in their own practice during the week, they've thought about it … if there's ever any doubt about that, I always adopt a 'command' strategy … Partly because I just think that it's sort of my responsibility as well. You know. But it's very – so much nicer when –
When you don't have to.

(Burwell 2005, p. 211)

A contrasting view is provided by a student interview from the same study: in this particular case, the student seems to regret her teacher's commitment to 'discovery' strategies. Once again, the interviewer's speech is indicated by italics.

Sometimes I wish that he would just give me a few more technical tips, because I know he knows what I am struggling with and sometimes I think he just doesn't want to say 'You've GOT to do this'. Sometimes he will say 'You could try doing this, or this', but [he] doesn't necessarily recommend a certain way of doing things.
Why do you think he doesn't?
I think he likes to get his pupils to experiment with different ways of practising to find the way that best suits them.
Oh, right. He doesn't want to dictate.
Yeah. I would prefer to be dictated to.

(Burwell 2005, p. 209)

Jørgensen (2000) has offered some useful observations on the issue of responsibility for student learning in Higher Education. Prevailing attitudes to educational philosophy 'with roots in the enlightenment and earlier' seek to lay that responsibility at the feet of the student (p. 67), but Jørgensen points out that not all students want the kind of independence that senior practitioners – whether philosophers, teachers or researchers – might want for them (p. 70). The readiness to accept responsibility might depend on each student's personality and maturity, as well as ability in the subject. That reflective teachers are often aware of this is demonstrated in one of the responses to a questionnaire administered to teachers and students at SEU. After responding to a series of questions about his use of verbal strategies in lessons, the teacher added 'All of the above strategies assume [that students have] a high level of ability in decision making, regarding music at least, but in my experience this is rarely the case. Students need to be taught first how to make decisions about their music. Without this skill most of the above would seem to be useless' (Burwell 2003a, p. 13).

Vocabulary

It seems that performance studies in Higher Education might involve learning not only performance skills, but decision-making skills, perhaps problem-solving skills, and the ability and willingness to take responsibility for independent learning. At the same time, students presumably learn to discuss their subject, and learn through discussing their subject. Music is a nonverbal art, however, and it is notoriously difficult to articulate some aspects of musical performance and education. This has been discussed above with reference to research focused on modelling, and in Chapter 2; a good deal of recent research has been devoted, too, to exploring the vocabulary used to discuss the ineffable in music. The problem is usefully explored by the musician and philosopher Reimer, reflecting on an instruction he was once given, in a band rehearsal: 'Once more with feeling' (Reimer 2004, p. 4).

> I had no idea that his apparently simple instruction to me raised issues so complex that many of humankind's most important thinkers had struggled with them in search of a resolution ... I did what my novice performer's instincts told me to do – the only thing I knew how to do – I placed more emphasis on what the notes of that melody seemed to want to do, where they seemed to want to go and how they got there. Feeling their melodic tendencies more concentratedly and making them more apparent by the way I sounded them, I felt in myself a deeper sense of union – of the music as part of my undergoing – than I had the first time. When I finished the director stopped the band again, looked at me for several seconds, and said, 'Lovely, first clarinet. Very musical. Let's go on.' (Reimer 2004, pp. 4–5)

As an experienced professional, years after the event, Reimer is able to articulate his thinking about the meaning of 'playing with feeling', but for a 16-year-old in an educational setting the band leader was able to elicit the right kind of response using a few simple words. Howard argues that such verbal gestures – along with some physical gestures – are not imprecise, merely because they lack specificity; something that defies precise description might nevertheless be precisely discriminated (Howard 1982, p. 72).

In research at South England University it was found that metaphor is often used by teachers to discuss such ineffable features of instrumental teaching and learning, as interpretation and technique (Burwell 2006). This seems particularly true of singers, who must appeal to their students' imaginations to help them learn to control and operate an 'instrument' which is hidden from view (p. 345). Barten (1998) calls for the use of more motor-affective metaphors in music instruction, explaining that,

> metaphor does more than relay information. It also serves a clear rhetorical function, insofar as the instructor tries to influence or persuade students through capturing their attention and imagination, making the experience memorable, and possibly getting students to accept the directive through humor. (Barten 1998, p. 95)

Tait and Haack (1984) classify verbal behaviours slightly differently, suggesting that three distinct kinds of vocabulary might be useful to music teachers: professional, experiential and behavioural, with the last group further divided among thinking, feeling and sharing (pp. 78–83). The attitudes of teachers and students to verbal strategies of various kinds have already been noted in the discussion above of studies by Laukka (2004) who divides teachers' behaviour among modelling, language emphasizing felt emotion, and the use of metaphor, and by Woody (2000) who distinguishes between 'encouraging felt emotion or extramusical meaning' and 'teaching musical concepts' as strategies for encouraging expressive performance (p. 19). Woody has also explored the vocabulary actually devised by teachers, by asking ten music professors to devise some verbal instructions that might help students to develop their expressive approach to three different melodies. His findings highlight a 'remarkable similarity among the music instructors' chosen images and metaphors', suggesting that the professors shared, to some extent, both a repertoire of expressive devices and a vocabulary through which to evoke them (Woody 2002, p. 222).

Woody has employed some of the images provided by the professors in a further study, in which he asked 84 university music students to employ them in their practice sessions, reflecting on and recording the thought processes and other activity involved (Woody 2006b). Generally, and perhaps obviously, the students differed in the degree to which they continued to think in terms of the images given, or translated those into 'musical sound properties' (p. 134). These are presumably equivalent to what Tait and Haack labelled professional language, and to what Davidson meant when he asserted that American musicians 'prefer to discuss music in terms of its primitives, its basic elements' (1989, p. 96). Perhaps more important, students who had greater experience with private instruction were more inclined to translate their thinking in this way, apparently reflecting their acquisition of the vocabulary and the ability to apply it, in individual lessons. The most experienced students of all, however, reversed this trend: Woody suggests that 'the most experienced subjects in this study may have dwelt on and developed the emotional aspects of the imagery because that is what engages a translation process that has become automatized for the most part' (p. 135). While this study casts another light on the processes of cultivating the skills involved in expressive performance, it is also a further reminder of the variety among individual learners and their experience, and the effect that this might have on any processes observed.

The use of metaphor in lesson dialogue may depend to some extent on the cultural traditions behind the instrument and musical style studied. Both Davidson (1989) and Benson and Fung (2005), whose research is discussed above with reference to modelling, found that teachers in China, whether giving lessons on the yang ch'in or the piano, tended to employ metaphorical language more than their American counterparts. In research at SEU, with a sample of 67 instrumental and vocal lessons recorded on video for observation, it was found that vocal teachers made the greatest use of metaphor: it was suggested that this might be due not only to the problem that the instrumental apparatus is hidden from view, but to the fact that singers typically deal with poetic or dramatic texts in addition to purely musical issues (Burwell 2006). The same study however found many examples of instrumental teachers using metaphor, though this was far more common for instruments associated with the conservatoire tradition than with, for example, commercial music or jazz (p. 340).

Although there may be no more precise way to discuss some aspects of music than through metaphor, the effective use of this or any type of vocabulary depends on a shared understanding between teacher and student. Among lessons filmed at SEU one example was found, of a verbal exchange where such an understanding seems to be incomplete. The example shows student comments in italics.

> So what's all this about? It's quite a different piece to the Telemann.
> *It's got the different groupings over the bar line*
> Yes, what happens to the key, the plan of the piece.
> *It's the same, you get B flat –*
> Starts G major-ish – two flats and back into one sharp, but it doesn't develop harmonically or thematically. What markings does he put with each key change.
> *Dolce e espressivo*
> That's it, now what happens when the B flat major happens
> *Meno dolce*
> What does that mean
> *More?*
> Less, I would think, dolce. How are you going to do that?
> *Colour*
> Yes, well done, well observed. We haven't started talking about colour in classes. I will. This piece is all about colour. You need to show the keys in the different sections. So what could you do for the G major bits?
> *Umm*
> What sort of colour comes to mind.
> *Nothing heavy something light*
> Can you think in terms of colour?
> *Not really, no*
> Yellow or white
> *A more pure tone*
> Yes, then a bit darker. Can we have another shot at where you come in.
>
> (Burwell et al. 2004, p. 12)

It seems, in this extract, that the student has already learned enough to know that 'colour' is an appropriate answer to the teacher's question, but it also seems clear that she has not yet learned enough about the meaning of that answer, to put it into effective use. Without a satisfactory verbal response from the student, and perhaps feeling the pressure of having a research camera in the room, the teacher resorts to asking for a further performance attempt, even though the student is apparently unsure of what she should be attempting. This illustration adds resonance to Woody's finding, that instrumental students need first to acquire a vocabulary and the skill needed to apply it, before expressive language can be put directly to use (2006b, p. 134).

Summary and Reflections

As with the literature focused on modelling, research into verbal behaviour in instrumental lessons is only gradually distinguishing itself from research into classroom teaching. Behaviours found conducive to learning in that context, variously characterized as the discovery approach (Marchand 1975), the learner-oriented climate (Verrastro 1975) or student participation in decision-making (Petters 1976), do not always translate easily into the context of individual instrumental lessons. The rate of teacher approvals and disapprovals often seems to be different, and to be perceived differently in terms of lesson effectiveness (Yarbrough and Price 1989; Speer 1994). The teacher's use of a commanding style of speech, too, is not always a simple matter, and is often accompanied by explanations that may involve either verbal or performance behaviours (Young et al. 2003).

The focus of any research study also defines its limits. Research seeking to establish the relative contributions of teacher and student has shown that teachers tend to dominate lesson dialogue (Burwell 2003a; Burwell et al. 2004), but it should not be assumed that the student remains inactive while the teacher is talking, any more than she does while the teacher is modelling. Some research has shown that sequences of teacher instruction, drawn from classroom research, may often be incomplete or incorrect in instrumental lessons (Yarbrough and Price 1989), but other research, aimed at interpreting observational data inductively rather than seeking preconceived sequences, shows that teachers sometimes engage in scaffolding behaviours in a freer and perhaps more subtle order (Kennell 1992; 1997; 2002; Burwell 2005). Students must learn to participate in such processes, learning to talk, and through talk, and there is some evidence suggesting that they must also internalize the patterns and vocabulary involved (Woody 2002; 2006b; Burwell et al. 2004).

One procedural limitation in the study of verbal behaviour should be noted. Research studies have measured verbal behaviours by calculating the amount of time spent on them or the wordage devoted to them, once again quantifying only what can be reliably quantified. In research undertaken at SEU, for example, it was found that teachers dominate lesson dialogue, and that the larger proportion of dialogue is devoted to the discussion of technique (Young et al. 2003, p. 47). Indeed, in a sample of 67 lessons, a moderate negative correlation was found between the wordage devoted to technique and interpretation (Burwell 2006, p. 337). This might seem to contradict the estimate given by students (Lindström et al. 2003, p. 38) and teachers (Laukka 2004, p. 52) that approximately half of their lesson time is typically devoted to expressivity. Perhaps what is at issue here is not the subject but the methodological approach taken in investigating it. The significance of any verbal behaviour cannot be entirely measured by timing or counting it; and conversely, when asked to estimate the proportion of a lesson devoted to expressivity, it seems possible that participants might conflate their sense of its importance with the amount of time spent. When Reimer was asked to play 'once more with feeling', the effect was akin to dropping a pebble into a pool of water, evoking an immediate response and expanding through circular ripples that were still taking effect, through his philosophical reflections, many years later. In instrumental teaching, this ripple effect can be created by concise gestures that can be verbal, physical or musical; and each will be refracted by the individual student's understanding of the language. Although it might seem to defy measurement, the context represented by the variation among the personal characteristics of individual musicians must be implicated in both the process and outcomes of instrumental teaching and learning, and will therefore be considered next.

Studies focused on Personal, Interpersonal and Social Attributes

Literature

Research into instrumental teaching and learning has been relatively slow to focus on the variety among individuals involved, and on what each participant brings to the lesson. This no doubt reflects the course of the 'quiet methodological revolution' documented by Denzin and Lincoln (2005, p. ix). Case study research is not inherently qualitative but it does draw attention to what can be learned about particular cases, and qualitative approaches allow researchers to focus on issues, 'complex, situated, problematic relationships', rather than the 'information questions' characteristic of experimental studies (Stake 2005, pp. 443–8). It is the increasing use of and confidence in qualitative approaches that supports the development of research into the personal, interpersonal and social attributes of participants in instrumental lessons. This discussion, of research focused on such attributes, ranges from systematic studies in which some generalizations have been attempted, through to case studies addressing the behaviour of individual participants.

    Among the studies to be considered here, the earlier work tends to be characterized by coding, quantification and an interest in evaluating lesson effectiveness. Schmidt (1989), noting a lack of previous research of the kind in the context of individual lessons, compares aspects of lesson behaviour with personality variables, among 43 instrumental teachers in an American college. Behaviour is coded using a system of categories close to that used by Kostka (1984): approvals and disapprovals, task-related talk, modelling and questions (Schmidt 1989, p. 262). Personality is gauged through a self-reporting exercise based on Myers-Briggs Type Indicators (p. 259). The findings suggest that four behaviours are related to the teacher's personality: approvals, rate of reinforcement, use of modelling and pace of instruction. Schmidt suggests that this might help in clarifying the relationship between teacher behaviour and lesson effectiveness, and help teachers to become more aware of the need for flexibility and sensitivity in dealing with the needs of individual students (p. 269).

In a complementary study Madsen, Standley and Cassidy (1989) investigate the behaviour of student music teachers in the classroom, with reference to 'intensity', a construct closely related to both 'magnitude' and 'enthusiasm' (p. 85). Intensity might involve 'eye contact, closeness to students, volume and modulation of voice, gestures, facial expressions, and pacing' (p. 86). To use these effectively, the authors conclude that it is important for student teachers to develop their social awareness (p. 92). Hamann, Paul and Lineburgh (1998) also study the social attributes of 138 student teachers, including music education majors, and compare teaching effectiveness with a social skills inventory, finding that 'emotional expressivity', 'emotional sensitivity' and 'social control' are positively correlated with classroom success (p. 96).

Emotional expressivity and sensitivity are dependent on the use and awareness of nonverbal communication (pp. 96–7), highlighted in a more recent study focused on individual instrumental lessons. Kurkul (2007) asserts that there have been few previous attempts to link the study of instrumental teaching and learning with aspects of psychology and communication (p. 328) and suggests that his work is the first known empirical study which has 'placed its emphasis solely on exploring the nature of nonverbal behaviors and various aspects of nonverbal communication in one-to-one music performance instruction' (p. 356). His study, involving 60 instrumental teachers with 60 college-level non-music majors, explores the possible links among nonverbal behaviours, nonverbal sensitivity and ratings of lesson effectiveness. All three are assessed through the use of coding systems, drawn or derived from 1970s literature on communication and instrumental teaching and learning (p. 330, p. 333, p. 339).

Kurkul's study gives rise to a number of interesting findings. Although the assessment of lesson effectiveness is an important component of the exercise, and although there is a high level of agreement about this between the researcher and three independent evaluators, the match between teacher and student perceptions of lesson effectiveness is relatively poor (p. 344). Nonverbal sensitivity – the 'ability to decode nonverbal cues conveyed by the face, body, and tone of voice' (p. 333) – is higher among these instrumental teachers than for 'norm groups of US teachers' (p. 353); this attribute is not related to teachers' own assessments of their lesson effectiveness, but it is strongly related to their students' assessments of the same lessons (p. 353, p. 359). There is no clear relationship between nonverbal behaviours and nonverbal sensitivity (p. 355), or between nonverbal behaviours and lesson effectiveness (p. 352).

Kurkul points out that the results might have been different had the students not been non-music majors, because 'music majors can sometimes be motivated by a variety of factors that lead them to keep studying with a particular teacher, regardless of the teacher's teaching or communication skills' (p. 356). This notion is supported perhaps in Sosniak's account of American concert pianists, arguably representing a pinnacle of advancement, who reflect on their own main teachers in mixed terms of awe and esteem (Sosniak 1985b, pp. 421–2). There has been some evidence too that teachers regard the personal needs of students as changing with age and expertise. In a questionnaire study by Mills and Smith (2003), asking 134 teachers for their views on effective teaching in schools and in Higher Education, 'teacher enthusiasm' emerges as the highest-ranking hallmark for the lessons of children, but that ranking drops to 11 in the context of Higher Education, where 'teacher knowledge' seems to be the most important feature (p. 9). In a study based on interviews with 257 children, Davidson et al. (1998) concur that in the early stages of learning, 'personal characteristics are important to promote musical development, [while] in the later stages it becomes more important that teachers be perceived to have good performance and professional skills' (p. 155).

While few would suggest that it is irrelevant whether a student at any stage of development finds her teacher enthusiastic, it seems unlikely that a simple link can or should be made between this and lesson effectiveness. Kurkul's failure to find a link between nonverbal behaviour and the student's perception of lesson effectiveness would seem to reinforce this point; his surprise at this finding (2007, p. 352) perhaps rests on the assumption that nonverbal behaviour would be taken as an indicator of enthusiasm – or the lack of it – and that students would consider that an important feature of good teaching.

Although Kurkul's study does seem unique in the degree to which it focuses on nonverbal behaviour in the context of instrumental teaching and learning, there is a cohesive body of literature on nonverbal communication which may help to cast further light on this issue. Research into doctor-patient dyads, for example, might be relevant to the consideration of the teacher-student interaction. In this context, patient satisfaction is normally considered to depend at least in part on rapport with the doctor; rapport has in turn been linked to positivity and 'interactional synchrony' between individuals, and to nonverbal behaviours such as 'smiling, nodding, high levels of eye contact, and forward trunk lean' (Koss and Rosenthal 1997, p. 1158). Koss and Rosenthal however failed to find a link between patient satisfaction and either positivity or interactional synchrony, in a study of 48 medical consultations in an American hospital. Since these were returning patients, they might have established working relationships with their doctors previously, and their satisfaction 'may be related more closely to their physician's task-oriented communication than it is to their physician's socioemotional skills'. The authors cautiously suggest that patient satisfaction might be multi-dimensional in nature (p. 1162).

Support for this word of caution would seem to come from Riggio and Feldman (2005), who in a volume devoted to applications of nonverbal communication warn that '[T]here is no dictionary of nonverbal communication. Given the great range and variety of nonverbal cues, only very few are "translatable" into their verbal counterparts' (p. xiii; italics original). The interpretation of nonverbal behaviour might be influenced by cultural differences, circumstances and the variety among individuals. Even so, there is a good deal of agreement about 'bodily signals' that can be usefully decoded, if they are interpreted with due regard for the context. Attitudes toward other people can be gauged, for example, through the interpretation of the following signals for affiliation, or liking:

proximity:	closer; forward lean if seated
orientation:	more direct, but side by side for some situations
gaze:	more gaze and mutual gaze
facial expression:	more smiling
gestures:	head-nods, lively movements
posture:	open with arms stretched towards other [versus] arms on hips or folded
touch:	more touch in an appropriate manner
tone of voice:	higher pitch, upward pitch contour, pure tone, etc.
verbal contents:	more self-disclosure.

(Argyle 1988, p. 88)

Behaviours suggesting affiliation or positivity might seem to be related to teacher approvals, though studies which quantify approvals, such as Colprit's account of Suzuki violin classes, tend to confine their definition of approval to the verbal evaluation of student performance (2000, p. 216). Davidson's more descriptive account of the Chinese yang ch'in lesson makes an occasional reference to personal gestures, as in the following example:

'Make a bigger contrast,' [the master] encouraged, this time showing [the pupil] what he meant on the instrument. She tried again and was rewarded with a smile. (Davidson 1989, p. 87)

We might imagine that the master's tone of voice influenced Davidson's choice of the word 'encouraged' to describe his instruction here; and that the student seemed to receive the smile as a sign of approval.

Other nonverbal signals are noted in a case study undertaken by Nerland (2001; 2006; 2007), based on a series of observations of lessons in a Norwegian academy of music. Nerland draws on a social-constructionist theoretical framework to conceptualize instrumental teaching as a discursive practice, enacted 'through the words and actions of the persons involved; through the material resources and tools used; and through the ways in which the activities generally are organized in time and space' (2007, p. 401). The two cases characterized in this study, already mentioned in Chapter 2, represent different discursive practices, and evidence for this is drawn not just from what the teachers say but from how they use proximity in their nonverbal behaviour. One teacher, whose approach is very much focused on concert performance, typically simulates that by sitting five metres away while his student plays (2001, p. 5); the other, in contrast, takes an approach focused on preparation for an orchestral career, and typically sits beside his student so that they can address problems in a collaborative manner (p. 11).

Nonverbal behaviour can reflect, then, participants' views of the aims of their lessons together, in the broader context for example of professional performance. It is also possible that nonverbal behaviour might constitute a more explicit feature of the performance skills being acquired. Davidson in his yang ch'in study (1989) offers a vivid description of the use of physical gesture as a more or less deliberately framed aspect of a modelled performance:

> Approaching the ending, [the master] made a ritard, slowing down into the last note. In the motion of playing the last note, the rebound of the mallet appeared to lift his arm, continuing the time of the ritard until the movement congealed into stasis. He froze, creating the illusion that the final note was still sounding – making the last note appear to sound longer than was physically possible. Suspense. He broke the pose, and we applauded his appropriate sense of theatrical gesture, his reminder that this was after all a performance medium – and his demonstration that he was, after all, a prize-winning performer. (Davidson 1989, p. 88)

The nonverbal aspects of this demonstration no doubt help to make it more vivid and memorable for the student, resembling the rhetorical function that Barten ascribes to the use of metaphor (1998, p. 95). Davidson's interpretation of the event also suggests that the gestural display is an intrinsic part of the performance itself, and thus part of what the student is there to learn. Potter (1998) names gesture as one of the channels through which performance rhetoric is realized, along with technique, technology, semiotics, dress codes and the expression of sexuality (p. 158). The visual aspects of musical performance have been the subject of a number of studies by Jane Davidson (for example, 2002; 2007) and its significance has been demonstrated in a recent experiment conducted by Juchniewicz (2008). In this experiment, a single recording by Horowitz of a Chopin *étude* was linked with visual recordings of another pianist, deliberately varying his degree of body movement; the recordings in which he moved most freely were most highly rated by 112 viewers. The author concludes that 'the addition of physical movement only amplified the listeners' perception' of phrasing, dynamics and *rubato* (p. 424). Perhaps the yang ch'in master in Lyle Davidson's 1989 study was not merely showing off to his invited audience; he may have been employing physical gesture to teach a rhetorical aspect of performance and to amplify the communication of the ineffable aspects of musical expression, to his student. Once again, parallel to the dual roles of both performance and verbal behaviour in lessons, the student may be simultaneously learning to use gesture in performance and learning to perform through gesture.

Summary and Reflections

Although they have not often been made the focus of research studies, the interpretation of nonverbal behaviours can add a further dimension to the understanding of what happens in instrumental lessons. Any such interpretation needs to be made with care for the context of each lesson setting, and the individual characteristics of participants: even where indications of personality and personal enthusiasm are perceived by either participants or researchers, they might not be linked unambiguously to the perception of lesson effectiveness (Kurkul 2005; Koss and Rosenthal 1997).

Among personal attributes, an important variable may be what students want from their lessons. Research at SEU has shown that even within a single context – instrumental lessons conducted as part of a degree programme in a university music department – students can differ widely in their attitudes. Hence one student, quoted above, 'would prefer to be dictated to', while another complained, 'I want more self-discovery, exploring different ways of doing things. I don't want to be told that there is a definitive way' (Burwell 2005, p. 209). The teacher's approach, verbal or nonverbal, and conscious or unconscious, is always subject to interpretation by the student, and her own previous experience and current goals will influence her perceptions of what is effective and appropriate.

Its sensitivity to context, and the range of individual variables that that entails, suggests that the assessment of lesson effectiveness should always be approached with caution, and that at this early stage of development for research into advanced instrumental teaching and learning, it may not be the most useful way of driving research. Thus Jørgensen (2009), addressing quality improvement in institutions of Higher Education music, warns that '[the] one-to-one teaching situation is a complex context, and we must be careful not to draw normative conclusions and give cast-iron recommendations about what is right or wrong' (p. 111). Rather, research findings to date, slowly and carefully derived through a range of approaches and with a range of aims and points of focus, have given rise to certain recurring themes that, more fully developed, may take their place in a tentative characterization of the subject as a whole. The three themes discussed above – embracing aspects of performance, verbal and nonverbal behaviour – interact in complex ways within the instrumental lesson, and in the next chapter these will be considered in the broader context beyond it.

Chapter 4
Framing Instrumental Lessons

In Chapter 3 it was suggested that the focus of any research study can be viewed as articulating both its scope and its limits; and that in seeking ecological validity, it is important to take account of the 'multifaceted reality' of the subject, 'even if the research's prime focus may be on one particular aspect of that reality' (Welch 2007, p. 23). Such an account might involve drawing links among the aspects considered, within or among individual research studies; it might also involve viewing those aspects in the context of broader settings.

Since research into instrumental teaching and learning represents a relatively new field of inquiry, it is perhaps not surprising that much of the literature in which these links are made, or contextualization attempted, date from the twenty-first century. This coincides with methodological developments in sociocultural research – alongside psychology and education – in which it was suggested, by the late twentieth century, that the 'individual is a traditional but wrong unit of analysis' (Matusov 2007, p. 307). While the appropriate unit for analysis will presumably depend on what the researcher wants to investigate – each study articulating its own scope and limits – this shift of emphasis has drawn more attention to the sociocultural framework of any area of study, as an area ripe for investigation in itself, and to the interdependent nature of the subject and its sociocultural context.

Although explicit links can be made between the lesson and issues external to it, a further layer of interest may be brought into focus by changing the lens through which the subject is viewed, or the 'planes' of analysis (Rogoff 1995, p. 141). Matusov explains:

> Although the research focus can be on the individual's participation in a given activity, this participation and this activity cannot be fully described and understood without the researcher's consideration of interpersonal relations and the entire community spread over physical and semiotic time and space. This consideration constitutes the 'background' of the study while the research focus on the individual's participation constitutes the 'foreground'. Similarly, interpersonal relations can be studied in the foreground of the study while keeping in the background consideration of individual contributions and institutional practices and norms. (Matusov 2007, p. 324)

These methodological developments, and the ways in which they may be interpreted and applied to instrumental teaching and learning, are explored further in Chapter 5. Here, the literature review is loosely divided into two parts, according to the strength of the lens applied to the subject. All of the studies discussed here help to frame the instrumental lesson by looking at features which are evident and influential in the lesson but which reach beyond it. The first part of the discussion addresses studies that do so on a personal level: these make links, for example, to the student's practice and performance, the interpersonal relationship between teacher and student, and both participants' views of the broad processes in which they are involved. The second part of the discussion addresses studies that view the instrumental lesson on a broader plane: these frame the lesson by focusing on issues of institutional authority, musical cultures, the music department and the university degree programme.

Personal Frameworks for the Instrumental Lesson

Links to the Student's Independent Work

In an early phase of research into instrumental teaching and learning at SEU, examining verbal dialogue transcribed from 27 individual lessons, some surprise was expressed at the apparent infrequency of references to the work undertaken by the student either before or beyond the lesson (Burwell, Young and Pickup 2004, p. 31). Three settings for student work were represented in a pyramid structure shown in Figure 4.1, indicating something of the time spent, the intensity of work undertaken and the nature of assessment involved in each.

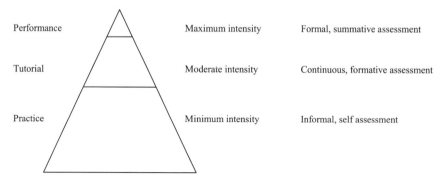

Performance	Maximum intensity	Formal, summative assessment
Tutorial	Moderate intensity	Continuous, formative assessment
Practice	Minimum intensity	Informal, self assessment

Figure 4.1   A graphic representation of three components in Performance Studies (Burwell, Young and Pickup 2004, p. 31)

It was argued that the instrumental tutorial should represent a link between the student's independent practice and the performance, typically assessed through examination at the end of the academic year; but – in the absence of any evidence to the contrary – without effective links to those settings, the lesson might become 'self-contained, dominated by the charismatic teacher and his own agenda, and focused on mastery of the instrument' (p. 31). Efforts have been made, since, to encourage a more fluid dynamic among components of the Performance Studies modules in the Music Department at SEU, first by supporting a staff development programme through which tutors can engage more easily with one another as well as the curriculum, and second by developing a series of performance seminars which provide students with an intermediate platform between the practice studio and the concert stage (p. 32). The effective distance between instrumental teachers and the curriculum, as determined by the institution, remains however a characteristic problem for the design of performance studies courses in Higher Education (Presland 2005, p. 247; Gaunt 2008, p. 236).

A recent study at the Royal Conservatoire in The Hague has attempted to make a more thorough examination of the links between individual instrumental lessons and student practice (Koopman et al. 2007). Consistent with the research at SEU, Koopman et al. found little evidence of explicit instruction concerning practice, in the lessons they observed. Their study was characterized by multiple methods of data gathering, including video recordings of lessons and practice sessions; six student participants kept logbooks reporting on their practice, and completed questionnaires, while their teachers were interviewed about the conduct of lessons. This triangulation of data gathering methods revealed several inconsistencies between what the researchers observed and what the participants reported of their own perceptions and experience.

Although the researchers may have seen no 'explicit communication about the aims of practice and training' in the observed lesson interactions, for example, the students' perception was that these were 'for the most part, clear enough' (p. 387). This claim would seem to be supported by the direct relationship which was observed between lesson instruction and the student's behaviour in the practice room, even if that behaviour often lost focus and concentration during the week following each lesson (p. 386). On the other hand, the student practice observed tended to be dominated by what the researchers felt was a relatively ineffective, 'trial and error' approach, and this once again they linked to the apparent failure of some teachers to explicitly address strategies of executing and regulating practice, during lessons (p. 390). The unwillingness of some teachers to address the learning process explicitly is clearly regretted: Koopman et al. suggest that teachers might regard the development of these skills as the students' responsibility (p. 389), and in asserting that 'the master makes use of his personal strengths – superior knowledge and inspiring qualities – rather than taking the self-effacing role of servant to the learning process' imply that the attitude is immodest (pp. 391–2).

The authors call for a strengthening of teaching methodologies, in a way that respects the unique nature of learning in the arts (p. 392). While this seems a sound recommendation, it is worth examining the issues on which the authors base their conclusion, in a little more detail. First, the use of the term 'master' would seem to refer to apprenticeship, but the reference in this context would seem to have little meaning in itself. Apprenticeship is not an intrinsic part of the argument presented by Koopman et al., and the reference would seem to rest on assumptions that recur in the literature on instrumental teaching and learning, as discussed in Chapter 2. It should perhaps be added that the study by Burwell et al. (2004) quoted above rests on the same implicit assumptions. What the apprenticeship situation is taken to represent, here, are two issues that can usefully be separated: the tacit nature of the skills involved, and the dominance of the teacher.

According to Koopman et al., 'individual practice mirrors the proceedings in the lessons' (p. 392) with students therefore reproducing behaviour that is more or less systematic, according to the nature of their lessons. That performer-teachers vary in the level of prescription they offer their students is supported by Gaunt (2008), based on interviews with 20 teachers in an English conservatoire; if we can assume that this in turn reflects the performer-teacher's own behaviour in practice, then the variety is further supported by Hallam (2001), based on interviews with 22 professional musicians. Although professional musicians appear to have highly developed metacognitive skills, however, the behaviour they reported varied widely: 'Of the twenty-two musicians, seven appeared to be low in "natural" organization, ten were moderately organized in their practice and five considered themselves to be highly organized and efficient in their practice' (p. 33).

If a substantial proportion of musicians have succeeded at a professional level without feeling able to report a highly efficient approach to practice, perhaps being highly efficient is not essential, and perhaps what is essential is tacit in nature: if this is so, it might be argued that the acquisition of the essentials may not always be observable. Koopman et al. do report that two of the teachers they interviewed recalled using explicit instruction in practice skills for first-year students, so that by second year it was unnecessary to discuss them unless problems arose (p. 385). The flaw with this approach could be that ineffective practice might not present itself as a specific problem during a lesson, and yet might curb the long-term success of all but the most exceptional.

At the same time, and particularly if the teacher is dominant in other respects, the student's practice may represent the principal space in which she can develop her own judgement, and the 'trial and error' approach is presumably necessary at some points in the development of self-regulation. Whether the teacher is dominant is determined in this study by noting the initiatives taken by participants, in 'bringing up topics' (p. 381) or referring to the student's 'homework' (p. 383, p. 385). In lesson observations such initiatives were usually the prerogative of the teacher, with the student only occasionally the dominant partner, more likely to be active when homework was at issue (p. 390). Student views however tended to conflict with this evidence, and their questionnaire responses suggested that '[s]tudents saw themselves as taking more initiative than what we concluded from our observations' (p. 383). Although Koopman et al. do not discuss possible reasons for this apparent conflict, it seems likely that the felt importance of the student's practice and lesson contribution does not lend itself easily to observation, given that there are many ways to be active in a lesson apart from engaging in overt behaviours. As previously remarked, in the discussion of observational studies focused on modelling, an apparently inactive student might be listening, thinking, reading or learning. Koopman et al.

themselves acknowledge that 'teaching and performing is intentional behaviour, and if one wishes to reconstruct what actually happens during these sessions, one cannot dispense with this aspect' (p. 376).

Student Attributes and Perceptions

That the student experience of instrumental teaching and learning cannot be fully ascertained through observational studies is argued by Reid (2001), who therefore draws on phenomenography to analyze interview data obtained from 14 conservatoire students. Reid explains that this method 'does not look at how people behave in certain circumstances but looks at how people experience, understand and ascribe meaning to a specific phenomenon' (p. 26). In particular, she examines the variation in students' conception of learning (p. 27) and proposes a hierarchy of five categories to describe that variation. This is a subtle and interesting paper which perhaps reflects as much on the students' conception of themselves as on instrumental lessons; here however only the material most relevant to lessons will be highlighted. Table 4.1 is derived from Reid's descriptive categories, extracting all of the references made to the teacher: it is worth quoting these references in full, because together they demonstrate a continuum of possible roles that the teacher might represent.

If these categories provide an insight into the variation in students' conception of what instrumental teaching and learning is about and how it functions, then they also provide an idea of how difficult it must be to assess the scope and limits of the teacher's contribution. Although each category represents an increasingly sophisticated view of learning, the teacher is arguably equally important in all of them: what clearly changes is the role in which she is cast. The wide variety among student perceptions suggests that the teacher's role in the learning process cannot derive solely from her own intentions, whatever the nature of her own expertise and personal attributes.

Although they may vary in sophistication, Reid's informants are not classified according to their instrumental expertise, and while it seems clear that their conception of learning must affect their lesson behaviour, there are no links made in this study between the student's conception of learning and for example examination success. Research at SEU has however drawn some connections among student characteristics and their behaviour in lessons. The examination of a sample of 67 instrumental lessons, observed on video, revealed that the students' contribution to verbal behaviour, measured in wordage, tended to increase gently with the student's age, year of study and ability, measured either through subsequent performance examination marks or through final degree results (Burwell 2003a, p. 11). An exception occurred at the lower end of the scale of examination results, where it was found that students who were weakest in this respect often contributed with surprising energy to the verbal dialogue in their lessons; it was speculated that the cause of their ironic lack of success might need to be sought beyond the lesson itself (p. 7).

Table 4.1   Categories describing the ways students experience learning. From Reid (2001)

Categories describing the ways students experience learning	*Descriptors referring to the role of the teacher*
Learning an instrument	[Students] rely on their teachers to organize their repertoire and practice schedules (p. 29). The views and advice of the teacher play an integral role in the students' notion of learning. The students rely on, and respect, their teacher's advice, which inhibits experimentation with technical or musical elements. This does not enable the students to look beyond the technical aspects of musicality which are evident in the following categories (p. 30).
Learning an instrument and some musical elements	The focus is on the acquisition of technical skill combined with a dependence on their teacher to choose repertoire and organize practice schedules (30). Instrumental and notational techniques are practised focusing on advice that has originated from the teacher (p. 31).
Learning musical meaning	Students reflect on their teacher's advice on technique and stylistic interpretation of music. [They] reflect on [the] teacher's advice about the stylistic interpretation of the music and then choose how to use the advice. … Both the teachers and students are contributors to the development of the sound (p. 32). Students understand learning to be an integration of the teachers' ideas with their own with the students having the autonomy for making the final choice about 'what works and what doesn't and why it works and why it doesn't' (p. 33).
Learning to communicate musical meaning	Students reflect on their previous experiences with similar music and combine their own musical views with that of their teachers to develop an informed view of the musical meaning to be communicated (p. 34).
Learning to express personal meaning	Learning is not confined to the lesson time or their official time as students, but learning about the world and themselves through reflection on their experiences becomes the basis for lifelong learning (p. 35). Teachers function as advisers, guides, mentors and friends, but the content and the direction of the learning experience is determined by the students (p. 36).

The influence of student characteristics and views on their own learning, which must imply something of the limits of the instrumental teacher's influence, is further investigated by Hewitt (2004) in an interview study with 14 university students. This study is focused on students' ability, self-confidence and effort, seeking the students' own perceptions of and explanations for these aspects of their learning. The role of 'significant others' is only one of three influences cited, alongside assessment and previous experience; and the teacher is only one of the significant others mentioned, alongside peers and parents (pp. 46–53).

All of these studies, focused on student attributes and perceptions of instrumental teaching and learning, overlap to some extent with a paper by Burland and Davidson (2002), which represents part of a longitudinal study of the lifespan development of young musicians. For this paper the researchers conducted telephone interviews with 20 participants who had previously been identified as being 'talented': the aim was to discover differences between the 14 who had become professional musicians, with the 6 who had not. As with Hewitt's 2004 study, the influence of other people was found to be among the key themes to emerge from these interviews. The professional musicians reported positive relationships with peers, parents and teachers, who represented 'opportunities for learning, and for inspiration and motivation'; the non-professional group reported such relationships in negative terms, and – again consistent with Hewitt 2004 – this seemed to have affected their view of their own abilities and experiences (Burland and Davidson 2002, p. 126). Other people however were by no means the only influences distinguishing the two groups. Both reported a mixture of positive and negative experiences with institutional settings, but it seemed that the professional group had been able to develop coping strategies to deal with these (p. 128); and although the non-professional group was motivated by the enjoyment of music, the professional group demonstrated 'a powerful intrinsic motivation' to pursue a musical career (p. 129). Interestingly, the professional musicians alone seemed to perceive music as a vehicle for communication (p. 130), a finding that resonates with the more sophisticated levels of students' conceptions of learning, in the hierarchical model proposed by Reid (2001). Burland and Davidson themselves propose a 'tripartite model of success', depending on positive experiences with others and institutions, methods for coping, and the impact of music on each informant's self-concept (p. 134).

Teacher Attributes and Perceptions

Although many of the studies focusing on instrumental teaching and learning seek teachers' views of what happens in individual lessons, it is relatively rare that their own backgrounds are investigated, though these must have a more or less direct influence on lesson dynamics. Mills (2003) broadly characterizes teachers of performance in nine conservatoires and 13 universities or university colleges in Britain, but her study tends to focus on employment rather than professional issues.

More recently Gaunt (2008) interviewed 20 performer-teachers in an English conservatoire about a range of issues concerning the teaching of performance, including their own fundamental aims as teachers in the institution. Kingsbury argues that the core of individual lessons in the conservatoire system – the 'studio-centred social organization in the conservatory' – is focused on solo repertoire and technique, in spite of the fact that '[a]lthough it is only occasionally spoken aloud, there is a general understanding that only a small minority of the graduates of the conservatory will be able to make professional careers as performing musicians' (Kingsbury 1988, pp. 56–7). The aims articulated by Gaunt's informants, however, while endorsing the emphasis on vocational skills, embrace a wider range of views:

> [T]eachers focused on a fairly wide range of instrumental/vocal and musical skills that would provide students with the tools for finding work within the music profession in some capacity or other. In other cases, the focus was on a highly specific career, such as being a concert soloist or an opera singer. Other teachers were more concerned with supporting and developing an emerging artistic voice with each individual student, which might lead to a number of different pathways within music. Some teachers emphasized the broad educational potential of engaging with the heritage of classical music. A further group focused on lifelong learning skills such as self-directed work, self-discipline and motivation. (Gaunt 2008, p. 220)

That conservatoire teachers acknowledge a wider range of possible aims for their students than preparation for the profession is endorsed in a study by Purser (2005), who also used an interview study to explore the views of six instrumental teachers. In a preliminary questionnaire, the informants divided their preferred lesson aims among 'preparation for the profession; maximisation of student potential; [and] providing a broad musical education', which seemed to suggest that 'the differences between them were essentially a matter of emphasis' (p. 289).

Purser's informants agreed that 'students need to be taught to teach themselves' (p. 293), and although her interview schedule does not mention it explicitly, 11 of the 20 tutors interviewed by Gaunt also referred to student independence (2008, p. 221), offering a good deal of specific evidence to show how they set about facilitating the development of student autonomy (p. 224). The variety of aims expressed by teachers was matched by a variety of lesson strategies employed (p. 225) and lesson content (p. 227); the variety among teachers' approaches to student practice (p. 237) has already been noted.

In spite of what seems an abundantly healthy range of approaches to instrumental teaching, there seem to be some reservations in Gaunt's account of the conservatoire teacher's role. Although many teachers had apparently raised the issue of student independence themselves, for example, 'it was not clear whether this was considered to be a personal attribute or a quality that could specifically be developed through the learning processes of one-to-one tuition' (p. 225). The responsibility for student learning is an issue that has already been raised, and would seem to be an important one in the context of Higher Education (Jørgensen 2000). In Purser's study, two of the teachers interviewed asserted that their own role would change alongside the student's development: 'students should not be taught to be independent while they still need the strong support of their teacher, [as] this was an aspect to reserve for the final years at a conservatoire' (Purser 2005, p. 293). This assertion runs parallel to the gradual withdrawal of advice about practice strategies, reported by Koopman et al. (2005) and discussed above.

A further potential concern arose in Gaunt's study when the informants, asked to talk about the 'typical elements and structures of a lesson', reported what seemed to be a widely accepted procedure: the lesson may or may not begin with a warming-up session, with 'a brief chat, followed by the student performing or playing through some repertoire, study or technical exercises, and teacher feedback leading to detailed technical and musical work' (2008, p. 226). Gaunt remarks on an apparent lack of variety among teachers' approaches, though she suggests that the procedure might embody 'a key quality described by the teachers [as] the ability to react in the moment to what a student presented, to respond to their performance and facilitate development' (p. 226). This responsive procedure – as opposed to the formal structure that might perhaps be more characteristic of classroom teaching – has been observed in some of the previous research at SEU where episodes resembling what Gaunt calls 'improvisatory responsiveness' were identified and admired (Burwell 2005, pp. 206–8). Gaunt however asks whether this kind of approach might represent 'tradition and habit, unquestioned over many years as generations of apprentices have become the next master teachers' (2008, p. 226).

Gaunt also notes that her informants displayed 'scarce knowledge of, or engagement in, the wider context of learning beyond the one-to-one lesson' (p. 236) and that those whose positions were limited to one-to-one tuition had little contact with other teachers or course leaders. She calls for the professional isolation of these teachers to be addressed, not least through support in 'generic areas of teaching'. In this she is supported by, for example, Koopman et al. (2007, p. 392) and Rostvall and West (2003, p. 224). Once again the interview informants in Purser's study also provide something of the teacher's view of this issue: they report that the only major influences on the development of their teaching have been their own conservatoire teachers and their own experience of teaching, with reflections on self-teaching playing some part (2005, p. 295). When asked about the possibility of developing formal ways of sharing or discussing their approaches to teaching, their responses are cautious, with one informant finding the prospect 'simply intimidating' (p. 296). Purser nevertheless concludes:

> [I]t is hard not to draw the conclusion that some forum for sharing experience and modes of good teaching practice would be beneficial. ... This is essentially the situation – working, as they do, largely in isolation – in which most new and many developing conservatoire teachers find themselves. ... It would surely be useful to find a way of making the pool of accumulated wisdom more readily available, for example through training, in order to avoid some errors that must occur from time to time, but also to provide new instrumental teachers and the research community with a source of ideas and current thinking about teaching at this level. (Purser 2005, p. 298)

The Interpersonal Relationship between Teacher and Student

While it seems clear that the perceptions and attributes of both teacher and student are significant background influences on the conduct of instrumental lessons, the teacher-student relationship is a still more salient theme in research to date. Among the most important studies to highlight this theme are several focusing on the lifespan development of musicians, relying on interview data that has been collected in a variety of ways. One study takes a longitudinal approach by returning over a period of time to interview up to 257 young musicians in England: an early product of this research is the paper by Davidson et al. (1998) and the most recent is the paper by Burland and Davidson (2002) cited above. The much-cited study by Manturzewska (1990) characterizes lifespan development through the analysis of data collected from 165 professional musicians in Poland, aged 21 to 89; another by Sosniak (1985a; 1985b) relies on the reflections of 24 American concert pianists, accounting for aspects of their musical careers. All of these bear witness to the central importance of the teacher-student relationship, which – as discussed in Chapter 2 – might easily be traced to master-apprentice traditions.

Several recent studies have been explicitly focused on the teacher-student relationship behind instrumental teaching and learning. Hays, Minichiello and Wright (2000) propose mentoring as a way of understanding the relationship: they trace the concept to the quasi-parental role taken by Mentor in Homer's *Odyssey*, through the education of gifted children in the 1960s, to an academic orientation in the 1970s (p. 3). At SEU the term is most commonly applied in the Education Faculty, to the supervision of student teachers, and it appears that this usage is common elsewhere in England. Thus Williams et al. characterize mentorship in terms of teacher education, and assert that one of its key functions is to support reflection:

> Reflection is a much over-used term within teacher education and space does not permit an analysis here of its various meanings. Suffice to say that reflection is used here to refer to aspects of mentor-student interaction *which provoke thought on the part of students* so that they are actively involved in their own learning rather than receiving information or guidance passively. All the mentors [interviewed in our study] referred to this in some way during interviews. Most students also mentioned it, although some did so critically, either because they wanted more of this kind of help or because they would have preferred to be told what to do. (Williams et al. 1998, p. 229; italics original)

There is a clear resonance in this description with both apprenticeship and previous remarks about the teacher-student relationship. In the context of instrumental teaching and learning, Hays et al. go further, to describe mentoring that involves 'an exclusive relationship' that extends 'beyond the normal teacher/ student interaction', in the sense that mentoring 'implies more of a commitment to the relationship' (2000, p. 4). On the strength of a study based on interviews with

15 members of music faculty staff in Australia and America, Hays et al. tend to characterize mentorship not only in terms of the mentor's teaching, but also her personal attributes:

> ... patience, perception, openness, care, genuine interest in the student's welfare, sensitivity to other people's needs, honesty, commitment and professional integrity. (Hays et al. 2000, p. 6)

This rather tall order requires that the mentor 'takes responsibility for the total development of the protégé' (p. 6). The possible functions of the relationship are listed as being either psychosocial or career-orientated (p. 7) and it represents a significant influence on the student's developing sense of identity, 'affecting his/her conceptualisation of self, and goals in life' (p. 8). These general, though remarkable characteristics are supported by Presland (2005) who collected data about the teacher-student relationship by interviewing 12 piano students in an English conservatoire. In descriptions by both Presland and Hays et al. however the personal aspects of the relationship are conflated with the commitment of both participants to their subject. The nature of the subject, too, implies a degree of emotional involvement:

> All felt that the intimacy of the relationship developed over time – but how? For most [of the students interviewed] the key to this was simply the gradual revelation of their personalities through their playing. [One student] articulated this well, speaking of playing as 'an intimate and transparent picture of all you are'. (Presland 2005, p. 242)

Support for this rather poetic characterization of the situation comes from Nerland and Hanken who argue that the 'participants will inevitably grow close to one another ... partly due to the fact that musical practice at such a high level requires the personal involvement of the performers' (Nerland and Hanken 2002, p. 183). They suggest that the performers 'abandon themselves to the musical subject' (p. 183) and, as previously quoted with reference to the master-apprentice relationship, 'both student and teacher must expose themselves emotionally, and therefore they grow closer to each other on a personal level' (p. 180).

So far, so good; indeed, this seems a unique and ideal picture of a setting for teaching and learning. The picture does not necessarily fit neatly with the variety already demonstrated, among the attitudes and personal attributes of teachers and students; and the tendency to conceptualize their relationship in terms of the student's benefit perhaps disguises the fact that although the student may have one significant mentor, the teacher presumably has a great number of students. Can the instrumental teacher be all things to all students? Gaunt reports that some are wary of an excessive or inappropriate investment in the teacher-student relationship, remarking that students can 'put all their eggs into the one basket, which is you' (2008, p. 230). The degree of formality seems to be the prerogative of the teacher, but 'the intensity and emotional demands of the one-to-one relationship' were sometimes felt (p. 234).

Given the difference in numbers between teachers and students, it might also be asked whether every student can have an instrumental teacher who becomes a mentor figure. This question is not often squarely addressed in the research literature, though answers may be sought perhaps in its omissions. Manturzewska (1990), describing the master-apprenticeship relationship as 'paramount for the entire future career' of her informants, mentions only in passing that this involved working with 'the teacher-master (*if the musician was lucky enough to find one*)' (p. 134; italics added). It seems, although no more is said about it, that a student might survive to professional maturity without having such a figure in her musical life. Research into this subject is inevitably skewed, however, by its dependence on either student musicians or professional musicians for information: it is obviously difficult to identify people who have been student musicians but who have failed to become professional. The longitudinal study by Burland and Davidson (2002) is therefore rare and valuable in this respect. It will be recalled that the young musicians in their study who did not become professional, in spite of being found 'talented', reported their relationships with significant others in negative terms (p. 126).

There is a paucity however of substantial reports of problematic teacher-student relationships. Presland, in a personal aside in her interview study with conservatoire students, mentions some limits on the relationship with her own conservatoire professor:

> I admired my professor tremendously and looked forward greatly to my lessons, but I regarded them as an opportunity to absorb as much information and advice as I could, rather than a chance to enter into dialogue and discussion. (Presland 2005, p. 240)

Hays et al. (2000) are able to offer evidence of 'negative mentorships' only by reporting the reflections of teachers, rather than current student complaints, and most of these reflections seem to have been offered as general impressions, rather than reports of direct experience (pp. 8–9). Perhaps it is the complex and personal nature of the relationship that prevents students articulating any personal problems they might perceive with their teachers; Presland estimates that less than 5 per cent of the piano students in the conservatoire she has studied request a change of teacher, each year (p. 246). Whether the proportion of problematic teacher-student relationships is actually higher would seem to remain, for the moment, an issue resting on speculation and anecdotal evidence.

Summary and Reflections

It seems that the personal attributes and attitudes of participants that underlie their engagement in instrumental teaching and learning are potentially complex and significant. Explicit links between the instrumental lesson and the student's work beyond that context – in either independent practice or performance activity – have been sought in a number of studies, but the findings are sometimes qualified by the suggestion that the participant's views of such links may be distinct from the researcher's observations (Koopman et al. 2007). Although these distinctions or even contradictions might be attributable to limitations in either the participant's understanding or the research methods employed, it also seems possible that both perspectives might eventually be incorporated into a more richly textured conception of the subject.

The investigation of the views of individual participants would therefore seem to offer an important opportunity to enrich our understanding of lesson interactions. Research in this area has already shown that teachers and students are likely to vary in their understanding of their own roles and responsibilities, and indeed their understanding of the aims of instrumental teaching and learning (Reid 2001; Burland and Davidson 2002; Gaunt 2008; Purser 2005). In the light of the complexity of these contextualizing links, which may be viewed in terms of both connections and disconnections, it would be difficult to argue that any one participant, or any particular aspect of the situation, is responsible for the nature of lesson behaviour. Jørgensen (2009) goes so far as to ask whether it should be assumed that 'whatever change does occur in [music students in Higher Education] can be attributed to institutional attendance rather than other sources of influence'. More specifically:

> How can we be sure when we attribute a change to a specific circumstance, for instance by saying that 'This student played so well because her teacher is so good'? My concern is to caution our tendency to attribute simple causes to effects, because life is complicated and whenever something changes it [will] probably have many causes … (Jørgensen 2009, p. 180)

In the context of instrumental teaching and learning, the personal characteristics that each participant brings to the lesson, including the varying sophistication and maturity of students, are likely to drive their perceptions of the situation, arguably as much as the lesson interaction itself. The relationship between teacher and student too might be implicated in lesson behaviour: although the importance of this relationship may vary, with some students seeing their teacher as only one among a number of 'significant others' while others see the teacher as a mentor or even a master, it seems clear that the success of this relationship may have a significant effect on the success of the enterprise as a whole (Hewitt 2004; Burland and Davidson 2002; Hays et al. 2000). Perhaps regardless of its level of importance in any particular context, the teacher-student or master-apprentice relationship must entail power relations, as in any apprenticeship situation (Lave and Wenger 1991, p. 64), and these are sometimes described in terms of the teacher's personal attributes. The fact that power is invested in her, however, makes the teacher's authority not just an interpersonal but an institutional issue. This will therefore be discussed in the next section.

Sociocultural Frameworks for the Instrumental Lesson

Institutional Authority

While there is widespread agreement on the importance of the teacher-student relationship in instrumental teaching and learning, and its nature has been vividly and even passionately described on a personal level, a broader and more impersonal view of this subject can help to frame it in terms of the social and cultural circumstances that support and to some extent define it. Nerland and Hanken argue that the teacher-student relationship has an institutional construction:

> We can say that the positions as teacher and student are *institutionally regulated* in the sense that the norms, expectations, and rules of behaviour are shaped by the institutional culture in which the teaching-learning activity takes place. In order to understand teacher-student relationships in higher music education, it thus is necessary to broaden the perspective so as to include the cultural conditions under which such relationships are constructed. (Nerland and Hanken 2002, p. 167; italics original)

Institutional rules of behaviour are not unique to music education, and some of these are implicit in any educational setting. Cazden for example remarks on the institutionally constructed rules of speaking in school rooms:

> In traditional classrooms, the most important asymmetry in the rights and obligations of teachers and students is over control of the right to speak. To describe the difference in the bluntest terms, teachers have the role-given right to speak at any time and to any person; they can fill any silence or interrupt any speaker; they can speak to a student anywhere in the room and in any volume or tone of voice. No one has the right to object. But not all teachers assume such rights and few live by such rules all the time. Given teachers' rights inherent in their institutional role, *speaking rights* here refers to the ways by which students get the right to talk – to be legitimate speakers – during teacher-led group activities. (Cazden 2001, p. 82; *italics original*)

Of course, instrumental teaching and learning is not predominantly conducted in group settings, and the student in Higher Education will have left some of the habits of her schooldays behind her, but Cazden asserts that all discourse is regulated by cultural norms, even if it must be recreated in every case through a collaborative improvisation – much as jazz musicians improvise within agreed structures (p. 40).

The authority granted teachers by institutions of education may influence nonverbal lesson behaviour as well as speaking rights. Authority can be considered as an element of the generic issue of dominance and submission, which may be found in a range of settings for human relationships, including the workplace and the military as well as institutions of education. Previously, a widely accepted list of signals for liking was quoted in the context of the personal, interpersonal and social attributes evident in instrumental lessons (Argyle 1988, p. 88): here, a similar list outlines the signals that may be taken to express dominance in an established hierarchy:

spatial position:	height, e.g. on a raised platform, or standing (though sitting is a sign of status on some formal occasions); facing a group; taking up more space
gaze:	in an established hierarchy, less gaze, but relatively more looking while talking; when trying to establish dominance, more gaze and staring other down
face:	non-smiling, frowning; face with mature adult features
touch:	asymmetrical touching of other
voice:	loud, low pitch, greater pitch range, slow (high-pitched, rising pitch contours), low resonance, more interruptions, small latency, more talk
gestures:	pointing at other, or his property
posture:	full height, hands on hips, expand chest; in established hierarchy – relaxation

(Argyle 1988, p. 97)

In practice these nonverbal behaviours are highly dependent on context, and will vary according to social, cultural and personal characteristics, including for example gender. Women, often taken to be of lower power and status, may 'emit fewer dominance signals than men; they take up less space, are shorter, look more, smile more, have less loud, more high-pitched voices, and interrupt less' (p. 99).

The authority invested in the teacher may also be seen as an aspect of the power relations implicit in the apprenticeship setting, as discussed in Chapter 2, and this has given rise to some anxiety among practitioners and researchers. Hays et al. discuss the possible drawbacks of mentoring relationships in instrumental teaching and learning, describing 'a negative mentorship [which] usually is a result of a controlling power base perspective rather than a guiding teaching style that fosters independence, professional growth, analytical thought and holistic personal development' (Hays et al. 2000, p. 8). Although only one of their informants refers to direct experience with such a 'dominating personality', there is evidence elsewhere of what seems to be power abuse within the teacher-student relationship, with Sosniak in an example previously quoted reporting the remarks of a professional pianist whose main teacher 'would just intimidate you out of your mind' (1985b, p. 421).

A broader and more positive view of authority has been attempted in several highly reflective studies focused on instrumental teaching and learning. There is an important difference, for example, between being authoritative and being authoritarian: Howard argues that 'instructional commands are conditional and prudential in the sense of, "If you want to learn how to do this well, then you must undertake the following"', and he suggests that it is the responsibility of the adult learner 'to find and to follow authoritative sources of expertise' (Howard 1992, p. 67). Seizing on this, Riggs (2006) asserts that an authoritative approach is quite different to the 'external control' that is characteristic of authoritarianism, and might actually support the development of student independence. Excessive external control would seem counterintuitive in the light of the undergraduate's stage of development, but with an authoritative approach the teacher can offer 'information, experience, [guidance] and encouragement' as they pass through this period of maturation. Riggs draws on research into musicians' personalities to support this claim (pp. 180–81).

There is indeed evidence to suggest that during adolescence, musicians seem to pass from a phase of being submissive in personality, to being dominant and imaginative, these being characteristic of independence and of the personalities of professional musicians (Kemp 1996, pp. 55–7). Kemp emphasizes however that his own research methods place some constraints on the reliability of his findings. His study, examining the apparent shift from dependence to independence in young musicians, was not longitudinal but relied on data collected from three different age groups: the shift therefore might have been due to 'a dropping-out (or de-selection) of those who were: (1) finding it increasingly difficult to maintain motivation; (2) uncomfortable with the demands being made upon them; [or] (3) having difficulty maintaining progress' (p. 58). Kemp further suggests that apparent changes in personality might be attributed to the student's changing position within the educational institution:

> [I]t is possible that the trend towards independence [reflects] not only the demands of teachers at different points, but also the different climates of the various educational institutions. In other words it may be revealing the shift of emphasis from skill acquisition routines to a more autonomous regime of personal decision-making, particularly for the more talented. (Kemp 1996, p. 58)

In their essay on the institutional construction of teacher-student relationships, Nerland and Hanken describe authority 'as a crucial and productive resource in the teacher-student interaction' (2002, p. 168). The instrumental lesson is conceptualized as a person-centred apprenticeship, in that the master embodies the profession (p. 174); the setting, because of its institutional nature, is described as a public place rather than one that fosters private intimacy (p. 183); and students seeking induction into the profession actively support their teacher's position of authority (p. 172). The last claim is endorsed by Nielsen, in his investigation of 'apprenticeship' in a Danish academy of music, who observes that 'it seems [that] the students themselves maintain the teachers' authority, just as much as the teachers' (Nielsen 1999, p. 124).

On a personal level, instrumental teachers may deliberately play down their authority, and Gaunt for example reports teachers 'going for a drink after a lesson or performance, [or forming a] friendship/patronage outside of the [institution]' (Gaunt 2008, p. 234). Nerland and Hanken, after interviewing teachers in Norway about their personal reservations toward institutional authority, argue that authority 'appears to be rooted in the students' ambition to learn from interaction with their teachers' (2004, p. 5). The relationship may appear to be characterized by equality, 'from the outside', but 'students both wish for and expect dominant authority to be allocated to the [teacher's] position, and they deliberately subjugate themselves to their teacher's perspectives because they trust what the teacher stands for, and assume he or she can initiate them into the profession' (p. 6).

Whatever the teacher's personal reservations, authority is not a personal property that can be simply laid down; it is inherent in the cultural systems of the institution and perhaps of the subject itself. Nettl, in an ethnomusicological study of American schools of music, describes theirs as a 'quasi-religious system' (Nettl 1995, p. 144), with authority invested in artefacts as well as human figures:

> [It is] instructive to look for the godlike in the pantheon of great masters who have scriptures (the manuscript, the authoritative, scholarly urtext edition reflecting the earliest sources, and the authentic performance); who are served by a priesthood of performers and musicologists; who are celebrated in and surrounded by rituals such as concert, rehearsal, lesson, and practice session; and who are commemorated by controversies regarding the authenticity of manuscripts, letters, and portraits. (Nettl 1995, p. 15)

It seems that quite aside from the personal attitudes and characteristics of the participants, authority is an element of the power relations inherent in apprenticeship situations, and researchers observing lesson interactions will be witness, whether it is the focus of their study or not, to teachers and students negotiating their way through this deeply seated and complex issue.

Musical Cultures

In his anthropological study of the conservatory as a cultural system, Kingsbury claims that the fundamental aim of the institution is to perpetuate itself (Kingsbury 1988, p. 57). It might have seemed more obvious to describe its fundamental aim as serving music; but although the curriculum tends to define music in terms of itself, even that can be viewed as a social product:

> Since what music 'is' is itself contingent on social situation, the inescapable conclusion is that far from being ultimately or essentially asocial in nature, music is at bottom a cultural integument of social interaction, a cultural fabric in which social process is clothed. (Kingsbury 1988, p. 160)

That the very definition of music is contingent on the social situation is perhaps most obvious when the approaches to music in different cultures are compared. Over the last generation, conservatoires have begun to embrace instruments and musical styles which have previously had no long tradition within formal institutions of education (Laukka 2004; Lebler 2007; Parsonage, Fadnes, and Taylor 2007), and this is even more evident in the University sector of Higher Education. At SEU for example music students may pursue various degree programmes and the Music Department offers a degree in Commercial Music as well as the Bachelor of Music degree; even within the BMus, the principal study instrument may be orientated toward classical, jazz or popular music.

It seems reasonable to assume that the range of musical traditions informing contemporary degrees in music manifests itself in a range of behaviours among practitioners, and this in turn will presumably affect behaviour within instrumental lessons. A good deal of information about musicians' attitudes to musical expertise, and how they might differ with various musical traditions, comes from a questionnaire study undertaken by Creech et al. (2008). It should be noted that the demographic of the 244 informants does not provide a neat match for the student body at SEU, in that about half of the classical musicians involved were professional rather than students, while the non-classical musicians were chiefly undergraduate; in addition, the students involved seemed to belong to degrees focused on their principal musical genre rather than one with mixed content, as at SEU. The non-classical musicians in the study were engaged with popular, jazz and Scottish traditional music (p. 216).

In this detailed and careful study, Creech et al. warn that dichotomies between classical and non-classical musicians are by no means clear-cut, though they note that '[a]ll of the musicians in this sample evidently considered themselves to have been influenced profoundly by social factors and in particular by musical role models and interaction with other musicians' (p. 231). In spite of some common attitudes, however, with the informants in broad agreement for example about the importance of performance standards and the development of coping strategies (p. 218), there were many clear contrasts between the two groups. Classical musicians were conspicuous for their high regard for musical and technical excellence (p. 218), for example, and in contrast with the tendency of non-classical musicians to acknowledge the influence of other performers, academic lecturers and peers, they regarded instrumental teachers, parents and county ensembles as being most influential (p. 226). Creech et al. suggest that a useful way of conceptualizing the influences felt by musicians participating in various overlapping traditions is Bronfenbrenner's Ecological Systems Theory, which maps individual development against social systems of increasing scope (p. 217).

Several researchers have helped to characterize the behaviour of musicians performing in folk genres, outside formal institutions of education, including Cope (2002) who conducted telephone interviews with six musicians who had participated in a folk festival, and Kamin, Richards and Collins (2007) who interviewed 12 professional folk musicians. In both studies there seems to be an emphasis on relatively informal, peer learning. It should not be assumed however that the approach to learning taken by musicians in non-classical traditions is to be uniquely found outside educational institutions. Folkestad argues that learning is broader than this:

> [I]t is far too simplified, and actually false, to say that formal learning only occurs in institutional settings and that informal learning only occurs outside school. On the contrary, this static view has to be replaced with a dynamic view in which what are described as formal and informal learning styles are aspects of the phenomenon of learning, regardless of where it takes place. (Folkestad 2005, p. 284)

Folkestad emphasizes that what is learned and how it is approached are interconnected, and the subject content therefore mediates certain approaches, that may be found either inside or outside the institutional context (p. 283). Previous research at SEU has offered some evidence showing that the relatively informal approaches taken to learning in non-classical music have penetrated the instrumental lesson within the institution, in terms of the distribution of talk between teacher and student (Burwell 2006). Among 67 instrumental lessons, it was found that in classical instrumental lessons (n = 32) the student spoke very little, contributing an average of 10.3 per cent of the total wordage; in lessons given on instruments outside the conservatoire tradition (n = 23) the far more talkative student contributed an average of 26.3 per cent of the total wordage. Singers (n = 12) lay somewhere between the two. In addition, the non-traditional instrumental students were more likely than the classical students to engage in off-task dialogue (Burwell 2006, p. 338). This particular finding would seem to tie in neatly with the attitude among classical students reported by Nerland and Hanken: that they will learn through subjugating themselves in an interaction with a dominant authority (2004, pp. 5–6).

The historical nature of cultural influences is highlighted in a study by Callaghan (1998) who conducted interviews with 50 voice teachers working in the Higher Education sector in Australia. Using methods derived from Grounded Theory, Callaghan examines the approaches taken by teachers, which she argues are all ultimately derived from the seventeenth-century *bel canto* tradition (1998, p. 25). This means that they shared a concern with tone and breath control, aural and mental skills, and learning by sensation, along with the use of kinaesthetic, visual and aural imagery in teaching these skills. The teachers had developed their approaches primarily by drawing on their own experience, and were keen to address the individual needs of their students (p. 30). Callaghan identifies one category of approach in which, in addition to these shared features, a particularly strong sense of tradition is evident:

> Traditional teachers ... are distinguished by the fact that they teach vocal technique through imagery and emphasise 'beautiful tone' and naturalness.

> These teachers have been classified as 'traditional' to link their teaching approaches to those common at the time of their training, in the 1940s or early 1950s. Their emphasis on 'beautiful' tone and 'naturalness' demonstrates links to the oral tradition. (Callaghan 1998, p. 28)

The approach taken by these teachers however falls short of offering physiological explanations for vocal technique, which, along with an emphasis on 'appropriate rather than beautiful tone', seems characteristic of teachers associated with music theatre or contemporary commercial music (pp. 29–30).

In terms of lesson content and vocabulary, the distinction among teachers' approaches, traditional or modern, again has some resonance with the study by Burwell (2006) at SEU, where singers and conservatoire and non-conservatoire instrumentalists were found to behave rather differently. Among 67 observed lessons, for example, the proportions of verbal dialogue devoted to various areas of study suggested that singers were discussing technique more than instrumentalists, with non-conservatoire instrumentalists discussing technique least of all (Burwell 2006, p. 338). Parallel to this, singing teachers too were the most likely to employ imagery in lesson dialogue, and non-conservatoire instrumentalists least; conservatoire instrumentalists were closer to singers in their occasional use of imagery, and in actually singing during lessons, to make or illustrate their points (pp. 339–41).

The Music Department

As remarked above, the Bachelor of Music degree at SEU embraces a wide range of musical traditions. Although differences have been distinguished in the approaches taken by teachers associated with those traditions, it seems possible that any or all of them might have been influenced by one another. The isolation of instrumental and vocal teachers, even within a single institution, has been previously mentioned but the recent cultivation of formal staff development events at SEU, alongside instances of peer observation and informal networking, have begun to facilitate the sharing of interests and concerns among individual teachers. At the same time, students who pursue Performance Studies modules are brought together regularly in practical seminars, in which mixed groups of students are supported in practising and discussing performance: the exchange of practices and views, here, might perhaps filter back in some ways, to their individual lessons.

Although the influence of distinct musical cultures may be felt within the Music Department, within the University the Department may be seen to have a distinct culture of its own, the result perhaps of the hybrid traditions of the university, informal musical practices and the conservatoire. The traditions in place are further complicated by the rapid transformation of South England University itself. While modern universities and conservatoires essentially date from the nineteenth century (Weber; Nielsen 1999), SEU was founded as a teacher training college in the 1960s. From the mid-1970s music was offered as part of a combined subject degree in education, and eventually degrees in music as a single subject became available. The achievement of full university status made the influence of that tradition explicit; the original emphasis on education as a subject area remains however significant to the institution as a whole, and is also felt within the Music Department. The Head of Department until 2006 was originally engaged at SEU as a member of the Education Faculty, and another member of that faculty was a member of the research team which began to study instrumental teaching and learning in the Music Department, in 1998.

Froelich (2002) has offered a useful sociological account of the approaches taken to education, in the distinct traditions of teacher training and music. In an institution where musical performance is only one of a number of courses of study offered, he asserts that the students tend to perceive the musical construct more strongly than, for example, the educational construct. This assertion is supported by several other researchers, who report that musical performance tends to attract a disproportionate degree of motivation among students, regardless of their specific career paths (Nielsen 1999; Jørgensen 2002).

Between the traditions of the music school and the teachers' college, Froelich proposes a series of contrasting 'rites and rituals'. The music institution is characterized as a relatively closed community, with entry subject to audition. Cultural elitism is standard, with the individual instrumental teacher the 'significant other', and the preferred model the 'master-apprentice approach'. In the teachers' college, however, cultural egalitarianism is standard, with the teacher regarded as the objective dispenser of knowledge in a classroom setting, and the preferred model, the 'discovery' method. Because performance is skill-based, learned experientially, music students enjoy an 'insider routine' of practice and 'insider status' from performance; for education students, the first priority is the acquisition of professional knowledge, with experiential skill to be acquired, only later. It is interesting, in the light of research suggesting that instrumental students take an apparently passive role in their lessons, that learning through performance is held to be participatory in nature and instills a sense of active learning in the music student, whereas the education student learns by 'on-looking', which instills a sense of being a bystander (Froelich 2002, p. 153).

The course of study identified by each student of the Music Department at SEU can be highly individual, and within that the Performance Studies module might vary in its importance, from being the main point of focus for some students to a relatively minor subject for others. This variety presumably means that it is less likely that students will take a unified view of teaching and learning, than they might if they were all pursuing similar aims and to a similar extent.

The character of the University Music Department, embracing such diversity, may be usefully compared to the more unified character of the Danish Academy of music described by Nielsen in a thesis framing that institution as an apprenticeship (Nielsen 1999). Nielsen asserts that there is an agreed, underlying aim for Academy students, with becoming a solo performer the 'paradigmatic trajectory' of the institution (p. 77, n. 50): he interviews a teacher who explains that '[the piano students] know that they will not become a Rubinstein but it is still Rubinstein who drives them on' (p. 113). In contrast, although the range of possible aims among students in the University Music Department is wide, aspiring to solo performance must be comparatively rare. This has been explained in setting the scene for a research study in the department:

> Graduates of the music department tend to be capable people rather than concert artists, and while the proportion of graduates moving on to either full employment or postgraduate study is high, their range of career destinations is characteristically wider than that of conservatoire-trained musicians. (Burwell 2005, p. 201)

An important difference between the Music Department and the Academy is that the prestige of the solo recital tends to make that the focal point for successful students in the Academy, whereas in the Music Department, students at all levels are far more likely to appear in ensemble situations. The nature of internal performance platforms, too, would seem to be different. Although Nielsen describes the Academy as a safe environment, where students can gain performing experience in 'sheltered conditions' (p. 192), he also reports that students can be particularly nervous about playing in this situation, 'because the audience there are musicians and therefore critical and know the music'. Students can become '*paralyzed* with fear' (p. 189; original italics) and it is in effect the Academy and its 'particularly critical discourse of classification which helps create the nervousness' (p. 188). Nielsen also argues that the high pressure associated with internal concerts is 'a way for the profession to *control* its own production of pianists' (p. 73; italics added). This has resonance with Kingsbury's discussion of the conservatory as a cultural system, in which he asserts that 'the culling of students perceived as less talented, less accomplished, or less "musical" is generally accepted as necessary and inevitable in conservatory life, even if this is accomplished in an unpleasant fashion' (p. 105).

In comparison, the Performance Studies modules in the Music Department at SEU neither labour under nor aspire to the ideal of the solo concert artist as a goal for their students. Internal performance seminars are explicitly designed to support students overcoming performance anxiety: sessions are closed, class sizes start small, and conduct is largely informal, only gradually beginning to resemble the public concert forum as students gain confidence and expertise. Although the Department is supportive of individual students able and wishing to pursue instrumental skill to highly advanced levels, the broader emphasis is on participation more than performance.

Finally, in the Academy, the authority accorded the main instrumental teacher suggests a clear separation, within the community of practice, between teacher and student. The emphasis is on solo performance, and although the teacher's reputation depends on his solo career, no mention is made in Nielsen's thesis of teachers performing in the institution itself. In contrast, the concert calendar of SEU shows a free mixture of teacher- and student-led activities, with collaborations common particularly among teachers and senior students. In outstanding cases, participants in this community of practice – perhaps reflecting its collegiate heritage – have moved from being students undertaking undergraduate and postgraduate degrees, to joining the staff of the Department. The clear separation between master and apprentice, implicit in Nielsen's study of the academy, becomes less clear in such cases. In some ways this might be regarded as having a closer resemblance to apprenticeship as a community of practice than the academy as described by Nielsen: Lave and Wenger for example propose a perspective that focuses on the potential movement of the individual 'from entrance as a newcomer, *through* becoming an old-timer with respect to new newcomers [rather] than a teacher/ learner dyad' (Lave and Wenger 1991, p. 56; italics added).

The University Degree Programme

In terms of a broad context, then, the institutional ancestors of the Music Department at SEU include apprenticeship, the conservatoire, the teacher training college and the university. Added to these are the musical cultures that do not have a strong tradition within formal institutions of education, such as jazz and popular music. In terms of a more local context, the formally structured undergraduate degree programme may be characterized as a frame for instrumental lessons.

The emphasis on individual teaching in the Music Department implies that in some ways, what happens within instrumental lessons is separate from the programme validated by the University. In the light of the information presented in Mills's review of institutions in Higher Education music, it seems that the amount of instrumental tuition provided in the SEU BMus programme lies between that offered by conservatoires and other universities (Mills 2003 p. 51; Burwell 2005, p. 201). In the conservatoire setting, where the provision of instrumental tuition is more generous, Presland suggests that 'there is a danger, given the roaming nature of visiting professors, that staff will tend to work in their own educational and musical worlds, perhaps unwittingly accentuating the division between instrumental lessons and general musical education in the minds of their students' (Presland 2005, p. 247). At SEU the staff development programme for visiting instrumental and vocal teachers is designed to help them keep abreast of the institution's musical activities and curriculum design, and although there may be some tension between the aims published for the degree programme and the aims felt within the instrumental teacher-student dyad, the scope that this offers for individual tailoring, according to the strengths and interests of participants, is generally viewed in a positive light.

Even so, what the Bachelor of Music programme is or can be, may be viewed from the perspectives of either the University's formally structured programme or the contributions of visiting instrumental staff who represent varying musical traditions and practices and who enjoy a certain amount of autonomy within the institution. The variety available is perhaps more obvious to visiting staff than the coherence of the programme, and for this reason the handbook for instrumental and vocal teachers includes background material describing 'A university degree in music' (Burwell 2009). This document emphasizes the breadth of skills involved in such a degree, additional to instrumental expertise, alongside the concepts of widening participation and lifelong learning, both prioritized in the University's Strategic plan. In contrast to concert performance as the paradigmatic trajectory of conservatoire students, it is noted that the range of career destinations for university graduates is a wide one, and that the degree in music is well designed to support that. A Head of Department is quoted as arguing that '[the] major qualities sought by employers in industry were those exemplified in music education: flexibility and adaptability; motor skills; self-awareness and confidence; cooperation; the ability to marshal relevant information to make decisions; and the ability to use initiative' (Hancox in Pugh and Pugh 1998, p. 5).

Student independence is a highlighted issue in the same handbook, and a sketch is offered to show how student learning is scaffolded in the Performance Studies modules: this is intended to show what background elements might inform individual instrumental lessons:

> The written component of the performance modules tests students' ability to reflect on their work, but perhaps more importantly, it poses a series of carefully ordered tasks which provide a guideline for the kind of thinking students should be undertaking. Thus first year students for example are asked to give an account of their current stage of development regarding performance, and to outline the personal goals they have agreed on with their individual tutors. Later, more specific challenges ask them to interrogate their own standing in terms of the decisions being taken, in terms of practice strategies, repertoire choice, and critical self-evaluation. Some will be able to demonstrate a high level of independence at an early stage; others, less accustomed to the kind of thinking expected in higher education, will need to begin by examining the advice offered by their instrumental tutors, and trying to understand the judgement behind it. Certainly we encourage students to think that their individual tutors will welcome questions, and to negotiate with them an individually-tailored course of study. (Burwell 2009, p. 3)

While students are encouraged to engage in this way with their tutors, the tutors in turn are encouraged to take a flexible approach 'to the needs of a wide range of students, with varying levels of ability, independence, and musical ambitions' (p. 3).

A limited amount of research has been conducted into the experience of music students within English universities. Pitts (2001) investigated the transition from secondary school to university, and the effect that had on young musicians in terms of their sense of identity and expertise; in another study (2003) she used a small-scale questionnaire to investigate the 'hidden curriculum' felt by third-year undergraduates. The university framework for the Music Department investigated was evident in findings that seemed generic across various subject areas: thus diversity among teaching styles, friendliness and responsibility for learning were themes equally prominent in both the Music Department and the Chemical and Process Engineering department (p. 290). Six out of the eleven music students however also described their Department as being 'cliquey' (p. 286), a characteristic perhaps more typical of a conservatoire than a university (for example, Kingsbury 1988, p. 37). Within the same university, Dibben studied the sociocultural experiences of music students through a survey and interviews, and emphasized the importance of the role taken by performance in students' identities and sense of belonging (2006, p. 102).

Although the amount of research focused on music students within the University sector remains limited, a good deal of research has been focused on the student experience in universities in general, with work undertaken since the 1970s usefully summarized by Entwistle (2007). Introducing his subject, Entwistle proposes that teaching and learning in Higher Education should be seen as an interaction among the teaching-learning environment, the subject matter and student characteristics (p. 1). The teaching-learning environment encompasses a range of features, including 'the various teaching activities, the learning materials made available, [and] the support provided by tutors or demonstrators, as well as the assignments students are required to complete and the assessment procedures adopted' (p. 8). A degree of alignment or congruence among these features would seem to be important in supporting effective teaching and learning (p. 8, p. 10).

The subject matter is itself a crucial element within the interactive system of teaching and learning, and individual subject areas evidently have their own distinctive teaching methods, reflecting 'an inner logic of the subject and its pedagogy' (pp. 13–14). This appears to be particularly true of subjects closely related to specific professions, such as musical performance. Schön (1983; 1987) has addressed the relationship between professions and institutions of education, and Nerland and Hanken (2004) refer to a tension that can exist between the professional field and the conservatoire, creating a double position for the institution:

> Institutions for higher music education occupy important positions in the field of arts and musical performance, while being situated at the same time in the field of education. This double positioning implies that different sets of values, standards and forms of 'symbolic capital' are brought into play, and that these different, and in some cases even conflicting, sets of values offer participants in higher music education divergent ways of understanding and looking at their institutional practice. (Nerland and Hanken 2004, p. 8)

Within any subject-specific pedagogy, certain characteristics are consistent throughout the curriculum, so that the student must learn for example to 'think like a lawyer' or 'think like a physician' (Shulman, in Entwistle 2007, p. 14). This clearly resonates with the notion of learning as participation in a community of practice, as described by Wenger (1998).

Finally, the student's perception of the teaching environment and the nature of the subject matter will inevitably have an effect on the learning that takes place, largely because this will have direct bearing on her approach to studying (Entwistle 2007, p. 6). The conceptualization of undergraduates' approaches to study has been qualified and refined over a generation of research. One influential account of it identifies three broad categories: a 'deep' approach which involves transforming with the intention 'to understand ideas for yourself'; a 'surface' approach which involves reproducing with the intention 'to cope with course requirements'; and a 'strategic' approach which involves organizing with the intention 'to achieve the highest possible grades' (Entwistle 2005, p. 19). A later adaptation of this theory suggests that these approaches be reframed, so that deep and surface approaches are seen to operate on one dimension, while on another the strategic approach is regarded as 'achievement motivation' and can be associated with either of the main approaches to studying (Kember, Wong and Leung 1999). The ideas put forward by this research, and the focus on student perceptions, are parallel to Reid's 2001 study, previously discussed, which proposed hierarchical categories to characterize music students' conceptions of learning.

Summary and Reflections

Implicit in studio-based instrumental teaching and learning is a complex web of social and cultural links that may be regarded as framing lesson interactions. Teacher and student enact, to some extent, roles that are laid out for them by the institutional setting, itself a cultural system; and in particular, the authority invested in the teacher represents the power relations inherent in any apprenticeship situation (Lave and Wenger 1991, p. 64). Although an authoritarian approach to lessons might have negative consequences (Hays et al. 2000, p. 8; Sosniak 1985b, p. 421), there is evidence suggesting that an authoritative approach in teachers is often sought and maintained by students, and it has been argued that in some settings authority is an invaluable teaching resource (Howard 1992, p. 67; Riggs 2006, pp. 180–81; Nerland and Hanken 2002, p. 168). The roles taken by teacher and student may be evident in their lesson behaviour, verbal and nonverbal, even if the cultural setting that provides them may be no more than a background feature of studies focused on lesson observation (Matusov 2007, p. 324).

The university music department is likely to rest on an ancestry of various musical cultures, some of which are associated with a long tradition within the conservatoire while others have been associated more often with the 'informal' learning characteristic of musical styles such as jazz, folk and popular music. The conservatoire culture and associated behaviours have been characterized by, for example, Kingsbury (1988) and Nielsen (1999; 2006), and the 'informal' cultures by Creech et al. (2008), Cope (2002) and Kamin et al. (2007). In addition, the institutional heritage of the music department is likely to include traditions drawn from the university, conservatoire and teacher training college. All of these formal and informal traditions may be blended in various ways among teachers and students with individual learning histories, and it seems possible that they will be evident in both personal and interpersonal behaviour (Burwell 2006; Froelich 2002).

Although there may be little previous research focused on university music departments (Pitts 2002; 2003; Dibben 2006), there is an extensive body of research and scholarship focused on the student experience of learning in the university, and in this broad context it has been argued that teaching and learning represents an interaction of the environment, the subject matter and the characteristics of individual participants (Entwistle 2007, p. 1). The cross-currents implicit in the instrumental lesson might therefore be regarded as working both horizontally – through participant identities, the present situation and the resources in hand – and vertically – drawing on participant histories and ancestries as well as their aims and aspirations for the future.

Summary: Researching Instrumental Teaching and Learning

In building the conceptual framework for the current study, the main sections of each chapter have been summarized, with occasional reflections offered. Here, the interrelationships among sections, and between the literature reviews and the lines of inquiry yet to be reported, are clarified, and some salient issues, including gaps in the literature, highlighted.

The first two research questions for this study ask how lesson interactions are undertaken in the studio, and how that might vary with individual participants. Within the study, these questions are most closely related to the epistemology of skill and to the investigation of lesson behaviour (Chapter 3). Studies of lesson behaviour have been divided according to their focus on modelling, verbal behaviour or the individual attributes of participants; in the current case study, these will be loosely matched by a layered investigation of performance, verbal and nonverbal behaviours, respectively.

The third research question asks how lesson interactions are contextualized, and within the study, this is most closely related to apprenticeship and to studies that effectively frame instrumental lessons (Chapter 4). Broadly, lessons might be contextualized through the consideration of apprenticeship as a social framework; of musical traditions as a cultural framework; and the university music department as an institutional framework. Like all communities of practice, these are complex and overlapping, and while lesson behaviours are conceptualized in layers, these might more usefully be conceptualized as intersecting planes that imply a multidimensional model of activity.

For the current study, in the terms used by Matusov, lesson interactions represent the 'foreground' of interest, while the frameworks for them represent the 'background'. Insofar as the individual may be the 'traditional but wrong unit for analysis' (2007, p. 307), the behaviour observed in instrumental lessons is regarded as a collaboration, with the behaviour of each participant contingent on that of the other, while the intersecting contextual frameworks play an essential role in lending ecological validity to the description and interpretation of the collaboration.

In the discussion of research focused on either lesson interactions or the frameworks around them, there have been a number of recurring themes providing rich food for thought. The various conceptions of authority, for example, have been related to details of asymmetrical behaviour within the teacher-student dyad, on one hand, and the broad traditions of apprenticeship on the other. Imitation is another complex theme, that might be conceptualized as highly specific lesson behaviour led by demonstration, or as collaborative participation in a community of practice.

Such ambiguities suggest that what the researcher finds will depend on the strength of the lens used for observation. It might further be suggested that the findings will depend on the longitudinal boundaries of the study: the teaching and – even more – the learning that might be observed in an individual instrumental lesson might only represent one small component in the pyramid structure of the student's learning career (Burwell et al. 2004, p. 31), since so much more time and effort is presumably invested outside the studio setting, and since the effects of lesson interactions might be felt more expansively long after the lesson has ended (Reimer 2004).

In addition to the strength of the lens and the time scale, the perspective adopted by researchers may further affect the nature of findings. Indeed, some of the gaps in the literature could be associated with a failure to take multiple perspectives into account: thus, for example, the tendency in some observational studies to seek preconceived lesson behaviours might lead to the assumption that a participant not engaging in those behaviours must be inactive. It seems clear that teachers dominate verbal behaviour, for example, but there has been little research asking what the student might be doing while the teacher is talking, nor how the student's behaviour might be implicated in that of the teacher. Perhaps parallel to this is the issue of demonstration: although this activity and its role in lessons has been explored by philosopher Howard (1982; 1992), empirical researchers have yet to fully explore how this is undertaken, and how the teacher's behaviour might be implicated in that of the student.

The perceptions of participants provide another possible perspective on studio-based instrumental learning. Indeed, the investigation of individual perspectives seems an important area for further research, given for example the wide variety of student conceptions of learning analyzed by Reid (2002) and the mismatch between participant and observer perceptions of lesson activity noted by Koopman et al. (2007, p. 383). It is worth reiterating that although wordage or performance may be counted or timed, the significance of lesson behaviours must be difficult to measure meaningfully without reference to the perceptions of lesson participants. A meaningful evaluation of lesson activity, too, must be difficult, given that the perception of effectiveness in teaching and learning has been found to vary, among students, teachers and expert observers (Siebenaler 1997, p. 18; Kurkul 2007,

p. 344); and that the perception of lesson effectiveness has been found to alter when observers focus their attention on the teacher, the student or both (Duke and Prickett 1987, p. 27).

The issue of evaluation, and the need to approach it with caution (Jørgensen 2009, p. 111), recalls the further need to handle with care any theoretical premises brought into research focused on instrumental teaching and learning, from other contexts. The short history of research in this area has often been characterized by the identification, testing and eventually adaptation of assumptions drawn from the literature related to either general education or group and rehearsal settings, with the attention to 'local' particulars needed to enhance validity (Lincoln and Guba 1985, p. 42).

The current study is not evaluative in its aims, but seeks to interpret a close observation of a closely bounded case study, with due regard for context, in an effort to enhance understanding (Stake 2005, p. 445). The approach taken to fieldwork design in the study is more fully addressed, in Chapter 5.

Chapter 5
Fieldwork Design

This chapter introduces the case study which, through video observation and semi-structured interviews, explores two clarinet lessons, undertaken within the normal course of Performance Studies in the Music Department at SEU. It is divided into two broad sections.

The first offers some reflections on the theoretical perspective, and elements of the conceptual framework for the study. This includes the fieldwork design and the position of the researcher, both of which are implicated in the aims of the study and in the methods adopted. Indeed, the position of the researcher, along with the potential influence of the researcher on the researched, is perhaps one of the chief threats to validity in qualitative studies (Maxwell 2005, p. 108).

In the second section, the research methods will be outlined, with remarks about the relationship between the methods adopted and the previous literature reviews, the selection of the case for study, the research tools used for data collection and the approach taken to data analysis and interpretation. The chapter concludes with a brief summary showing how the methods are related to the research questions.

Theoretical Perspective

Fieldwork Design

This discussion begins with some remarks about the characterization of the research problem, which is a fundamental task for the researcher and which feeds into all other aspects of fieldwork design. Maxwell characterizes the research problem as part of the conceptual framework for any study:

> … it identifies something that is *going on* in the world, something that is itself problematic or that has consequences that are problematic. Your research problem functions (in combination with your goals) to *justify* your study, to show people why your research is important. In addition, this problem is something that is not fully understood, or that we don't adequately know how to deal with, and therefore we want more information about it. (Maxwell 2005, p. 34; italics original)

The research problem is contingent not only on the nature of the subject, but the perspective of the researcher. It is assumed that the researcher's perspective might be individual, without being unique; and yet there are no ready-made problems in instrumental teaching and learning: these must be framed, explored and justified by the researcher herself. It has been remarked that it remains relatively rare for performer-teachers to undertake research themselves (Mills 2007, p. 76), partly perhaps because of the particular range of professional interests and opportunities required for the task. Even among performer-teachers, however, the characterization of research problems might not be easily agreed, because of the nature of the subject.

Pring writes about 'publicly agreed bodies of knowledge' that lie behind other subject areas in education: 'the theories, propositions and explanations which have accumulated through enquiry, criticism, argument and counter argument, [and which] have survived testing and criticism'; the credentials of the body of knowledge depend on their being 'public property', open to challenge and refutation (2000, p. 80).

From the perspective of the performer-teacher-researcher, this leaves studio-based teaching and learning with particular problems. It would be difficult to argue that there is a body of knowledge shared by instrumental teachers, not least because – as previously discussed – their individual knowledge has been developed in relative isolation. The subject is rarely supported by a shared regime of formal training that might serve as a framework or even a starting point for professional practice; this, along with a blurred distinction between professional and amateur, is what led sociologists Fredrickson and Rooney (1990) to argue that music as a whole has failed to become a profession in the modern sense. A lack of cohesion is also evident in employment conditions, since teachers are typically engaged on a private or part-time basis. Even the characteristic one-to-one setting of lessons serves to underline the isolated nature of individually developing practices.

The difficulties involved in discussing musical skills and the acquisition of them, explored at some length in Chapter 2, would also seem to work against the establishment of a publicly agreed body of knowledge specific to instrumental teaching. The complex skill of the performance teacher is to a significant degree nonverbal in nature; her practice is typically conducted through demonstration, and through language designed for coaching and feedback more than explanation; and her skill is likely to be unique in some ways, since music teaching, no less than musical performance, can involve artistry and individuality.

Studio-based instrumental teaching and learning, then, generates particular problems for the researcher, which arguably require the development of an individually tailored conceptual framework, implying a highly specific selection and use of research tools. The theoretical perspective adopted for the current case study is more fully discussed elsewhere (Burwell 2012). Here, it is noted that the premises of the current study place it under the broad umbrella of Social Constructionism (Burr, 2003). These include a critical stance taken toward Postpositivism; a focus on interaction among the participants observed, in the conviction that knowledge is sustained by social processes (p. 4); and an assumption that like all human action, this will be historically, culturally and institutionally situated (Wertsch 1991, p. 119; Säljö 1997, p. 5). The concerns of social constructionist research are explained by Mehan:

> [The tradition is concerned with] how the stable features of social institutions such as schooling, science, medicine, and the family are both generated in and revealed by the language of the institution's participants ... People's everyday practices are examined for the way in which they exhibit – indeed, generate – the social structures of the relevant domain ... Inferences about social structure are permissible only when the workings of the structure can be located in people's interaction. (Lave 1993, p. 20)

Schön (1987), drawing a contrast between constructionism and objectivism, embraces the former as better suited to interrogating professional artistry, as practitioners, '[t]hrough countless acts of attention and inattention, naming, sensemaking, boundary setting, and control, [make] and maintain the worlds matched to their professional knowledge and know-how' (p. 36).

In the current case study, the practice of studio-based instrumental learning is explored with reference to two individual lessons. The interactions among participants are studied through a micro-analysis of lesson behaviour, and this is enhanced by the consideration of interviews with participants, who discussed their own perceptions of the lessons shortly after they were filmed. Their 'insider perspectives' also help to frame lesson behaviour, by drawing links to the activity, attitudes and understanding that lie behind it, and to establish a sense of context within the social and cultural institutions that surround it.

Position of the Researcher

Maxwell (2005) describes the conceptual framework of any piece of research as the theory behind it, however tentative or incomplete it may be. It includes, but is not synonymous with, the literature review, and in broad terms comprises a 'set of concepts and the proposed relationships among these, a structure that is intended to represent or model something about the world' (p. 42).

The conceptual framework will be fundamentally influenced by the researcher's basic beliefs, which are implicit in the process of inquiry, guiding the choices of problem, paradigm to guide the problem, theoretical framework, major data-gathering and data-analytic methods, context, treatment of values already resident within the context, and format for presenting findings (Guba and Lincoln 2005, p. 198). Far from trying to neutralize the researcher's 'bias' – particularly as personal experience can be used to facilitate insight and understanding – it is necessary to remain keenly conscious of it, and to ensure that readers have the opportunity to evaluate the research in the light of that explicit context.

My own conceptual framework must be influenced by a range of prior experiences. These include formal study in a conservatoire as well as universities, covering a range of performance-based and academic work. As a performer I was one of those student musicians whom Manturzewska calls lucky enough to find a 'teacher-master' (1990, p. 134): this was a concert pianist of international renown, whose position in the broad community of practice rested more conspicuously on his performing expertise than on his teaching. In addition to performing professionally, myself, I have been a teacher of performance both in a conservatoire and in a university music department. A further insight into the profession was gained when I acted informally as assistant to my 'teacher-master' over a period of several years.

Within the institutional context – chiefly the university – my roles have included curriculum design in Performance Studies, as well as Instrumental Teaching and Learning; I have conducted research into both of these within the university music department, publishing journal papers and speaking at conferences; led or contributed to staff development activities for other teachers of performance; and as a member of the core academic staff, had some experience in management roles.

In conducting research within the Music Department at SEU I was to some extent a participant observer, being a member of the department as a community, known to all of the teachers and students who were observed and interviewed. Although this study is focused on individual clarinet lessons, which generally lay outside my own professional remit, I had often acted as piano accompanist to clarinet students in their concerts and performance examinations, and had attended their individual lessons in preparation for such events.

As previously remarked, the participant researcher's familiarity with the environment might be seen as an advantage, particularly in identifying and understanding themes drawn from observations and interviews, but this vantage point must also qualify aspects of the research undertaken. One of these aspects is the effect of the researcher on the researched, and in this respect it should be noted that both the participants and the members of the original research team at SEU were all members of the same academic community. Particularly in interviews, student participants might be influenced by their perception of us as familiar academic lecturers, piano accompanists or as more senior members of the social community in the Music Department. Teacher participants might be influenced by their perception of us as teaching colleagues, fellow performers or as academic staff associated with course design and management. It would be difficult to argue that either students or teachers would not feel that, in being observed and interviewed, they were being evaluated in some way. This potential influence on participant behaviour would presumably be complicated by the presence of the research camera in lessons, and although participants were later invited to comment on the perceived effect of the camera, all of these influences should be acknowledged as potential sources of influence on the data.

Familiarity with the environment might also lead to the researcher overlooking aspects of the subject that are so much part of 'normal practice' that they are taken for granted; and although the participant researcher might have some specialist insight to offer, the interpretation of data cannot be value free. To some extent these effects may be countered through the use of research tools which can help to create some distance between the observer and the observed. These are identified in the Method below.

Method

The Case Study and Data Collection

The methods employed in this study may be related to issues identified in the epistemology discussed in Chapter 2 and the literature reviews in Chapters 3 and 4. It has been argued that studying individual issues, participants or behaviours in isolation may undermine the ecological validity of any study: thus early experimental research in instrumental teaching and learning has often involved making compromises in authenticity in order to collect quantifiable data; systematic observations, by seeking preconceived behaviours, have entailed comparable limitations. The reviews of literature – on skill, apprenticeship, lesson interactions and frameworks for instrumental lessons – have helped to highlight a number of important issues pertinent to further research: interactive behaviour is involved, with the behaviour of one participant implicated in that of the other; the views of participants may be important in triangulating the meaning of any observed behaviour; the nature of the subject matter suggests that different lesson behaviours, such as performing and talking, might be implicated in one another; and the various frameworks that might be positioned around lesson interactions suggest the sensitivity of all lesson behaviours, to context.

These considerations suggest that a small-scale broadly qualitative case study approach is appropriate to the aims of the current investigation. Obtaining rich data from the micro-analysis of two instrumental lessons, using both qualitative and quantitative tools and allowing categories for analysis to emerge from the data, supports the study of interaction among participants and different kinds of behaviour. The case study approach, as previously mentioned, is well suited to taking the insider perspectives of participants into account (Lincoln and Guba 1985, p. 27). It also permits research 'when the boundary between the "case" (the phenomenon being studied – or the unit of analysis) and its context is not clearly evident' (Yin 1998, p. 237) and is therefore appropriate, too, to the study of the instrumental lesson as positioned among intersecting social, cultural and institutional planes.

The current case study is nested, in that the data has been drawn from a larger project investigating aspects of instrumental teaching and learning in the Music Department at SEU. This work, at times involving a team of researchers, involved the collection of data over an extended period, through successive phases of video observations, of individual and group lessons; questionnaires concerning participant biographies, areas of study, teaching strategies and student practice; and semi-structured interviews with teachers and students, reflecting on observed lessons as well as their broad approaches to instrumental teaching and learning (Young et al. 2003; Burwell et al. 2004; Burwell 2005; 2006; Burwell and Shipton 2011).

In particular, the data mined for this study represents two different methods of data collection. The first of these is video observation. The camera might represent the metaphorical presence of the researcher, potentially influencing lesson behaviour; but this presence is arguably removed to a certain distance, and there are obvious advantages in being able to capture aspects of participant behaviour in a 'natural habitat' (Heath 1997, p. 198).

The second method of data collection is the use of semi-structured interviews. Interviews have been used at various stages and in various ways in the department's research programme, but the data to be examined here is drawn from a set of 27 interviews with students and teachers, conducted shortly after their lessons were filmed. Much of the interview schedule was devoted to the discussion of the lessons that had taken place, usually only hours or even minutes before. This meant that neither the interviewer nor the interviewed participants had the opportunity to review the video data before meeting for discussion, but it had the advantage of ensuring that the lessons were fresh and immediate in the participants' minds. In addition, the absence of video prompts would arguably prevent participants from focusing chiefly on explaining visual evidence, and thus encourage a freer discussion that might include reference to personal impressions, attitudes and feelings. The interview schedule included both specific and open-ended questions that would position the interviewed participants as both informants and respondents (Yin 1998, p. 237).

The interviews began by addressing aspects of the participants' biographies. The teacher was asked about his formal qualifications, the number of years he had been teaching, and the number of years he had been teaching in Higher Education; the students were asked for information about their current courses, how long they had been playing the clarinet, and how long they had been studying with this particular teacher. The student participants were also asked for their approximate ages. More importantly, in an effort to establish a triangulation of meaning, the participants were invited to discuss the lessons that had been captured on video, shortly before. This included some discussion of what had taken place during the lessons, as well as the context represented by their individual biographies, the broader course of study currently under pursuit, and their sense of the musical future for each of the students. All participants were invited to comment on the effect of the research camera in their lessons.

It is acknowledged that these discussions, like all qualitative research interviews, would not serve to validate the researcher's interpretation of the observed lessons, partly because the interview itself is a 'construction site for knowledge' (Kvale 1996, p. 14), a conversation in which the interviewer is implicated as much as the interviewed. Rather, the interviews would themselves provide evidence to be interpreted, arguably an alternative to the concept of validity (Denzin and Lincoln 2005, p. 6) and a way of enriching the data collected through observation. This, according to Maxwell, is the meaning of 'thick description' as the term was originally coined by Ryle and Geertz: 'description that incorporates the intentions of the actors and the codes of signification that give their actions meaning for them' (2005, p. 111, n. 1).

Ethics and the Identification of Participants

Consistent with the protocols established by the Research Governance Framework for SEU, the study was focused on participants who were not classified as being particularly vulnerable, were involved only through informed consent, and were assured of anonymity in reporting; the topics under investigation were not classified as being particularly sensitive.

Participants were initially identified when teachers in the Music Department at SEU responded to a call for volunteers to be involved in the department's research programme, and helped to identify volunteers among the students. Because the participants were assured of anonymity, no video evidence has been directly used in reporting. Research outcomes were made available to participants through access to published papers, and through a series of staff development events at which research presentations were delivered and discussed. In the course of the larger project, 19 instrumental and vocal teachers were eventually involved, and were filmed giving a total of 67 lessons to individual students and 10 lessons in group settings. The processing of data tended to be focused on drawing generalizations from this relatively large pool: the video evidence was initially transcribed with a particular focus on verbal dialogue in lessons, with some annotation of other behaviour, including incidents of performance and other activity (Young et al. 2003; Burwell et al. 2003; 2004).

For this project, the identification of the case study within a case study was made through purposeful selection. Although a strength of case study research is its ability to address contextual conditions (Yin 1998, p. 237), the emphasis here would lie on understanding the particular case rather than on generalization: an intrinsic rather than an instrumental case study (Stake 2005, p. 445). The work of one teacher was selected for further examination. It had become evident through the larger research project that the expertise of this teacher was sophisticated and wide-ranging, an impression agreed by research colleagues (Pickup and Young, 2010). The data in hand included video observations of five lessons given by him, along with a substantial and articulate interview: the choice of this teacher therefore seemed to offer an opportunity to learn, more important in an intrinsic case study than the typicality of the case (Stake 2005, p. 451).

The degree to which the selected teacher was typical of those who participated in the department's research programme should nevertheless be addressed. The range of experience among the 19 participating teachers was 1–38 years, with 1–32 years in Higher Education: with 23 years in both, this teacher had rather more experience than most. He represented the slight majority of 11 male teachers, and a rather stronger majority of 13 teachers who had no formal teaching qualifications. In approaching teaching and learning, no one instrumental teacher could be regarded as being entirely typical of the Music Department, since it had emerged that individual teaching within the Performance Studies course included a wide range of practices varying among, for example, singers and instrumentalists, or instrumentalists within and outside the conservatoire tradition (Burwell 2006). Even so, the conservatoire tradition was well represented in the department, and the clarinet – this teacher's specialty – popular among the university's music students. On the whole, it seemed that the case could be considered relevant, if not entirely representative, in the Music Department and in universities and conservatoires elsewhere.

The choice of student participants was subsequent to the choice of teacher. The two lessons selected for the current study were filmed on a single, continuous tape one morning during the Trinity term, a few weeks before the final performance examinations were scheduled. The fact that they were filmed consecutively provided some consistency in the time of day as well as the stage of the academic year. The two students also had some personal features in common, belonging to similar age brackets (22–29 years) and to the third year of the degree programme, and achieving similar academic results in that they both graduated with second class degrees. There were other personal features, too, that provided interesting contrasts, particularly within the performance course, with one student an outstanding player and the other achieving results closer to the course average. The intention however was not to compare lessons in order to identify the components of outstanding student success: to do so on the strength of only two lessons would be naïve. Such an aim would also limit the scope of the research, since comparison in a case study is likely to obscure any information not conducive to it (Stake 1995, p. 454). Rather, it was felt that investigating two lessons could provide something of a stereo effect which could enhance the dimensions of the study.

Data Collection and Analysis

Denzin and Lincoln suggest that the use of multiple methods in qualitative research, or triangulation, allows for a 'simultaneous display of multiple, refracted realities' (2005, p. 6). In this study triangulation appears in the use of interviews with participants to complement the video observation of their lessons, and in the use of multiple tools for the transcription and analysis of the evidence.

If, as discussed above, the term 'thick description' properly refers to the incorporation of actors' intentions rather than the amount of detail provided (Maxwell 2005, p. 111, n. 1), 'rich transcription' is perhaps a more appropriate term for the approach taken to data from the observed lessons. The transcriptions were devised in distinct layers, with verbal, nonverbal and performance behaviour treated as subunits for analysis (Yin 1998, p. 237) to be notated and coded separately. The systematic inclusion of all three layers would arguably provide an enriched account of the lesson interactions, thus enhancing the reliability of the description (Peräkylä 1997, p. 207), particularly in that some of the subunit behaviours would be more conscious – and more consciously controlled – than others (Argyle 1988, pp. 3–4).

As previously discussed, the third research question in this study, asking how lesson interactions are contextualized, represents the background of the case, while the first and second, asking how instrumental teaching and learning is undertaken, and how that might vary with participants, are in the foreground of interest (Matusov 2007, p. 324). Within the foregrounded lesson interactions, the lesson behaviours, verbal, nonverbal and performance, are regarded as embedded subunits and are analyzed largely through quantitative strategies; more broadly, the lesson descriptions and interview data are regarded as framing those subunits, and are interpreted qualitatively. The combination of quantitative and qualitative strategies is characteristic of what Yin calls 'embedded' case studies, which might involve quantitative data and analysis at the subunit level with a more qualitative treatment of the main unit of analysis (1998, p. 238).

The observed lessons had already been transcribed, with verbal dialogue, incidents of performance and occasionally other nonverbal behaviours noted, and some timings provided for the sake of orientation. Now, in Excel spreadsheets, the original transcriptions were divided into columns representing timing, and for each participant, the verbal contribution, performance behaviour and nonverbal activity.

The notation of verbal dialogue was very much refined through the use of conventions drawn from conversation analysis (for example, Wooffitt 2005) to indicate overlaps, emphasis and changes in volume. Initially, descriptive comments were added to note the occurrence of interesting features of the verbal behaviour, and patterns began to emerge that were eventually treated as formal categories. These were coded to indicate the varying functions of speech. The wordage and proportions of wordage were calculated for teacher and students, and for each verbal function; in all, this accounted for 98.3 per cent of the total wordage in the two lessons.

Similarly, a range of nonverbal behaviours was noted, and as patterns began to emerge, coded and described. To identify patterns, it was necessary to move back and forth between the data and its analysis, as repeated incidents began to suggest new subunits or categories; some categories emerged in the notation of the second lesson that necessitated a further review of the first. At times, it proved helpful to observe nonverbal behaviour in silence: the loss of aural information perhaps served to focus attention more closely on what could be seen.

To enrich the transcription of performance activity, each incident was timed to the second, and again colour coding was used to identify distinct categories, depending on the strength of the resemblance between the nature of the noted behaviour and concert performance. Because the categories were identified during the examination of data rather than being fixed before data was collected, they are explained as they arise in the discussion of findings, in Chapter 6.

The lesson observations on video represent the central source of data employed in this case study. The interviews with the three participants were mined more selectively, chiefly because although the original interview schedules addressed issues that are of central concern in this study, they also included prompts specific to areas of study and teaching strategies. These were issues that were of concern to the research team at the time (Young et al. 2003, Burwell et al. 2003), but have less relevance in the current study. Some discussion, too, of other individual students and their work would be of limited interest in this context.

Summary

The method is summarized here with reference to the research questions first given in Chapter 1. The broad aim of this study is to examine the interaction between teacher and student as they engage in studio-based instrumental teaching and learning, foregrounding lesson interactions against a contextual background. Specifically, the research questions ask:

1. How is instrumental teaching and learning undertaken?
The conduct of instrumental teaching and learning is examined through the micro-analysis of two consecutive clarinet lessons given by an expert teacher. These are captured in 105 minutes of videotape, transcribed in detail with specific reference to verbal, performance and other nonverbal activity. The three subunit behaviours are distinguished according to their function, which will be explained further in the discussion of findings to follow. The behaviours and their functions are analyzed through a mixture of qualitative and quantitative strategies: they are coded and summarized through the use of descriptive statistics, and identifying relationships among behaviours interpreted.

2. How does the conduct of instrumental teaching and learning vary with participants?
Points of comparison are drawn between the two lessons in order to examine the variation of behaviour among different participants. The comparisons help to distinguish the students from each other, and to add a further dimension to the picture of the teacher's lesson behaviour.

3. How is the interaction between teacher and student contextualized?
A sense of context for the lesson interactions is examined through the semi-structured interviews with the participants. These are cross referenced with the lesson observations, to take participants' perceptions of their own activity into account; they also offer some explicit discussion of the participants' biographies and their perceptions of the personal and broader contexts of their lessons together.

A Note on Reporting

In the reports that follow, consideration of the interview data is used to frame the more detailed examination of the two instrumental lessons. Thus Chapter 6 begins with an account of the broad context of instrumental teaching and learning, drawn from the interview with the teacher; while Chapter 7 is concluded with material drawn from the interviews with all three participants, as they reflect on the observed lessons.

The participants are given pseudonyms:

Teacher	Timothy
Student A	Andrew
Student B	Beth
(Student C	Catherine)

Quotes from lesson transcriptions are presented with the following conventions:

Abbreviated material is indicated by … dots.

A short pause in speaking is indicated by , a comma.

A longer pause in speaking is indicated by – a dash.

Louder words are indicated by CAPITALS.

Words given emphasis are underlined.

Timings from the transcription of the lessons are given as minutes:seconds.

Specific behaviours and functions of behaviour, coded in lesson transcriptions, are introduced and explained as they arise in the discussion of findings.

Chapter 6
Lesson A

Introduction and Context

The account of the research findings is divided into several separate sections. The case studies of the two individual lessons are considered in Chapters 6 and 7 respectively, and within those chapters each lesson is examined in terms of three behaviours: spatial, performance and verbal. Interview data is used to provide a frame for the pair of chapters. As a preface to Lesson A, an account of the interview with the teacher, Timothy, provides a broad – but gradually narrowing – sense of context for the individual case studies. Following the description of Lesson B in Chapter 7, reference is made to the interviews with all three participants, as they reflect on their lessons today, in the context of the students' past experience and future prospects.

Timothy's interview may itself be contextualized by biographical information about him that is available in the public domain. Timothy is a distinguished professional performer on the clarinet. He has taken a particular interest in performing contemporary music, but he also frequently performs many of the standard works of the clarinet repertoire. His website lists 19 CD recordings, ranging from Mozart through to Maxwell Davies, and a recent review describes him as 'a true master of his instrument', his playing 'technically and musically flawless'. When his lessons were observed Timothy had been teaching clarinet in Higher Education for 23 years.

In a substantial and articulate interview, Timothy offered his reflections on a wide range of issues connected to the instrumental lessons observed, sometimes exceeding the scope of the questions put to him. In this respect the interview revealed a strong sense of context, taking a broad view of the profession and of music education. When comparing his work in Higher Education to a recent visit to a secondary school, he spoke terms of 'a satellite map of the world':

> It was as if you had zoomed in on your computer map and you could see the details of the coastline and the general outline of the country. ... All the same things seem to come out in terms of technique, it is just that one is looking under a bigger and bigger microscope.
>
> (Excerpt 6.1 Interview with Timothy)

Accordingly, Timothy's reflections are framed here in a series of increasingly strong lenses: musical culture, music education, Higher Education, the degree programme and lesson strategies. The final, most narrowly focused lens is

Timothy's characterization of individual students, which will be addressed separately after the findings from their individual lessons.

Musical Culture

Timothy's view of musical culture is a broad one, and he characterizes the current state of the profession in England compared with developments in other countries. When asked to comment on the role of the Performance Studies course within the degree programme at SEU, he answers in far broader terms. The interviewer's speech is presented in italics here to distinguish it from Timothy's own remarks:

> *[Our Head of Department] tends to think that Performance Studies are central to the degree programme. What is your response to that?*
> I think they are a very important part. I wouldn't say that they were 'central', myself because of this changing world we are in. I think that putting this place into context with a sense of realism, if you consider that the specialist music colleges are churning out stock clarinet players, two fantastic players a year, sometimes it is a bit more.
>
> (Excerpt 6.2 Interview with Timothy)

Timothy goes on to place his work at SEU within this context, in which professional performance appears to be the yardstick for success. The profession, he says, 'is inundated with over-qualified people':

> But even so, if you think of South England versus the rest of the world – or the rest of the country – and the specialist places that are just concentrating on performance, it is already over.
>
> (Excerpt 6.3 Interview with Timothy)

'Versus the rest of the world' signifies that competition is in the nature of the profession, and it seems that for students at South England this is almost a competition that cannot be won. Auditions for any 'major job' are likely to depend on students being conservatoire graduates, but because of 'the sad state of affairs', even prize-winners from the main colleges are 'seriously contemplating giving up because they got so close to major appointments [but] not quite'.

The profession, in Timothy's view, lacks structure; he refers to promotion and retirement arrangements that are a normal part of other kinds of career, and to the fact that in music, senior practitioners are 'fighting against younger people' who have earned quick success by winning high-profile competitions. The answer is that 'music in this country … has got to become a little more like the [United] States, where the main structure of the profession is built round the teaching side, not round the playing side'.

Timothy expands on 'the way forward' for the music profession, which may be sought in a revival of musical culture at a fundamental level:

So my view is that we should get music, like in Hungary or Slovenia or probably Kosovo before the crisis, accepted so that every kid does singing in class from the age of four, and everyone can play an instrument by the time they are about ten in some way. But it means that if there's a concert, most people go. It is something they are interested in, just like everyone here wants to play football. There is no stigma about it being 'sissy': it is just a nice subject to do. …

So the way forward and the way to entice people into music as a profession is to make the main thrust of activity quality teaching, on the premise that it is a really good thing for everybody to get involved in, whether they are going to be professional musicians or not.

(Excerpt 6.4 Interview with Timothy)

Music Education

Timothy narrows his lens to discuss the teaching and learning of music in more detail. He refers to Aristotle's remark that those who can, do, while those who understand, teach; though he gives it in its more common – but misapprehended – form:

> [A]t the moment or certainly until a few years ago there was very much the feeling that those who could, were playing and those who didn't quite make it, took up teaching. I think we have all realized that we have got to do a bit of both to be really good …

(Excerpt 6.5 Interview with Timothy)

Timothy distances himself from the attitude implied here: 'there was very much' a feeling, but it was not necessarily his, and on the contrary, Timothy positions himself among those who now realize that both teaching and performing are necessary. Unfortunately he cuts himself off at this point, to resume his discussion of the lack of structure in the profession, so there is no development of the idea that teaching and performing might inform each other. Elsewhere however he touches on the relationship between the two sides of the profession, if more obliquely. When asked specifically about teaching, he frames his answer in terms of his own career as a performer, as shown in the extract below.

> *Can you tell me then what influences there have been on your development as a teacher?*
> Um, just being thrown in at the deep end. I started teaching when I was still in the Sixth Form because there was such a shortage at school and I was thought to be worthy of helping some youngsters through, so I learned the hard way! Since 1976 when I joined [a London ensemble] I suppose I have been thrown into the masterclass situation.

(Excerpt 6.6 Interview with Timothy)

Teaching then is something that Timothy first took up as a consequence of his performing success. He lists several further examples of his own teaching activity, in terms of what might be described as a portfolio career: he has led and run workshops, contributed to the educational work of charitable trusts, and helped other musicians develop their skills in the same areas. Indeed, he develops the theme of helping other teachers relatively fully, before briefly positioning himself as a teacher who might benefit from such activities:

> I spend a lot of my time going round the country doing INSET days for teachers who have to teach clarinet but are actually flute players or oboe players and this kind of thing. …
> *Apart from masterclasses and INSET courses –*
> Generally, I have done short two-day courses and that kind of thing but I am always open to suggestions. Having never done a formal teacher training qualification I just think it is so funny that in this country – my first job was at [another institution in Higher Education] and none of the staff I think at that time especially the Head of Department had any teaching qualification at all.
>
> (Excerpt 6.7 Interview with Timothy)

Timothy offers no further information about short courses he has done, rather than led, and although he is open to them, he offers no information about any specific suggestions that he might have found valuable in the development of his teaching. On the whole, his answers to this line of questioning are more expansive about the work he has done than about influences that he has embraced, and this would seem to imply that Timothy's development as a teacher has been predominantly experiential. In discussing formal qualifications, Timothy shifts his attention to take a slightly narrower focus on institutions of Higher Education.

Higher Education

It is clear that in spite of his own lack of formal qualifications Timothy's attitude to the value of teacher training is broadly positive. He declares when asked that 'it should be an essential ingredient of every music course', and he regrets that conservatoire training when he was a student did not include any mandatory element of teacher training. Once again however he does not expand on the essential value of such training: rather, 'I think it should be part of it, because you can't just be a performer these days unless you are fantastically well paid.' It is evidently assumed here that being 'just a performer' remains the preferred aim.

His assertions about the need for teacher training within performance studies leads Timothy to reflect a little further on the provision available from institutions of music education, during his own time as a student as well as in the contemporary setting at SEU:

[T]hings are very different now and the students at [South England] have a much better grounding in all sorts of ways. I suppose it is primarily a university course but I mean at the [conservatoire] back in the mid to early seventies, if you went to your piano lesson once a week and fudged your way through, you would get your [final qualification] with a few essays.

(Excerpt 6.8 Interview with Timothy)

The emphasis then in the 1970s was evidently very much on each student's main instrument; apart from a requirement to learn a second instrument, which need not be taken too seriously, the written element was minimal. Timothy perhaps assumes that a course focused on teaching would be grouped among those peripheral, text-based courses that were assessed by a few essays during his own time as a student.

Timothy is asked whether his approach to Higher Education differs from his teaching elsewhere, and it is now that he offers the idea of a satellite map being examined through increasingly strong microscope lenses: with students in Higher Education he expects to be able to address bigger issues. He is also asked about levels of motivation among students in Higher Education but, perhaps misunderstanding the question, he answers by comparing the attitudes of students such as Andrew at SEU to those he has seen in the contemporary conservatoire:

Do you notice any difference in terms of motivation between students here and outside Higher Education?
Um, there's no rhyme or reason to it. Some like Andrew [at SEU] really put some of the others who have been to the odd class at the [conservatoire] to shame because he is very very determined … [H]e is actually making use of every minute; and in other places I have been, people squander the time and don't seem to realize until it is all over. They very often come back to me after they have left the [conservatoire] and want to start again! 'I realize now what you were saying'. There is a lot of that sort of 'therapy', shall we say!

(Excerpt 6.9 Interview with Timothy)

Timothy describes the work he does at SEU as being 'one level below' the conservatoire, but allows that with the right attitude, university graduates might be able to do 'SOME playing and a lot of high quality teaching and will start to gradually change the world'.

The Degree Programme

It is perhaps a reflection of the relative isolation of instrumental teachers within educational institutions that Timothy has little to say in his interview about the degree programme itself, although as noted in several places above, the interview schedule includes a number of questions related directly to the Performance Studies course. When asked to comment on the centrality of this course to the degree programme, he responds with a broader discussion of the centrality of performance in the careers of musicians, even though measured against that yardstick – '[South England] versus the rest of the world' – the graduates of SEU have little or no chance of success. After some discussion, he does return to the original question, still without referring to the course itself, but to performance as a more general activity: because of the nature of the profession as he describes it, these students would be better dividing their attention between performance and teacher training.

Professional performance is apparently assumed to be the underlying aim of the course, and in the interview that aim is not qualified by reference to features of the local context, such as the particular nature of this institution and its students. Timothy suggests that students who are clearly unlikely to excel should be discouraged from continuing in performance activity. If the course is tacitly regarded as vocational, teachers will inevitably struggle with unsuitable students:

> I would think it would be more beneficial in the second year for the students to choose whether they want to perform, but for the teachers to say, 'That girl has really got something – she could really do something with performance'. And, 'That one, sorry, he works really hard but he would never do it. We both know it.' That is the *je ne sais quoi* that occasionally just happens. You can't teach that, can you? I think that is something I have noticed with the Performance option over the years that sometimes the ones to opt to do it, should not have and it is an uphill struggle for us teaching it.
>
> (Excerpt 6.10 Interview with Timothy)

In practical terms there are aspects of the performance course that have an impact on Timothy's approach to lessons. In particular, the proximity of performance examinations has an effect on lesson content and conduct. Timothy seems to feel, under the pressure of exam preparation, that the priority is to secure results, even if it means taking a more directive approach than usual. This is 'partly because it is getting close to exams, [and] I suppose one is anxious to get the information over.' He remarks that had the lessons been filmed at another time of year, other kinds of work might have been in evidence:

> If you had come and filmed in October, most of the lessons, even for the second and third years, have some sort of remedial work, revising breathing when something is going wrong after the long holiday, just forming bad habits, so reminding them of basic things. Obviously as things go through and we get nearer the exams the important thing is to be able fluently to play those pieces.
>
> (Excerpt 6.11 Interview with Timothy)

In other circumstances, Timothy would be more likely to take a flexible approach, inviting students to decide what work they would prefer to address in lessons, and to 'bring me the problems as they see them'.

Lesson Strategies

Narrowing the focus again to discuss more specific approaches to music education, Timothy touches on teaching strategies, highlighting particularly the importance of imitation as a tool. One of the problems commonly found in schools, he says, is that woodwind teachers often find themselves teaching instruments that lie beyond their own expertise, with flautists or oboists for example teaching clarinet to children without being able to demonstrate its use. Imitation, in Timothy's view, is as valuable in learning an instrument as it is in learning a language. In the lessons at SEU, too, Timothy clearly regards imitation as a significant resource, in spite of some reservations:

> You will see on the tape – hopefully without overdoing it – there are quite often times when I will (at the end of them having several goes at it) will play it to them, not to say I am doing it perfectly but just to hear a live instrument.
>
> (Excerpt 6.12 Interview with Timothy)

'A live instrument' is not what the students hear of themselves, but, presumably, a concert artist in person; Timothy is perhaps comparing that to recordings, which must be the kind of model more commonly available to students. Even so, demonstration is apparently something that he prefers to use in only limited amounts, 'hopefully without overdoing it'. Interestingly, too, Timothy's demonstration is not presented to the student as an initial aim, but is offered only after the student has had 'several goes at it'.

Asked how the filmed lessons compared to his idea of an ideal lesson, Timothy criticizes his own time management: today, two of his lessons overran, and he prefers to arrange for the student to 'play through a whole section at the end, to finish with, so it gives a sort of feeling of going out on a high'. He returns to this comment later in the interview, where he describes the conclusion to a lesson that would be ideal, psychologically:

> I would like a lot more smiles and for it to be paced better, so that whether you are participating or watching [the video], you would go out on a high because you have done this, they play this version, I say this and this and this and they try a few bits and then you end up encapsulating all those things and proving that, yes, the version that we go out with is better than the one when we came in.
>
> (Excerpt 6.13 Interview with Timothy)

Today, it seemed likely that certain aspects of the lessons were affected by the presence of the research camera. Timothy agrees that the camera did have some effect, in that the approach taken by both teacher and students was perhaps more serious than usual, with fewer jokes or 'banter'. Once again he explains himself in terms of psychology, showing a concern for the student's concentration and morale:

It just was more focused. It was like doing a masterclass where you are aware that you are trying to get certain things over and there is far less time-wasting. Inevitably, on a week-to-week basis, deliberately about half way through I break the tension, ask them how they are et cetera.

(Excerpt 6.14 Interview with Timothy)

'Trying to get certain things over' recalls the need, noted above, to secure good results in preparation for the imminent performance examinations, and it seems likely that the pressure represented by the assessment goal will have been exaggerated, so some extent, by the presence of the video camera.

Having drawn on Timothy's interview to contextualize his lessons through an increasingly focused series of lenses, we turn now to the lessons themselves.

Spatial Behaviour in Lesson A

Lesson A is given to Andrew, an advanced clarinet student: Andrew is in the 22–29 age bracket, and currently in the third and final year of his degree programme. He is a 'combined honours' student, meaning that his degree incorporates two subjects, Music and American Studies. Andrew has been studying with Timothy throughout his time at SEU, and in this, the last term of his degree, is preparing for his final examination-recital. His lesson is scheduled to be 45 minutes long. The account of Andrew's lesson is given, here, from three separate perspectives referring to spatial, performance and verbal behaviour. Later, some further light will be cast on the lesson by exploring the interviews with the teacher and student.

The room in which the lessons take place is approximately square, with the video camera in one corner pointed toward the opposite corner. In the centre of the room, and therefore in the middle of the shot, is a music stand. A sketch of the room's layout is shown in Figure 6.1, with the scope of the video camera indicated by dotted lines.

'Off stage right' is the door, and 'off stage left', a piano. There are narrow tables against both of the back walls in view.

The music stand forms the focus of a close triangle, with both participants normally facing it; the student Andrew stands to the left of the shot, giving his profile to the video camera, and the teacher Timothy stands to the back, almost facing the camera. Timothy has used the table on the right to set up his laptop, which has a computer programme that simulates piano accompaniment, and he has used the table on the left for his clarinet case. Although it is only 9.15 in the morning, Timothy has arrived very early and has been using the accompaniment programme to practice. In the few minutes before the filming started, Andrew has entered and used the top of the piano – off stage front left – as a table for his clarinet case.

The participants are in what might be called 'smart casual' dress, with open-necked collars; Timothy wears a suit jacket and Andrew wears an unbuttoned waistcoat. The teacher saunters a little, while the student is preparing his score

narrow table (left)

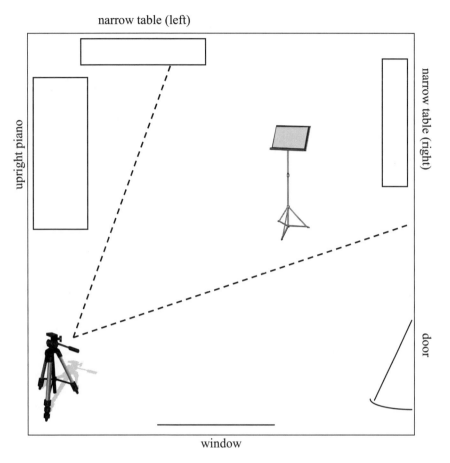

Figure 6.1   Room layout

and his clarinet, and conveys a relaxed but also rather authoritative demeanour. Timothy has his hands in his pockets for the first few minutes of the lesson, as shown in Table 6.1.

Table 6.1   Timothy's posture

	minutes: seconds
Both hands in pockets	0:30–1:24
Left hand only	1:24–1:43
Both	1:43–2:33

After two and a half minutes Timothy takes his hands out of his pockets and never puts them there again. Four minutes into the lesson he and Andrew adopt a relaxed but stable position, focused on the music stand. The simplified line drawing of this positioning, in Figure 6.2, comes from a 'still shot' from the video at 7:30.

Movement within the space is generally economical, to the point where the positioning shown above may be regarded as the 'default' for the participants. The minimal use of space seems to be in keeping with several features of the participants' spatial behaviour. There is a tendency to focus very much on details of the musical score, placed on the music stand at an early stage (1:21) and left there until the lesson is effectively over (45:52). Close attention is given to the clarinets themselves, too, particularly with regard to preparing the reed (2:28–2:48). While this is discussed, teacher and student together hold Andrew's clarinet, as Timothy uses his right index finger to mime the best way of scraping the reed. Aspects of clarinet fingering also require close positioning between the participants: Timothy often demonstrates or mimes fingering that Andrew is expected to observe, and when he wants to draw Andrew's attention to his own fingering, he moves in to touch the clarinet keys or the student's fingertips on them. Timothy actually touches Andrew's clarinet or fingers, to this end, 17 times during the lesson, though these instances tend to fall into episodes focused on the discussion of fingering: in the most salient example there are 11 'touches' in less than half a minute (14:12–14:35).

Relaxed concentration is shown by the two participants in their activity as well as their mutual proximity. During the first few minutes of the lesson Andrew

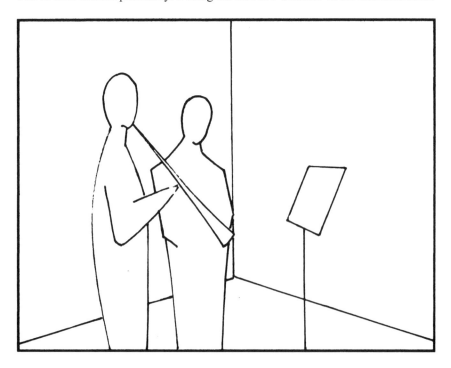

Figure 6.2   Spatial behaviour in Lesson A

prepares his clarinet and score in a businesslike manner: he does not take a stable position on camera until 1:19, when he is seen placing the score on the stand, opening it to the right page, inserting the clarinet's reed, tightening the ligature and adjusting the barrel (1:19–1:44). After playing a few notes lightly and quickly, he adjusts the barrel again (1:50). At this point teacher and student cooperate to examine, discuss and test the reed: this takes several minutes more, but from 4:00 the instrument is ready and the participants have assumed their 'default' position, ready to proceed with the lesson.

It seems that each is comfortable with this position, and there are few movements to suggest any lapses in poise. Andrew smoothes his hair with his right hand (0:23) and his left (1:59): he has just come in from outside. He rubs his leg in an isolated gesture after 6:27, but otherwise he makes no obvious gestures that are unrelated to the work at hand, until the lesson draws to an end. Then, in the closing minutes of the lesson, he toys with the back of his waistcoat (42:15), rubs the back of his neck (45:10) and flexes the fingers of his right hand (45:28). It is as if he is waking after a period of remarkable concentration.

Timothy too demonstrates considerable composure. After the first few, leisurely minutes, his posture remains upright and balanced, as it would be if he were performing, though he does not actually pick up his clarinet until almost halfway through the lesson (20:40). He rubs his face with his left hand, twice (7:38, 13:02): later he briefly mentions that he has had some dental work done the day before, and that this is still bothering him today (36:08).

In addition to being comfortable in their own physical conduct, it seems clear that Timothy and Andrew are comfortable with each other, in their use of space. The default position is one of businesslike intimacy, and at close quarters teacher and student typically gaze at the music stand rather than directly at each other. Often one of the participants moves in closer, usually to refer to the score; this does not lead the other to correct the distance between them, however, and on several occasions Andrew moves in toward the score when Timothy is already there (23:24, 35:44, 36:12).

The score is privileged, and in the default position it almost seems to be a third, silent participant in the proceedings. Teacher and student tend to look at it, even when they are not reading it; so for example when Andrew plays a few experimental notes to check his reed, his eyes are cast toward the music stand (1:47). When Andrew begins to perform more formally (4:10) Timothy watches the score, though it seems that he is not reading it, but rather listening intently while incidentally facing that point.

The score is often touched, and it is normally the teacher who touches it. This may involve a very brief gesture: Timothy touches the score for one second or less 15 times during the lesson. At times however Timothy continues to indicate specific points on the text over longer periods, and sometimes to rest his hand on the shelf of the music stand, at the bottom of the score, while discussion continues. On five occasions his hand remains more or less in contact with the score, for between 22 and 32 seconds. During the first half of the lesson Timothy touches the score with his hand or a finger, while during the second half, with his instrument now in his hands, he sometimes uses the tip of his clarinet to indicate the points under discussion.

Andrew does touch the score at times, particularly when asking a question about it (6:29, 9:05, 35:39, 36:25). On the whole, however, contact with the score remains the teacher's prerogative. Andrew apparently owns the score: he has brought it with him, arranges it on the stand at the beginning of the lesson and packs it away at the end of the lesson. While it is on the music stand, however, it is normally Timothy who makes physical contact with it. In all, he is in contact with the score for almost five minutes: 274 seconds using his hand or a finger, and 25 using the tip of the clarinet. Andrew, in contrast, makes contact for less than half a minute in total (17 + 8 seconds).

Touching the score normally involves moving slightly closer to the stand, even if a clarinet is used to make contact. It has been noted that this is evidently not taken to be an invasion of personal space, since it never provokes a mutual adjustment of the distance between teacher and student. The concept of personal space seems to change, however, when the student is actually playing his clarinet. This can involve different kinds of performing activity, which will be discussed later, but when Andrew is 'performing', Timothy stands back slightly in the 'default' position, to allow more space for it. This respect for the performance act is also reflected in the use of time: when Andrew is performing he typically takes a moment, standing very still, composing himself, even establishing a sense of occasion, before starting to play. Although these moments typically last only one or two seconds, Andrew spends a total of 73 seconds preparing himself in this way. It seems that this respect is directed chiefly at the student's performance, and not necessarily the teacher's. Timothy performs and indeed plays far less than Andrew, but when he does he is far less likely to take time to prepare or to establish himself as the performer, spending only one second on a single occasion (42:53).

Within his own space, Andrew normally stands still, particularly while he is playing. This is deliberate: performing success can be related to the overall posture of the performer, and Timothy criticizes one performance by remarking that the sense of line has been compromised, 'partly because you moved your feet in the middle'. When he is not playing, Andrew sometimes moves his feet. This seems an entirely natural way to maintain balance and relaxation, and he often does it immediately after he has stopped playing. Occasionally however the movement of feet seems to signal some slight discomfort. When Timothy asks him to demonstrate the sound of the reed he has chosen – having indicated smiling amazement at his choice – Andrew shuffles a little before playing (02:56). Later he shuffles again, while spontaneously criticizing his own sense of timing (18:46).

Elsewhere the movement of Andrew's feet is associated with a more positive release of feeling. When Timothy mimes a string pulling Andrew's finger away from the clarinet, Andrew rocks forward and back on his feet, laughing (18:11). Later he shifts his feet in smiling admiration of Timothy's playing (26:57, 32:57).

Timothy and Andrew both remarked in their subsequent interviews that there had been no off-task discussion during the filmed lesson, with 'fewer jokes than usual'. Even so, the lesson is generally good-natured, and although there is no explicit joking, smiling and quiet laughter are often in evidence. The lesson transcription shows 13 such gestures from Timothy and 9 from Andrew. The longest period in the lesson without smiling or laughter is about eight minutes (33:40–41:27), a period that includes some extended performing from Andrew (50 + 94 seconds).

The spatial behaviour of the two participants may be summarized as economical in scale. Teacher and student are close, comfortable and collaborative in their mutual positions, and their attention is directed toward fine details on either the score or the clarinet. The scale of the event is, of course, similarly minimal: although it is not cramped, the room is not large. The nature of the setting too calls for economy: teacher and student might have used the space far more freely and flamboyantly if they had been, for example, engaged in a public masterclass. It should be acknowledged that Timothy and Andrew might have felt constrained in their movements, today, by the presence of the video camera: although neither commented explicitly on this effect, Timothy mentioned in his interview afterwards that he had probably been 'subliminally' aware of the camera.

One further instance of economy might be noted: the soundscape of the lesson is generally quite constrained. The participants tend to talk quietly, with Timothy in particular rarely raising his voice above *mezzo piano*. The performance activity, focused almost entirely on the slow movement of Weber's *Grand duo*, also tends to be relatively quiet and expressive, with stronger dynamic levels used to create intensity rather than excitement. The clarinet, in the hands of an expert, can be used to reduce dynamic levels almost to zero, and control seems to be an important issue. At one point Timothy remarks that Andrew is 'worried now, having blurted it out' (6:42); at another he recommends 'that feeling of climax without blasting everyone to bits' (13:03); and at the other end of the dynamic spectrum he asserts that 'I doubt whether it will be audible, the last four notes, like that', because *pianissimo* has 'much more to do with attack and gentleness rather than decibels' (30:49, 31:00).

The nature of the soundscape is raised again in the two following separate sections: performance behaviour and verbal behaviour.

Performance Behaviour in Lesson A

Performance behaviour – referring here to all activity directly related to instrumental playing and singing – is to be found throughout the lesson, and over 45 minutes the clarinet sound may be heard for a total of 21 minutes 57 seconds, or 49 per cent of the lesson time. Most of the performance behaviour is contributed by the student Andrew, whose activity represents 89 per cent of the total.

Repertoire for the lesson is the second movement, *Andante con moto*, of the Weber *Grand duo concertante* Op. 48. During the lesson the whole movement is addressed, from beginning to end: the pace of the lesson is neatly gauged to match the length of the piece and the lesson, with the depth of study.

The performance behaviour may be divided among several different kinds of activity:

Rehearsal.   Sixty-six per cent of all performance time is spent on rehearsals of the *Grand duo*. This entails reading directly from the score with intent, as if performing on stage, even though all such 'performances' present only segments of the work, ranging from 1 through to 90 seconds in length. Andrew contributes 86 per cent of this performance behaviour. Twenty eight of his rehearsals are of less than 10 seconds' duration, while seven last 30 seconds or longer.

Preparation.   Although the length of the performed segments varies greatly, Andrew approaches them seriously, and indeed one of the features of his rehearsals is that they are typically preceded by a moment of preparation, as noted in the discussion of spatial behaviour above. Preparation involves more than merely taking an initial breath: Andrew stands still and poised, collecting himself and establishing a sense of performance before actually making a sound. Thirty-seven of his rehearsals are preceded by such moments, usually lasting one or two seconds, and in all he spends a total of 73 seconds preparing himself in this way.

Practice.   Fourteen per cent of the performance behaviour involves playing that is related to the *Grand duo* without being in any way a simulated performance. An illustrative example may be found at an early stage of the lesson, where Andrew has his first rehearsal, preceded by 5 seconds' silent preparation, and after 24 seconds' playing, strikes difficulty with an upward octave leap (4:32). Andrew stops rehearsing to repeat the leap three times, and then Timothy offers some feedback and advice before Andrew resumes rehearsing (5:18). Some more experiments with the same leap are made in another little practice session a few minutes later (6:47–7:08), this time with closer guidance from Timothy.

Exercise.   Thirteen per cent of the performance behaviour involves playing that is not directly related to the *Grand duo*. This includes the routine checks that both participants make when they first play their clarinets, or immediately after making any adjustments to the instruments' assembly. It also includes an episode where both participants withdraw from the *Grand duo* to exercise their tuning across the full range of the instrument (25:33–28:16). The intonation is checked, here, against an electronic tuner; later, similarly, teacher and student check their tuning against the piano.

The use of the piano constitutes the final mode of performance behaviour. At Timothy's request, Andrew plays several notes on the upright piano which is offstage left, so that both participants can check their tuning against that and against each other (40:19–40:41). It is perhaps of some interest that the clarinettists are not content to establish their tuning merely in relation to each other, but refer to both the electronic tuner and the previously-tuned piano in this way. The piano and clarinet are never heard together in either rehearsal or exercise behaviour, during this lesson, so there is no immediate reason for ensuring that the clarinets match the piano tuning: it seems that reference to this external framework is merely regarded as good practice.

The time spent on each mode of performance behaviour is summarized in Table 6.2.

Table 6.2   Performance behaviour in Lesson A

	Total time spent (seconds)	Timothy	Andrew
All performance behaviour	1317	164	1176
Preparation	74 (6%)	1	73
Rehearsal	871 (66%)	119	752
Practice	190 (14%)	4	186
Exercise	173 (13%)	40	155
Piano	10 (1%)	0	10

Nb. 23 seconds' exercise is shared by both participants playing simultaneously.

Distribution of Performance Behaviours

Table 6.2 gives the total duration of each performance behaviour, but does not show how they function in time. Table 6.3 illustrates how the performance behaviour is played out, in an example taken from the analysis of the first ten minutes of the lesson. Here, the various kinds of performance behaviour have been extracted from the lesson transcript to represent incidents of rehearsal, practice and exercise; time spent on preparation is indicated in parentheses. All of the performance behaviour in this extract is undertaken by Andrew. The duration of each incident is shown in seconds.

Some commentary on the activity here will help to recreate the texture of performance activity in the lesson. In the first incident, Andrew can be seen exercising and testing his instrument as he assembles it, over a period of slightly more than two minutes (1:47–4:01). This segment of the lesson involves the discussion of reeds, and teacher and student are listening carefully to the result of the reed that Andrew has chosen and prepared.

The first rehearsal incident is a substantial one, and is preceded by five seconds' preparation: this is the longest moment Andrew spends, in this lesson, preparing for a rehearsal, and it seems reasonable that it might take longer to initially put himself in the right frame of mind for the first performance of the day. Although a long moment of preparation precedes a relatively long rehearsal

Table 6.3   Example of distribution of performance behaviour in Lesson A

Time	Rehearsal	Practice	Exercise	Piano
1:47			3	
3:04			14	
3:50			2	
4:01			4	
4:06	(5) 24			
4:36		7		
4:51			2	
5:02	(2) 1			
5:17	(1) 43			
6:47		1		
6:49		12		
7:04		4		
7:10	(2) 5			
7:28	(2) 7			
7:43		2		
7:54	(2) 8			
8:26	(3) 22			
8:58		1		

here (5 + 24 seconds), it should also be noted that Andrew prepares himself before every rehearsal in the extract shown, and the length of the moment taken is not much compromised by the fact that some rehearsals turn out to be far shorter than others. His second rehearsal, for example, is prepared for two seconds, though Andrew only plays for one (5:02–5:05).

Under 'practice' Andrew may be seen withdrawing from his rehearsals to address issues that have arisen within them. The first rehearsal for example has ended with a mismanaged octave leap, already mentioned in the description of practice, above. On striking this difficulty, and without instruction from Timothy, Andrew stops to secure the lower note, and then to practice the octave leap three times. Timothy offers some feedback on the practice, to which Andrew responds with some exercise activity, checking his instrument again; then Timothy offers feedback on the preceding rehearsal, before the student begins to rehearse the same passage again. The practice and the accompanying feedback have been incorporated into the flow of the lesson, as if in parentheses.

The distribution of types of performance behaviour shows that Andrew and Timothy are able to move quickly from one to another, and on the whole the texture of the analyzed transcript shows a marbled effect. Even so, there are a number of episodes during the lesson where the type of performance behaviour remains consistent over rather longer periods of time. The longest ten of these episodes, ranging from 53 seconds to more than five minutes, are represented in Table 6.4. In this table, preparation is subsumed in rehearsal behaviour.

Table 6.4   Episodes of consistent performance behaviour in Lesson A

Time within the lesson	Length of lesson segment (seconds)	Type of performance behaviour	Duration of incidents in seconds: preparation shown in parentheses
1:47–04:05	138	Exercise	3, 14, 2, 4
11:22–14:11	169	(Preparation) Rehearsal	(2)18, (2)3, 3, 6, 4, (1)9, (2)3, (2)15
15:56–18:11	135	(Preparation) Rehearsal	(1)12, (3)3, 30, (2) 13, (2)5
20:52–22:55	122	(Preparation) Rehearsal	12, (2)11, (1)15, (2)14, 13, (1)14
24:20–25:13	53	Practice	2, 1, 4, 1, 3, 7, 1
25:33–28:30	175	(Preparation) Exercise	(2) 6, 13, 11, 8, 31, 10, 2, 22, 7, 19, 1, 1
29:07–30:28	81	(Preparation) Rehearsal	7, 17, 7, 14, 11, (2)1
30:33–34:18	225	(Preparation) Rehearsal	(1)15, 3, 3, (2)8, (2)22, 33, (2)31, (4)4, 17
34:35–39:38	303	(Preparation) Rehearsal	(1)1, 50, (2)94
42:53–44:25	93	(Preparation) Rehearsal	(1)33, (2)36
Average	149		

Reading Table 6.4 from left to right, for example, the first episode of consistent performance behaviour falls between 1:47 and 4:05, during which exercise is the only kind of performance activity; this includes four separate incidents of exercise, lasting 3, 14, 2 and 4 seconds respectively.

The most obvious feature of the table is the predominance of rehearsal as an extended activity. The less frequently pursued activities, practice and exercise, are each given a similar proportion of time, but this table shows that exercise is the more likely of the two to be pursued in longer episodes. Exercise tends to consist either of very short checks lasting as little as one second and often involving only a single note, or to constitute extended episodes of more than two minutes in duration. Practice, in contrast, tends to fall into episodes of medium length. The table also shows, incidentally, an exceptional occurrence of preparation used for an exercise rather than for a rehearsal (25:33): this is the only place in the lesson where such a space is given to exercise preparation.

The table does suggest, at a glance, that the performance behaviour of the lesson falls into two approximate halves, each beginning with a relatively extended period of exercise. To refine this impression and explore it further, the amount and nature of all performance behaviours is represented in Figure 6.3, which divides the lesson into five-minute periods.

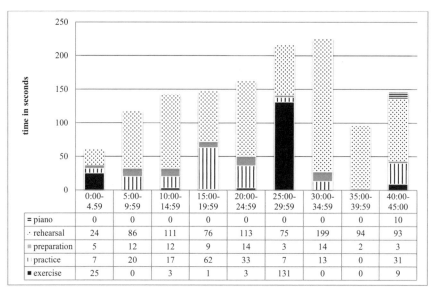

	0:00-4.59	5:00-9:59	10:00-14:59	15:00-19:59	20:00-24:59	25:00-29:59	30:00-34:59	35:00-39:59	40:00-45:00
▦ piano	0	0	0	0	0	0	0	0	10
∴ rehearsal	24	86	111	76	113	75	199	94	93
▪ preparation	5	12	12	9	14	3	14	2	3
‖ practice	7	20	17	62	33	7	13	0	31
▪ exercise	25	0	3	1	3	131	0	0	9

Figure 6.3   Distribution of performance behaviour in Lesson A

The time period 20:00–24:59 seems pivotal, dividing the lesson into two broad sections. It is in this period that Timothy first picks up his clarinet, and while this initially leads to an intensifying of rehearsal activity, it is followed by the most substantial exercise period in the lesson. It has already been noted, in the account of his interview, that Timothy normally likes to 'break the tension' halfway through a lesson, for example by pausing to 'ask [students] how they are'; this kind of behaviour has been constrained today by the presence of the video camera, but it seems possible that the switch to exercise activity might represent an analogous change of pace. If exercise does indeed represent a way of mentally relaxing, then the shading within the chart might be seen as an indicator of intensity, with the temperature of performance behaviour rising from rather cool piano playing – presumably the least gripping activity for a clarinettist – to rehearsal, the most intense and perhaps the most gratifying. In the time remaining after the central 'exercise break', rehearsal is given more emphasis at the expense of both practice and exercise; in terms of energy and concentration, it may be important that the intense rehearsal now has been preceded by an exercise break. The rise in rehearsal 'temperature' at this point may also be linked to the apparent commitment to deal with the whole of the *Grand duo* movement before the end of the lesson and to

Timothy's suggestion, noted above in the discussion of his interview, that an ideal lesson should conclude 'on a high' that can come from successful rehearsal.

Teacher Performance

Timothy does not pick up his clarinet at all until almost halfway through the lesson (20:40), and when he does it has a galvanizing effect on the soundscape. His first performance behaviour consists of exercising a few notes to check his instrument, and then rehearsing a segment from the *Grand duo* that has already been played by Andrew. The sheer quality of clarinet sound has already exhibited some variance: when Andrew is exercising his instrument his tone is only crudely focused and typically unmeasured, compared to the refined and deliberate tone of his rehearsals, but now the tonal quality enters a new realm. In Timothy's rehearsal the tone is conspicuous for its focused resonance, and the character of each note is clearly contextualized in the development of a long, limpid, legato line. Interestingly, Andrew responds to the demonstration, with no more prompting than 'Try it?' from Timothy, by rehearsing the same passage again, with a much more open and resonant sound. In this, he takes an immediate step closer to the exemplar, without quite matching his teacher's sound: Andrew is an advanced student of the clarinet, but Timothy is, after all, an artist of international repute.

Andrew is keenly attentive during Timothy's rehearsals, watching the score and engaging in silent fingering as his teacher plays, in six out of seven rehearsal demonstrations. In five of these he joins in with silent fingering within a few seconds of Timothy's starting to play, and in one, lasting 33 seconds, he participates in this way, throughout (32:24–32:57). The only rehearsal that Andrew does not shadow through the use of silent fingering lasts only 3 seconds (30:57–31:00): presumably in this case he simply does not have time to join in.

That Timothy should rehearse only after Andrew has practised and rehearsed the same passage is consistent with his remarks on demonstration, in the interview discussed above. True to his word, he never demonstrates a rehearsal, practice or exercise unless Andrew has tried it first, and with the exception of the Timothy's final rehearsal (44:52), the opportunity is immediately presented to Andrew, afterwards, to try it again. In this way demonstration has a responsive function as well as a stimulating one.

Timothy prepares for only one of his rehearsals, for one second (42:53), before a substantial demonstration of 33 seconds. Otherwise, his lack of preparation contrasts somewhat with the seriousness of the playing itself, and suggests an air of modesty, of minimizing his own importance in the interaction. Consistent with this impression is the fact that he tends to conclude his demonstrations rather unceremoniously, and the sense of performance is broken immediately afterwards, by talk. In places it seems that the demonstration is expected to speak for itself, and to elicit an immediate response, in kind, from the student; elsewhere, however, it seems that Timothy's quick switch from play to talk shows the musical thought merging fluently with the verbal, and in the following example the rehearsal functions as part of a rather exploratory sentence. Performance activity is indicated here in square brackets.

> 22:16   I want it much more sort of –
> 22:19   [Plays the phrase, with conspicuous *legato*]
> 22:32   – much more sort of, um, secretive sound somehow, you know, intimate, very much to yourself.
>
>   (Excerpt 6.15 Lesson A)

This merging of playing and talking suggests a close and possibly inseparable relationship between the demonstration and the verbal pointing that goes with it.

Andrew typically responds to rehearsal demonstrations, in kind – by rehearsing, himself – whether there is intervening verbal behaviour or not. In responding to exercise demonstrations Andrew takes a closer share in the activity, and occasionally there is some overlapping as both participants play at the same time (20:45, 25:41, 26:07, 40:21, 40:26). The central exercise episode (25:35–28:30) has been discussed above as a possible tension-breaker in the lesson, and it is interesting that the shared activity here has a competitive element. The episode begins with Timothy laying down a challenge for Andrew: 'Right – can you first of all play Es and As all the way up the instrument?' (25:27). Andrew attempts this, and then Timothy has a turn; Andrew joins in and tries to keep pace, but Timothy is able to carry on an octave higher than the student. There is some quiet laughter here and amid the subsequent attempts Timothy fetches the electronic tuner, and uses it to prove his own accuracy in the exercise. The challenge is reinforced by the strength of the demonstration: 'Pretty much bang on? You do yours again?' (26:58). Andrew is now allowed a further minute to improve his own efforts, with consistent coaching and feedback from Timothy. His reward is 'That's not bad' from a smiling teacher (28:16).

Student Performance

Although Andrew dominates performance activity, it is Timothy on the whole who directs it. At the beginning of the lesson, after some preliminary inquiries, Timothy identifies the material to be addressed. Andrew's speech is represented here in italics.

> 0:32   SO. You're doing – um, digital delay piece which you've already, you've recorded the sound track bit, have you?
> 0:45   *No, I've recorded all of it; it's all, it's all on one solo line, so –*
> 0:49   I see. Right. And er, Weber Grand duo –
> 0:55   *Mm hm*
> 0:56   second movement, and the Horovitz third movement. So er, well let's do some Weber shall we?
>
>   (Excerpt 6.16 Lesson A)

He also tends to command performance behaviours: after Andrew has independently checked his clarinet through exercise (1:47), for example, Timothy elicits a further test of the reed: 'Well just, just play a scale or two because it sounds a bit grotty' (3:01). Similarly, he elicits the first rehearsal, with an announcement 'Okay, let's try it' (4:00). This matches the establishment of the 'default position', described in the discussion of spatial behaviour: Timothy adopts a relaxed but commanding posture, standing back a little from Andrew's rehearsal position, weight equally distributed on both feet, and hands clasped either in front or behind his back.

Timothy's role in directing Andrew's performances does vary when rehearsals begin and end. The beginning of Andrew's rehearsals has been discussed above: they typically begin with a moment's preparation, but since Timothy's own rehearsals tend to begin without ceremony, it seems that the act of preparation has not come from imitating Timothy's lesson behaviour. Perhaps Timothy's concert behaviour is the hidden influence here. Andrew seems confident that Timothy will respect his preparatory moments, and certainly he never seems to feel rushed because of Timothy's presence.

The endings of Andrew's rehearsals are not given the same respect, and Timothy tends to take command in cutting Andrew's rehearsals off, typically by saying 'Yeah' or 'Okay' when he wants to halt the proceedings. Examples of this may be seen almost from the outset of performance behaviour. As noted above, Andrew cuts himself off after his first rehearsal, because of an obvious difficulty with the octave leap (4:34); but the next seven rehearsals are stopped by Timothy (5:04, 6:01, 7:17, 7:37, 8:06, 8:51, 10:17).

While Andrew is performing, Timothy continues to take an active role, even if that consists of intently listening, as noted above (4:10). He sometimes talks during performances, offering coaching, as well as offering feedback afterwards: these are described more fully under the discussion of verbal behaviour. His nonverbal behaviour during performances consists in singing and the use of gesture.

Timothy sings on ten separate occasions during the lesson, always briefly. On two occasions he sings to illustrate a point he is making verbally, as for example when he says 'Okay, you don't want a *dah* [sings]' (5:05). On the remaining eight occasions, Timothy uses singing to coach Andrew while he is rehearsing, using his voice to influence or steer Andrew's performance. It is interesting to note that Timothy does not sing less often after he has picked up his clarinet: indeed, seven of the ten singing incidents occur while he has the clarinet in his hands. It seems clear that Timothy does not regard singing merely as a substitute for the instrument.

Five of the singing incidents involve conducting at the same time, and Timothy uses either his hand or his clarinet to make conducting gestures on 21 occasions during the lesson. With a single exception, where Timothy uses a conducting gesture to illustrate his verbal explanation of a rhythmic figure (33:49), these constitute coaching, in that they occur while Andrew is rehearsing. Examples of the varying purposes of gestures are given in Table 6.5.

Table 6.5   Conducting gestures from Lesson A

Time	Purpose	Description
8:29	Drawing attention to specific difficulties	Difficulty with an upward octave leap has been identified and practised: when Andrew puts it back into context by rehearsing the passage again, Timothy conducts that specific leap, to illustrate and encourage the full support needed.
10:10	Clarifying rhythm	Timothy counts the beats aloud, saying 'Two, three' and illustrating this with his hand.
12:35	Eliciting stronger playing	As Andrew's phrase reaches its climax Timothy conducts the last three notes with a closed fist, increasingly emphatically.
19:19	Eliciting more delicate playing	As Andrew's phrase approaches an anticlimax Timothy coaches him by saying 'Gently', his hand making a calm but expressive scoop to match the arrival of the highest note.
44:09	Influencing the tempo	Here Timothy says 'Take your time' while conducting Andrew through an ornament.

The main features of performance behaviour may be summarized in terms of content, texture and structure. The three main kinds of performance activity are rehearsal, practice and exercise. On the road to Parnassus – the performance examination – rehearsal is the most intense activity. It is also the most dominant, and is typically preceded by preparation, regarded here as an aspect of performance in its own right. The texture of the performance activity has a marbled effect, switching from one kind to another easily and often quickly: practice and exercise are incorporated as activities parenthetic to rehearsal. They can also serve as markers for the structure of the lesson, which maps onto the study of the *Grand duo* but also suggests a response to the student's morale and concentration, through his guided navigation of the whole movement.

Although Andrew contributes most of the performing activity, it is directed by Timothy, who often initiates, sometimes conducts, and normally halts, Andrew's rehearsals. Timothy himself uses demonstration sparingly, always to notable effect. His own playing perhaps symbolizes the goal, lying even beyond the imminent performance examination, and relatively rarely glimpsed. Far more frequently, Timothy employs verbal behaviour in guiding Andrew, and this is discussed more fully in the next section.

Verbal Behaviour in Lesson A

The discussion of findings from Lesson A has already touched on its soundscape. In keeping with the close spatial behaviour, the sounds of the lesson are small in scope: the clarinet is perhaps more notable for its quieter dynamic range than for its power, the slow movement of the *Grand duo* is itself constrained in volume, and even the laughter of the participants is restrained and quiet and never simultaneous. Verbal behaviour too is generally *mezzo piano*, and Timothy in particular tends to be quietly, and precisely, spoken. Where the volume is raised it need only come to *mezzo forte* to have an effect: the lesson transcription highlights any speech that stands out in terms of volume, but the difference, in Timothy's lessons, is always slight and subtle.

Timothy, in coping with what must be an enormous amount of playing through his career, normally practises with a mouth guard devised from cigarette papers, to protect his lower front teeth. Andrew has adopted this habit, presumably influenced by his teacher, and he has his mouth guard in place before taking up the 'default' position on camera: it is only seen when he briefly removes it, mid-sentence (2:04) and replaces it soon after (2:29). The mouth guard may have a constraining effect on his verbal contribution to the lesson and certainly seems to reduce its clarity. Timothy has been using a mouth guard while practising prior to Andrew's lesson, but he removes this at the beginning of the lesson (0:11). Andrew sometimes mumbles – unlike Timothy, he does not always seem to feel the necessity of making himself clear – and sometimes hesitates, never matching his teacher's *moderato* fluency.

It has been noted that Andrew dominates performance behaviour; Timothy, for his part, dominates verbal behaviour, uttering 3611 of 4019 words in the 45-minute lesson. The proportions of each are almost perfectly inverse:

Table 6.6   Comparison of contributions to performance and verbal behaviour in Lesson A

	Performance (duration)	Verbal (wordage)
Timothy	11%	90%
Andrew	89%	10%

As with the analysis of performance behaviour, verbal behaviour has been divided into different kinds of activity, and the two participants undertake those activities in different ways. Since Timothy is the dominant actor now, the discussion of findings will begin with an examination of the functions of teacher talk.

The Nature of Teacher Talk

As might be expected, Timothy begins the lesson by saying 'Good morning' to Andrew, and ends it by saying goodbye and greeting the next student. Occasionally he makes an isolated exclamation such as 'Oops!' (28:57) or 'Yeah' (18:10), which do not serve any obvious purpose. Aside from such brief exceptions (44 words altogether) Timothy's verbal behaviour may be classified among four distinct functions.

Information.   Almost half of Timothy's verbal behaviour has the function of providing information. This represents 44 per cent of his total wordage in the lesson. The information is usually generalizable: it represents Timothy's knowledge or opinions, and has the clear potential to be applied in other situations, perhaps when Andrew is working independently, later. The information might refer to the nature of the instrument: for example, 'Now, in this area of the instrument it's going to be weaker' (8:53). It might refer to the nature of performance: for example, 'Well I think there's a danger that the player thinks too much, or hears too much of the, the core sound and you're blissfully unaware of all the extraneous sounds' (3:18). Or it might refer to musical principles: for example, 'Well it just says *dolce assai*; I mean, I would think a healthy *piano* there' (23:28). Very occasionally the information is off task, as when Timothy mentions some dental work he has had done recently (36:08), or has an organizing function, as when he notes that it is time to stop (45:21). Although Timothy is able to deliver information relatively fluently, he rarely speaks continuously for long: his speech is typically punctuated by short verbal or performance behaviours from Andrew, which will be discussed in more detail later.

Elicitation.   Almost a third of Timothy's verbal behaviour (30 per cent) is classified as eliciting a response from the student. This might involve asking Andrew for information: 'What sort of reeds are you using?' (1:51). It might also involve asking Andrew to perform: 'One more time?' (7:53). Eliciting does not always involve questions, however, and sometimes Timothy uses more direct instructions: 'Try straight on there' (7:08). Neither is what Timothy elicits necessarily simple, and at times he asks Andrew to engage in more challenging activity, as in the following extract. Andrew's interpolations are represented in italics, with overlapping speech marked by square brackets.

> 12.39   So that the rubato is kind of spread over the whole bar,
> 12:43   *[All right, yeah]*
> 12:43   speed it up as you go through there and then you can justify taking a little more time over the top few notes, to really ham that up. Okay?
> 12:52   *[Okay]*
> 12:53   Go from there.
>
> (Excerpt 6.17 Lesson A)

There are even places where what Timothy is eliciting is imaginative thought, for example, '[J]ust imagine someone's got a string and it's lifting off like that' (18:17), and 'Think about where, where it's actually going to change note' (18:28).

Feedback.   Measured in terms of wordage the next most important verbal behaviour from Timothy, representing 20 per cent of the total, is feedback. In this he offers his observations or analysis of Andrew's performance, immediately after he has played. This might involve correction: 'Still too slow on this, so it's one two three four five six dada<u>dum</u>' (13:47). At times this would be better described as criticism: '[Y]ou're <u>still</u> – old habits die <u>hard</u> – and you're bashing the down beats as <u>well</u>. So, the impact of the um accent is lost a bit' (11:10). More often however Timothy's feedback for Andrew is expansive and productive: the following example identifies a problem, diagnoses both the cause and the effect, and suggests the way forward.

> 6:04   This, partly because you moved your feet in the middle, you, you kind of lost the feeling of calm, there was a bit too much waggling around which, um, destroyed the line for me. If you could make that shape seamless and then this *con duolo*, I think you can really lay it on thicker there.
>
> (Excerpt 6.18 Lesson A)

Coaching.   Finally, Timothy's verbal behaviour can have the function of coaching: guidance, encouragement and advice given while Andrew is actually performing. This is hardly an opportunity for Andrew to take in subtle or detailed information, and such behaviours are therefore brief and direct in nature, comprising only 6 per cent of the total. A single example here encapsulates the varying intentions that coaching might have: while Andrew is practising, Timothy calls out further instructions, articulating the physical sensation that he wants Andrew to notice, and offers regular affirmation of his efforts. All of this speech overlaps with the performance:

> 6:49   Bit, bit more open.
> 6:50   That's it. And really push, down here. Yeah. You do need the, this – that's it.
> 7:00   Yeah. Feel that your diaphragm is pushing lower rather than –
> 7:05   That's right. Okay.
>
> (Excerpt 6.19 Lesson A)

The relative proportions of the four functions among Timothy's verbal behaviours are illustrated in Figure 6.4.

Although these proportions give a clear idea of the relative importance of each of these verbal behaviours in his overall approach to the lesson, the approach in practical terms often involves a close synthesis of behaviours, characteristic of Timothy's expertise as a teacher. In the following section the application of verbal behaviours is examined in more detail.

Distribution of Verbal Behaviours

Table 6.7 illustrates how the verbal behaviour is played out, in an example taken from the analysis of an exchange in the last few minutes of the lesson. In this

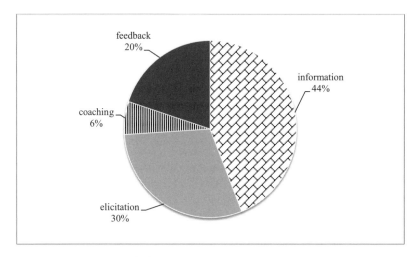

Figure 6.4   Functions of Timothy's verbal behaviour in Lesson A

table, the student's speech appears in italics, and performance behaviour is noted in a separate column.

This short sample shows Timothy moving quickly and easily from one kind of verbal behaviour to another, once again creating a marbled effect. His substantial rehearsal (42:54) offers a demonstration which is immediately pointed by the addition of verbal information; this is put into context by feedback referring to Andrew's own previous performance; further information is given to help set up Andrew's next attempt, and then that attempt is elicited. While Andrew is rehearsing the same passage that started this episode, Timothy offers coaching that consists of advice and support.

Although Timothy is quite adept at mixing these functions of verbal behaviour, there are episodes where he remains consistent with one of them, for rather longer. The longest of these episodes lasts for more than two minutes (35:44–37:54): during this time Timothy's verbal behaviour consists in giving information only. The length of the episode does not give an exact indication of the density of the information given, since it also includes remarks from Andrew, and performance behaviours: the wordage (263) helps to clarify the sheer amount of input Timothy gives, verbally, during the episode. Table 6.8 lists the longest ten episodes, during which Timothy's verbal behaviour remains consistent in function. Reading from left to right, for example, the first episode falls between 5:18 and 6:01, lasting 43 seconds, during which Timothy offers coaching only, using four words altogether.

The relationship between the length and the wordage of each episode clearly shows that coaching is the 'least dense' verbal behaviour: the figure given for the time spent (43) is larger than the figure for the wordage (4), by a ratio of more than ten to one. Because the student is actually performing during coaching, the teacher's exhortations must be concise and easily understood, and the language

Table 6.7   Sample of distributed verbal behaviour in Lesson A

Time	Classification	Verbal behaviour	Performance behaviour (seconds)
42:53			Timothy prepares (1)
42:54			Timothy rehearses (33)
43:27	Information	– and that's where it's going.	
43:28 43:31	Feedback	You gave everything on that top F *[Yeah, I know]* And then the, the actual cadence point was <u>quieter</u>.	
43:34	Information	I think it helps us if we're not blasting out totally – on the F, and keep something for those two. *[Right]*	
43:41	Information	So it'll be better in tune (unclear) as well *[Yeah]*	
43:44	Elicitation	Just try that section.	
43:46	Information	And then it's time to stop.	
43:47 43:49			*Andrew prepares (2)* *Andrew rehearses (36)*
44:02 44:09 44:11 44:25	Coaching	[Yeah lots of breath] [Take your time] [That's good. Now move it along again. Through, one two three, bom bom] [<u>That's</u> it, <u>that's</u> it, yeah.]	*Andrew practices (2)*

for coaching, illustrated in Table 6.7, is necessarily less prosodic than the other verbal behaviours. In addition, of course, the time during which coaching remains the prevalent behaviour is spun out by the performance it is supporting.

At the other end of the scale, the most intense verbal behaviour is found among episodes dominated by information. There is one episode of elicitation where the wordage outnumbers the seconds spent, by more than two to one (12:25–12:53), but in information episodes this is often exceeded, reaching a peak toward the end of the lesson where the ratio becomes nearer three to one (41:36–42:15).

A more graphic representation of the distribution of verbal behaviours may be seen in Figure 6.5. This representation is more refined, in that all verbal behaviour is included, regardless of whether it is consistent for long.

Figure 6.5 shows that the opening minutes of the lesson seem relatively leisurely: this is matched in Table 6.8, which shows that there are no extended episodes of consistent verbal behaviour during the first five minutes. It is also parallel with performance behaviour, previously shown in Figure 6.3, which was

Table 6.8   Episodes of consistent verbal behaviour in Lesson A

Time within the lesson	Length of lesson segment (seconds)	Type of verbal behaviour	Length of incident (wordage)
5:18–6:01	43	Coaching	4
9:09–10:00	51	Information	128
12:25–12:53	28	Feedback	72
13:14–13:40	26	Information	61
20:48–22:40	112	Feedback	106
31:00-31:34	34	Information	71
35:44–37:54	130	Information	263
39:38–40:12	34	Feedback	80
41:36–42:15	39	Information	125
45:10–45:43	33	Information	75
Average	53 seconds		99 words

least active during this time. The chart has two further features which appear parallel to the chart of performance behaviour. One produces a contrast: a trough is reached after the pivotal central episode (20:00–24:59) with verbal activity at its lowest point close to where performance activity reached its peak. The other produces agreement, in that the two broad divisions of the lesson show contrasting patterns of both performance and verbal behaviour. In verbal behaviour, after a 'slow start', the first half of the lesson remains relatively consistent in its patterns; in addition, Timothy seems to employ elicitation a little more freely now, than later. During the second half of the lesson the pattern is quite different, effectively producing an *accelerando* in the sheer amount of verbal activity and certainly in the amount of information being given. This process begins at the trough of activity that follows the central episode, and reaches its peak in the final minutes of the lesson. No doubt the high point of 'information density' here has a summarizing function for the lesson as a whole.

The Student's Role in Verbal Interaction

In the discussion of findings concerning performance behaviour, it emerged that although the student was responsible for most of the performing activity, the teacher's contribution was significant, both in directing the student and in performing himself, in rare but influential demonstrations. Complementing this, the following discussion considers Timothy's dominant verbal behaviour in the light of Andrew's role.

Andrew contributes only 10 per cent of the lesson wordage, and his verbal behaviour is typically concise, even monosyllabic. His speech acts – referring,

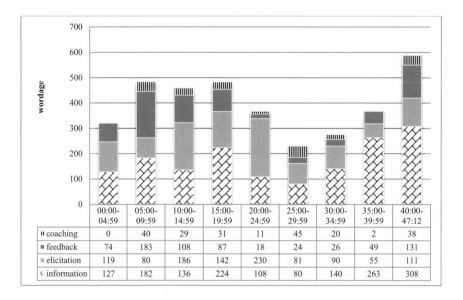

	00:00-04:59	05:00-09:59	10:00-14:59	15:00-19:59	20:00-24:59	25:00-29:59	30:00-34:59	35:00-39:59	40:00-47:12
‖ coaching	0	40	29	31	11	45	20	2	38
▪ feedback	74	183	108	87	18	24	26	49	131
▪ elicitation	119	80	186	142	230	81	90	55	111
‹ information	127	182	136	224	108	80	140	263	308

Figure 6.5   Distribution of Timothy's verbal behaviour in Lesson A

here, to any contributions that are uninterrupted by either Timothy's talk, or performance behaviour – are numerous, but short: there are 137 speech acts altogether and no less than 92 of these consist of a single word. 'Mmm', 'Umm', 'Yeah', 'Right' and 'Okay' are the most common, and on several occasions the word spoken remains entirely unclear.

The average wordage for Andrew's speech acts is 2.9, but of course, since such a high proportion of them consist of one word only, there are many cases where the wordage is greater. Figure 6.6 represents Andrew's contribution to verbal behaviour through the lesson, showing, for each five-minute period, the number of words uttered, the number of speech acts involved and the average wordage of each speech act.

Three features are clear from the chart: one, that Andrew's contribution is most verbose in the first five minutes of the lesson; two, that his contribution, in all respects, reaches a low point shortly after the central episode of the lesson; and three, that from this point through to the end of the lesson, Andrew's number of speech acts increases steadily, in spite of the fact that his total wordage, and therefore wordage per speech act, eventually falls off.

The trough of activity between 25:00 and 29:59 coincides with the lowest levels of Timothy's total verbal contribution, and his delivery of information in particular. It also coincides, as noted above, with the peak periods of performance activity between 25:00 and 35:00, and the use of exercise in particular. The swell in performance activity is boosted by the fact that Timothy is now playing, too, and it is hardly necessary to observe that neither participant can talk and play the clarinet at the same time.

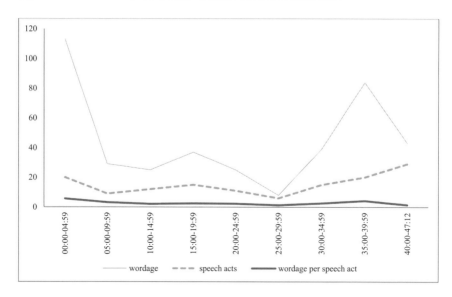

Figure 6.6   Andrew's verbal behaviour in Lesson A

If the low point of Andrew's verbal activity is associated with trends in performance behaviour, the remaining episodes of interest present more subtle patterns to be explored.

In the first five minute period of the lesson Andrew makes his greatest contribution to lesson wordage, with 113 words and 20 speech acts. It may seem paradoxical to assert that he does not achieve this alone, but there are several corresponding features of Timothy's verbal behaviour in this period which cast a significant light on Andrew's own behaviour. The teacher's use of elicitation, here, and in particular the use of questions, clearly plays an important part. Timothy asks a total of 43 questions during the lesson, and 9 of them fall within the first few minutes (0:00–2:28). These questions are simple in nature and do not provoke lengthy responses: one is a politely disguised instruction – '[L]et's do some Weber shall we?' (1:00) – but with the rest, the teacher is eliciting the information he needs to proceed with the lesson. In this way he checks what Andrew has prepared, where he has been practising and how he has prepared his reed, before eliciting any performance at all (3:01). If this is Andrew's peak period of verbal activity, it is once again Timothy who is directing it.

Timothy is doing more than directing Andrew, however, at this point. Andrew's speech acts tend to be neither lengthy nor fluent, and to encourage him to give information, Timothy offers brief, monosyllabic words of support. This kind of interaction is represented in a short extract in Table 6.9.

The supportive words – which may be described as back channelling (Argyle 1988, p. 111) – are not substantive, and appear to offer redundant agreements, even chiming in merely to echo Andrew's words. Their purpose however is clearly to encourage Andrew to continue, indicating interest and sympathy in quite a simple way.

Table 6.9   Verbal interaction in Lesson A

Time	Classification	Dialogue, *with student speech in italics*
1:51	Elicitation	What sort of reeds are you using?
1:54	Information	*Four.*
1:55	Elicitation	Fours! <u>Why</u>?
2:00	Information	*Well, I started – I seem to have upgraded ever since I started doing a little bit more practice.*
2:06	BACK CHANNELLING	Yeah
2:07	Information	*and three and a halves were getting really – weak*
2:11	BACK CHANNELLING	Yeah
2:12	Information	*Um, so I'm*
2:14	Elicitation	Where, where are you doing your practice? Are you always in bathroom-type rooms?
2:19	Information	*No, it's in [the Music Department] usually. Umm, but I usually – scrape them down a bit.*
2:25	BACK CHANNELLING	[Scrape them] down a bit yeah.
2:28	Elicitation	Where do you scrape them?
2:30	Information	*Well – around there.*

As it happens, Timothy never does this again in the lesson, but in Andrew's own verbal behaviour back channelling emerges as a dominant feature. In fact, this behaviour – with Andrew cooperating and encouraging his teacher to continue talking, by providing the kind of minimal response described here – lies behind the peak of Timothy's own verbal activity. During the last period of the lesson (40:00–47:12) Timothy's sheer amount of talk and provision of information reach their highest points; coincidentally, 25 consecutive speech acts from Andrew are classified as back channelling. Over the whole lesson, 106 of 137 of Andrew's speech acts (77 per cent) are classified in this way.

Of course, Andrew's speech behaviour does not have the same range as Timothy's, since it is never his role to offer either coaching or feedback. He does however employ elicitation in places, asking eleven questions during the lesson. Two of these are simple, as when he inquires at the end of his lesson whether there will be a class in the afternoon (47:00, 47:03). On three further occasions, he asks questions in order to check on advice or instructions that he has just been given, as for example when he says, 'So I hold that – ?' (24:24). More interestingly, Andrew's questions often seem to be preconceived, in that they tend to change the subject slightly, interrupting the flow of Timothy's own verbal behaviour. Interestingly, too, he often achieves the interruption in the same way as Timothy

Table 6.10   Verbal interaction in Lesson A

Time	Classification	Dialogue, *with student speech in italics*
23:09	Elicitation	Yeah. Make sure that B's low enough.
23:14	Information	It always comes out – comes out very sharp.
23:16	BACK CHANNELLING	*All right.*
23:16	Information	And then the instrument because of a reduction of, as you phrase off and reduce the air pressure obviously the pitch would go sharper.
23:24	BACK CHANNELLING	*[Right.]*
23:25	Elicitation	*What's, what's the er dynamic marking – still 'piano'?*
23:28	Information	Well it just says 'dolce assai'; I mean, I would think a healthy 'piano' there.

stops Andrew's performances, by interjecting a short, overlapping word to cut him off, before making his own assertion. An example is shown in Table 6.10.

That Timothy welcomes the interruption seems clear: his response here is brief at first, but after Andrew has put his advice into practice with a short, prepared rehearsal (23:34, 23:36) Timothy continues to address the issue that Andrew has raised, expanding his explanation by proposing the metaphor of a 'dandelion puff ball, floating by' (23:45).

Verbal behaviour in Andrew's lesson has been examined largely in terms of its functions. Timothy's verbal behaviour, which dominates, is itself dominated by giving information, though this is balanced to some extent by eliciting responses – in thinking, speaking or performance – from the student: the balance is effectively struck between giving and taking. Two further behaviours are more directly involved with Andrew's performance: coaching, in which instruction and encouragement are offered during the performance, and feedback, in which observations and analysis are offered afterward.

Andrew is clearly the junior partner in verbal behaviour, and never matches Timothy in terms of amount or fluency of speech. He does employ a number of similar behaviours, however. Through the use of back channelling he continually signals his interest and attention, and it seems clear that he has brought along a number of questions of his own, through which he elicits further information and feedback from his teacher.

The cooperative nature of the verbal interaction is in keeping with the closely collaborative nature of the spatial behaviour; and aspects of performance behaviour – particularly the lesson structure, falling loosely into two main sections – are reinforced by patterns of verbal behaviour. Timothy and Andrew, with an air of businesslike intimacy, seem to have developed considerable expertise in their work together. In interviews after their lesson was filmed, each was able to articulate his view of the other, of their professional relationship, and of the context of the lesson. Before the interview findings are examined, however, Lesson B will be discussed.

Chapter 7
Lesson B

Lesson B is given to Beth. Beth is in the 22–29 age bracket and currently in the third and final year of her degree programme as a 'combined honours' student, whose degree incorporates Music and Social Science. Beth has been studying with Timothy throughout her time at SEU and is now preparing for her final examination-recital, in a lesson scheduled to be 45 minutes long but which actually runs for an hour. The discussion of Beth's lesson will be divided among spatial, performance and verbal behaviour.

Spatial Behaviour in Lesson B

The layout of the room in which lessons take place has already been described and illustrated. There is some overlap between lessons. Beth enters the room during the closing minutes of Andrew's lesson – the door is heard to squeak briefly, at 44:43 – and first appears momentarily on camera at 44:47, placing two cups of tea on the table in the background of the scene and withdrawing toward the right to settle her belongings off stage.

Andrew does not leave the room until several minutes later – the door is finally heard to shut at 47:15 – and during the overlap between the two lessons Timothy divides his attention between the two students in interactions that remain quite separate. When his tea appears, Timothy thanks Beth immediately in a friendly tone and receives a prompt and polite response; but he and Andrew then proceed with their lesson discussion as if there had been no interruption and as if Beth were not in the room, for a further minute. When Andrew withdraws toward the left (45:54) Timothy turns to greet Beth more formally (45:57).

All three actors move efficiently and quietly in reconfiguring the scene. While Andrew packs his clarinet away and dons his jacket, partially out of view on the left, Beth settles her belongings off stage right, reappearing on camera at 46:09. The two students do not acknowledge each other, nor make eye contact: indeed, while she assembles her clarinet, Beth turns her back to both Andrew and the camera. Timothy, having confirmed with Beth that they will be working on a duet today, lowers the music stand for her, and fetches another which he places nearby, for his own later use. As Andrew leaves he and Timothy have a brief verbal exchange, agreeing on their next meeting; Beth ignores this as she carries on attending to the assembly of her clarinet, even playing through their talk to check her reed (47:05, 47:10).

Like Timothy, Beth is attired in 'smart casual' dress. Her blouse appears to be made of a sheer stretch fabric, meaning that it is semi-transparent and elastic in nature; her skirt is close-fitted and of mid-thigh length. Such items of clothing can give some little anxiety to the wearer, in that they have a tendency to slip slightly out of place, and although there is no evidence of this in the film, Beth makes adjustments to both items during the lesson, placing a hand on her blouse 5 times for a total of 15 seconds, and on her skirt 18 times for a total of 25 seconds. A further little preoccupation is Beth's hair, which is tied in a bunch at the back of her neck but not quite long enough to stay reliably in place, so that Beth raises a hand to touch or adjust her hair on 29 occasions (92 seconds). Occasionally she appears to deliberately remove some strands from the bunch before smoothing them back into position, and this takes longer: these occasions appear in Table 7.1.

Table 7.1   Instances of Beth touching her hair

Time	Duration of gesture, in seconds
53:01	6
65:28	3 + 1
93:10	9
102:23	13

More than this, Beth's busy hands tend to move to her face, which she touches on 58 occasions for a total of 384 seconds. Instances of this vary in nature and length, from an exasperated single-second slap on the forehead (55:23) to an extended episode in which Beth's hand remains on her mouth, toying with her lip, for 88 seconds (93:19). In all, Beth has a hand to her clothing, face or hair for a total of 516 seconds – around 8.5 minutes – and since her lesson eventually stops only moments short of an hour, this represents 14 per cent of her lesson time.

Self-touching is not unique to Beth, and during this lesson Timothy touches his own face 7 times, for a total of 12 seconds, and the back of his neck once, for 2 seconds. The reasons for Timothy touching his own face seem clear. Twice he touches his own mouth to illustrate a point he is making, as when he says, 'Don't curl your bottom lip in so far' (49:29) and 'You're still I think biting a little bit too much' (58:19). It will be recalled that Timothy has recently been to the dentist, and at 77:34 he brushes his left hand across his mouth; once he scratches his nose (56:46) and three times he puts his hand over his mouth to cough (47:05, 77:58, 84:37).

The use of space in Beth's lesson is relatively wide-ranging and changeable. Three of the contrasted positions adopted by Timothy and Beth are illustrated and described here. In the first the student is playing alone and the teacher observing, with some little distance kept between them. The simplified line drawing in Figure 7.1 is taken from 47:58, and is broadly representative of an introductory phase in the lesson where Timothy asks Beth to prepare for the rehearsal of her piece, through scale exercises.

This mutual positioning does not remain typical of Beth's lesson, largely because so much of it is devoted to the rehearsal with Timothy of duo repertoire.

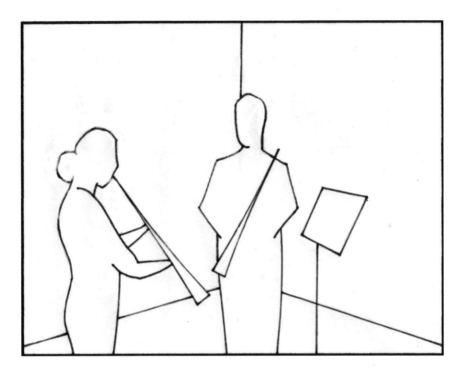

Figure 7.1   Spatial behaviour in Lesson B, example 1

The duo rehearsal begins after the introductory phase (56:12) and continues to dominate proceedings, in spite of several solo interludes, until the end of the lesson. The simplified line drawing in Figure 7.2 is taken from 83:34. The two music stands are closer together than the two players; rather than align them, Timothy has turned his own stand at an angle to Beth's. This might be a way of showing respect for her sense of personal space, or it might be so that he is more easily able to observe her playing.

These situations might be loosely regarded as the two 'default' positions for Timothy and Beth; even so, their use of space is relatively changeable and expansive. The third line drawing, in Figure 7.3, shows an example of a situation where Beth is to open a section of the piece alone, and Timothy steps back to lean on the narrow table against the wall. This is a pose of exaggerated relaxation, and it is associated with reassuring verbal behaviour: 'But I can kind of see the tension, before you start, worrying about it. Just, just play it very very, relaxed, and happy' (95:06). The simplified line drawing comes from 95:02.

Timothy remains in this pose for just 30 seconds, but he returns to it later. During the initial phase of the lesson he asks Beth to play a slow scale while walking around her own music stand, a practice strategy with which she seems to be familiar. To give her space to do this he stands back and leans against the table, smiling, for more than a minute (51:00–52:16), and when Beth passes

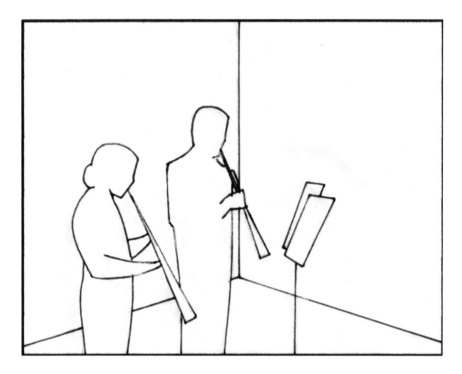

Figure 7.2   Spatial behaviour in Lesson B, example 2

between him and her music stand, he averts his eyes. Later, he returns to lean on the table for a further 28 seconds, while Beth plays (100:07) and when he stands upright again, he puts his left hand in his pocket for 13 seconds (100:36). These rather casual poses are also similar to one Timothy adopts during a discussion of the history of the work they are addressing, which provides a break from playing some 20 minutes into the lesson. Here, he rests his left hand on his own music stand, and his weight on one leg, giving the impression that he is actually leaning on the stand, for more than a minute (65:57–66:58). He does the same again later, for 16 seconds, while giving Beth some feedback on her performance (73:55).

The space that Timothy allows Beth – or perhaps more properly, that he and Beth establish between them – seems to carry over to the frequency of contact between them. He touches Beth's clarinet, only once, and for only one second (57:05). At 49:09 he steps forward to indicate a specific key on her clarinet, but his hand stops just short of it, and he withdraws it quickly.

Timothy's hand is in contact with either Beth's score or his own for 416 seconds during the lesson, largely because of the periods where he rests his hand on his music stand. Timothy's clarinet is used to make contact with the score for a total of 51 seconds: it seems that by extending his clarinet instead of making hand contact, Timothy is able to avoid trespassing in Beth's personal space.

Figure 7.3   Spatial behaviour in Lesson B, example 3

The handling of the score remains largely the teacher's prerogative. Beth touches the score relatively rarely and briefly: with her hand on four occasions (for a total 7 seconds) and with her clarinet on five occasions (12 seconds). As they work through their duet, Timothy fetches a pencil to mark their parts, and although Beth uses it once, for four seconds (77:00), this activity is dominated by Timothy, who writes on either Beth's score or his own, 15 times (90 seconds).

The use of a pencil in Beth's lesson is perhaps typical of a duo rehearsal situation, in which players sometimes need to compare the details of their individual parts. In addition, too, it seems that Timothy is working out some details of his own part as he goes along: his expertise is such that he need not have prepared it in advance of the lesson, and this means that he and Beth are working out their parts together. Although the duo rehearsal situation has Timothy and Beth collaborating, however, their physical attitudes are not always consonant.

The tendency to change among several different positions is an example of this, already noted in the illustrations above. A further example is the physical demonstration of good humour, by both teacher and student. One of the most conspicuous instances of this occurs early in the lesson. Timothy suggests that some warm-up scales would be helpful, and then pauses, widens his eyes and shakes his head slightly as if miming a thinking process – explicitly pretending to have to think hard – saying, 'Do um, oo, G major' (47:40). The joke here seems to be that the G major scale is fundamental to a particularly difficult section of the duet to follow, and that therefore he and Beth have worked on it before as preparation for that section, possibly more than once. Beth laughs.

Shortly after, when Timothy asks that the same scale be played while Beth walks around the room (50:53), the student's response further exaggerates the sense of comedy mime. While Timothy continues to explain, Beth laughs with less vocalization than physical show: although her clarinet remains on her bottom lip, she opens her mouth in 'laughing position' and holds this for 11 seconds, while she shifts on her feet, turning 180 degrees and back, as if reacting to a very good joke indeed. The scale of the gesture suggests that Beth is embarrassed to be asked to do this. She does not appear to need much explanation of how to do what Timothy is asking, suggesting that he has asked her to do it before; but this is presumably the first time he has asked her to do it in front of a video camera, and it seems possible that he is explaining it merely for the benefit of the audience that represents. As Beth walks, she takes 'giant' steps on straight legs, again as if participating in a pantomime.

These aspects of Beth's lesson are perhaps better described as comedy than humour, in that they do not seem to be simple expressions of good feeling. When Timothy says, 'Do um, oo, G major' he is pretending to be patronizing, but we do not know how the comment is taken, even though Beth laughs in response. There are a number of such comments, from both teacher and student, which have some little flavour of sarcasm. In the following selection of separate examples, the student's speech appears in italics, and 'action' in square brackets:

53:35   These tadpole things are crotchet rests! Ts. [Timothy smiles; Beth jiggles her head slightly in silent imitation of a laugh]

56:59   What's that meant to be? [Both play in response]

94:30   One of the big problems with, a word like 'andante', it's so vague anyway. What is 'walking pace'?
94:44   *I've got short legs remember.* [Both smile]

96:32   Sounds about a 'scherzando', this.
96:35   What's 'scherzando'?
96:36   Playful. Okay? So, it's got to sound, like teletubbies dancing, okay? [Timothy lowers his face to Beth as if telling a child a story; there is no response until he laughs himself, and she smiles a little, but continues looking at her score]
96:48   *I'll have to watch it.* [Turns to meet his gaze.]

(Excerpt 7.1 Lesson B)

Timothy and Beth each make 13 little jokes during the hour. Smiling or quiet laughter are conspicuous features of the lesson, with Timothy smiling or laughing on 15 occasions, and Beth 47. Although the sarcasm is always mild, and might in places be attributed to the researcher's conjecture, teacher and student seem equally likely to make little jokes at Beth's expense.

Consistent with this are some features that overlap with verbal behaviour. Beth vocalizes without words – 'Ow!' for example – on seven occasions, usually by way of remarking on something that has gone wrong, and once she cries 'Wha'?' as if the error is something that has happened to her rather than something she has done. Sometimes she speaks in a complaining tone – 'I know. I've forgotten it' (57:29) – and sometimes she blames herself aloud – 'I just went, "Ooh! That was stupid"' (77:13). Beth also apologizes, saying 'sorry' on eight separate occasions.

Timothy is perhaps falling in with Beth's behaviour when he makes jokes, now, and twice during the lesson he too makes nonverbal exclamations when something goes wrong, such as 'Ahh! That's my solo!' (102:18).

The spatial behaviour in Beth's lesson, effectively including any behaviour that is neither performance nor verbal, is characterized by a degree of tension. Although the rehearsal of a duo work means that the participants are placed in a cooperative position, a certain distance between them is generally kept; at times Timothy makes way for Beth by standing back against the rear table, and when he wants to make contact with the score he typically uses his clarinet rather than his hand, which allows him to avoid moving closer. This is not to suggest that there are any defensive postures adopted; rather, the observance of distance and avoidance of contact seem to be a matter of respecting personal space. However, while there are no signs of stiffness or dislike, the signs of relaxation and good humour often seem to be exaggerated, even deliberately demonstrated. Although neither Timothy nor Beth commented on it in their interviews after the lesson, it seems that the presence of the camera must have had some effect on their spatial behaviour, if only to highlight these features.

The discomfort apparent in Beth's posture and gestures suggests a lack of ease and fluency, and has its parallel in aspects of both performance and verbal behaviour, which will be discussed in turn, below.

Performance Behaviour in Lesson B

The clarinet is heard for a total of 28 minutes 43 seconds, or 48 per cent of the lesson time. Most of the performance behaviour consists in duo work: Beth and Timothy playing together contribute a total of 17 minutes 50 seconds, or 62 per cent of the total; Beth playing alone contributes a further 31 per cent, and Timothy alone, 7 per cent.

During the lesson Timothy and Beth work their way through the whole of the Mendelssohn *Konzertstück* Op.114 no 2. Although this was written for clarinet and basset horn, the basset horn part is commonly performed on a second clarinet, and this role is taken by Timothy. As the whole work is addressed, the lesson expands from the scheduled 45 minutes to a whole hour.

The performance activity in the lesson may be mapped against the structure of the *Konzertstück* itself. The piece normally lasts around eight minutes, though it should be noted that for much of it Beth is currently playing well below tempo. The structure falls into three short, connected movements. The opening phase of performance activity creates a preparatory ramp for the rehearsal of the first section: work on a scale exercise (46:29–52:12) becomes the foundation of the practice that follows (52:29–55:47) and that in turn becomes the foundation of the first rehearsal, from 56:12. The focus in the opening phase is the cadenza-like passage that concludes the first movement, and only after this has been addressed at some length do Timothy and Beth return to rehearse from the beginning. During the course of the lesson their attention is broadly divided among the consecutive movements, as represented in Table 7.2.

Table 7.2   Lesson B content

Movement	Time in the lesson
Presto	from 46:29
Andante	from 77:49
Allegretto grazioso	from 95:02 to 103:07

In terms of time spent, this gives approximate proportions 3:2:1.

The performance behaviour may be divided among several different kinds of activity.

Rehearsal.   74 per cent of all performance time is spent on rehearsals of the *Konzertstück*, and of the rehearsal time, 80 per cent represents duo rehearsal, with 15 per cent from Beth rehearsing alone and 5 per cent from Timothy. The length of rehearsals ranges from 2 to 149 seconds; there are fifteen rehearsals longer than 30 seconds, all of them duo work. Solo rehearsals are typically short, and only three of them exceed 13 seconds: two of these come from Beth (22 + 25 seconds) and one from Timothy (28). All three of these occur in the last phase of the lesson, while the *Allegretto grazioso* is being rehearsed.

Preparation.   On seven occasions, for a total of 12 seconds, rehearsals are preceded by a moment's pause, with Beth holding her clarinet in her mouth and looking ahead at the score. This seems to be unselfconscious, and may perhaps be a matter of checking that she is looking at the right spot before she plays. Twice, Beth waits in this position for two seconds while Timothy, having indicated the spot on her score, steps back into his rehearsal position.

Practice.   15 per cent of the performance behaviour involves playing that is related to the *Konzertstück* without being a simulated performance. There is an extended episode early in the lesson, lying on the 'preparatory ramp' between exercise and the first rehearsal, where Timothy guides Beth through some systematic practice of a passage she clearly finds challenging. This episode lasts for just over three minutes, which includes a total of 86 seconds' practice. Elsewhere, practice involves dealing parenthetically and briefly with a problem that has arisen during rehearsal.

Exercise. 10 per cent of the performance behaviour involves playing that is not directly related to the *Konzertstück*. This adds to a total of 183 seconds, of which 25 (14 per cent) are associated with setting up and checking the instruments at the beginning of the lesson, with five further checks of 1–3 seconds occurring later in the lesson. The remaining 151 seconds of exercise behaviour (83 per cent) come from the initial exercise of the G major scale, which is to support the practice and rehearsal of the challenging passage mentioned above.

The piano is used only once during the lesson, and for only 2 seconds. Here (73:37) Timothy draws Beth's attention to the last note of a phrase, which she has allowed to decay flatward; he asks her to play the note on the piano, presumably so that she can compare her intonation with the steadiness of a fixed-pitch instrument.

The time spent on each mode of performance behaviour is summarized in Table 7.3.

Table 7.3   Performance behaviour in Lesson B

	Total time spent (seconds)	Timothy alone	Beth alone	Both together
All performance behaviour	1737	114	547	1076
Preparation	12 (1%)	0	6	6
Rehearsal	1287 (74%)	60	199	1028
Practice	235 (15%)	49	162	42
Exercise	183 (10%)	5	178	0
Piano	2 (–)	0	2	0

Distribution of Performance Behaviours

The total duration of each performance behaviour shown in Table 7.3 does not show how those behaviours function in time: Table 7.4 shows how Beth's performance behaviour is played out, during the first ten minutes of the lesson. The breadth and consistency of the exercise and then the practice activity are immediately clear.

Table 7.4 represents much of the 'preparatory ramp' for the first rehearsal: there are only four more practice behaviours before duo rehearsal begins. Elsewhere performance behaviours switch more frequently, but this opening phase is by no means the only extended episode in which one kind of performance behaviour dominates. Indeed, as Table 7.5 shows, there are three episodes of unvaried performance behaviour that are longer than the initial period of exercise: these last for up to 8 minutes 30 seconds, and all of them involve rehearsal.

Table 7.4   Example showing distribution of performance behaviour in
              Lesson B

Time	Rehearsal	Preparation	Practice	Exercise	Piano
46:29				2	
46:36				11	
46:46				2	
47:05				1	
47:10				4	
47:19				1	
47:35				1	
47:38				1	
47:46				15	
48:09				2	
48:12				6	
48:21				10	
48:31				4	
48:57				6	
49:04				1	
49:06				2	
49:12				10	
49:24				5	
49:35				6	
49:43				4	
50:03				6	
50:12				8	
50:31				20	
51:12				18	
51:44				28	
52:29			2		
52:40			8		
53:26			11		
53:44			6		
53:55			1		
53:57			1		
53:59			1		
54:02			1		
54:03			4		
54:12			5		
54:20			5		
54:33			8		
54:42			7		
54:51			2		
54:59			7		

Table 7.5   Episodes of consistent performance behaviour in Lesson B

Time within the lesson	Length of segment (seconds)	Type of performance behaviour	Duration of incidents in seconds: preparation shown in parentheses
46:29–52:12	343	Exercise	2, 11, 2, 2, 1, 4, 1, 1, 1, 15, 2, 6, 10, 4, 6, 1, 2, 10, 5, 6, 4, 6, 8, 20, 18, 28
52:29–55:47	198	Practice	2, 8, 2, 11, 6, 1, 1, 1, 1, 4, 5, 5, 8, 7, 2, 7, 1, 4, 7, 3
58:25–60:01	96	(Preparation) Rehearsal	(2)5, 37, 37, 28
61:02–64:26	204	Rehearsal	49, 2, 10, 60
65:03–73:33	510	Rehearsal	(1)3, 3, 11, 13, 4, 14, 19, 16, 3, 20, 9, 7, 6, 5, 7, 6, 8, 9, 45, 2, 25
74:31–77:55	204	Rehearsal	149, (1)5
78:34–85:17	403	Rehearsal	3, 6, (1)3, 5, 3, 34, 9, 3, 40, 4, 4, 45, 37, 34
86:07–92:52	405	Rehearsal	37, 8, 20, 6, 54, 23, 5, 4, 2, 40, 22
95:33–96:32	59	(Preparation) Practice	4, 4, 10, (3)4, 3, 5, 2, 9
98:10–99:56	106	Rehearsal	5, 22, 28, 8
Average	*253*		

Work on the opening *Presto* movement occupies the first half of the lesson, with the initial sequence of exercise – practice – rehearsal culminating in the longest rehearsal of 149 seconds, at 74:31. At 95:33 another extended episode of practice begins, associated now with fresh work on the *Allegretto* finale.

The amount and nature of performance behaviours is represented in Figure 7.4, which divides the lesson into five-minute periods.

Process and Structure

Against Figure 7.4, it is easy enough to envisage the approximate proportion of time devoted to each of the three movements: the opening *Presto* broadly occupies the first six periods, the central *Andante* the next four, and the *Allegretto grazioso* finale the last two.

A systematic approach is taken to the *Presto*, and there is some evidence to suggest that the plan for this has been preconceived, so that each step feeds into the next. In the exercise phase Timothy asks for a G major scale, which – on B flat clarinets – is the relative major and ultimately the tonic of the *Konzertstück* to follow, and likely to be important. As previously noted, Timothy in a moment of comedy mime pretends that he cannot decide which scale he would like to choose, and Beth laughs; the inference is that G major has already been established between

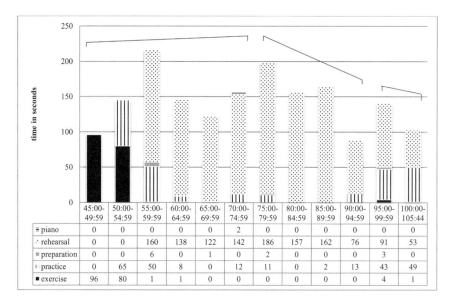

Figure 7.4   Distribution of performance behaviour in Lesson B

them as the inevitable preparation for the passage they are to address. Beth plays the three octaves that happen to match the range of the passage.

Having heard the scale in its entirety, Timothy now identifies a problem area, and sets about reducing it; first in size, by asking for just the top four notes, and second in focus, by concentrating for a minute and a half on establishing the correct fingering. He then feeds in a little more information by making a comment on embouchure, and then gently increases the size of the task by asking for the whole of the top octave. With this Beth's fingering again becomes muddled, and they pause to secure it in the context of the full octave, through simple strategies of slow practice and walking around the room. The next step is to return to the full three octaves, again with a little more information about support in the lowest octave, where the pressure on Beth's thinking seems minimal. Broadening the context again, Timothy searches the score for 'this horrible bit' (52:15) which Beth is now to attempt.

Several fresh complications undermine the attempt, in spite of the careful preparation. One, although neither teacher nor student mentions it, is that the passage does not proceed to the top in exactly the same way as the scale: there are several chromatic notes incorporated, now, which have not been prepared. Another is a problem with tonguing over the top three notes, which is discussed and practiced; and another is a change in note values, which become progressively slower toward the top, and which seem to take Beth by surprise. For several rather intense minutes, Timothy and Beth address these before returning to the issue of fingering, which has by now reverted to its original, insecure state. Once again a simple practice strategy is employed, repeating the difficult part correctly; this is intensified somewhat when Timothy asks for a certain number of correct repetitions, and further when he announces 'two penalty ones' (54:30) for each mistake. This is done smilingly, as if he is proposing a challenging game, which perhaps serves to offset the pressure of the task. Beth is not altogether successful in meeting the challenge, and although he declares that there must now be 'six extra ones', Timothy smiles again and relents, settling for just one more.

The next step is to begin the duo rehearsal of the passage. There is no performance activity for more than a minute, between the practice and the rehearsal, perhaps giving Beth a moment's pause before the fresh task begins. When it does begin it begins gently, with Timothy setting a pace that is perhaps half the usual performing speed.

The preparatory process has consisted of targeting a problem in its smallest components, and dealing with issues individually, securing each before adding more, and incrementally returning to the original context of the piece. Although this does not proceed altogether smoothly, with the participants sometimes returning to revise some issues, it does seem to support the subsequent rehearsal of the first movement. After almost half an hour's work the movement is rehearsed in its entirety (74:31–77:00) and although there are some little relapses from Beth, there is a clear improvement in the general coherence.

The broad move from exercise, through practice, to rehearsal, is clearly represented in the first six periods of Figure 7.4. The second movement is approached quite differently, with the next four periods in Figure 7.4 showing that performance activity is dominated by rehearsal. There is an arpeggio passage introducing the movement, which requires some practice and then solo rehearsal from Beth; thereafter, almost all of the performance activity consists in duo rehearsal. There are only three exceptions: Beth plays a two-second gesture alone, to check for rhythmic accuracy (85:56) and Timothy demonstrates two rehearsals, of four and then eight seconds (81:18, 86:48). It seems that the difficulties of this slow movement are not of the kind that requires technical exercise or practice.

With the finale, represented by the last two periods in Figure 7.4, performance behaviour becomes more freely mixed. Timothy asks for rehearsal in the first instance, but Beth seems reluctant to attempt the movement in this way, cutting herself off after three seconds (95:05) and allowing her tone to trail away after a further attempt of only four seconds (95:26). Guided practice behaviour ensues, here and elsewhere, but Timothy never abandons the intention of pressing ahead with rehearsal, and this phase of the lesson includes the three longest solo rehearsals. It seems that Timothy wants to press ahead, too, in identifying the character and tempo of the final version, though this apparently lies beyond Beth's grasp today. There is only one incident of duo rehearsal of the *Allegretto* (101:50) but Timothy twice demonstrates by rehearsing a passage, considerably faster than Beth's own attempts (97:20, 99:16); the second of these, at 28 seconds, is the longest demonstrated rehearsal in the whole lesson. He also discusses the character of the movement, referring to Mendelssohn's *A Midsummer Night's Dream* and playing a tiny excerpt of that (98:05).

Other Performance Behaviours

Over the course of the lesson Timothy sings on eight occasions, and uses conducting gestures thirteen times; with the first three of both, he sings and conducts at the same time. The use of conducting is complemented, because of the duo rehearsal, by the need for one player to cue the other on many of the entries. The first eight cues are given by Timothy, who gestures with his clarinet without exaggeration, to indicate the starting point and tempo. At 60:52 however Beth attempts to give the cue for a unison passage, herself. She makes a gesture with her clarinet that seems indecisive because it is large and loose, and because she abandons her first attempt to begin another. Timothy does manage to catch the entry point, but they stop to address the problem through brief, repeated demonstrations of the cueing gesture from Timothy. As first clarinettist, Beth should presumably be giving cues for unison entries as a matter of course, but such a pattern of behaviour is never quite fixed, and confusion recurs in several places. It seems that Beth has not altogether grasped the reason for giving cueing gestures: thus when Timothy gives the cue, Beth sometimes copies it at the same time (for example, 89:40, 90:48, 91:17); elsewhere, Beth makes a redundant cueing gesture for her own, solo entries (for example, 65:35, 67:03, 67:29). At one point, Timothy eschews cueing and counts an entry in (72:00) and perhaps relaxing because of this, Beth forgets to cue the following entry (73:00), which leads to some further explicit coaching on the subject. It seems that Beth has been given a clearer idea of how cueing is to be done, than of when she needs to take responsibility for doing it.

The main features of performance behaviour may be summarized in terms of content, texture and structure, with all three related to the work being rehearsed. The first half of the lesson, focused on the opening *Presto*, is the most clearly structured, with broad, successive swathes of activity leading up a preparatory ramp to duo rehearsal, and concluding with the longest duo rehearsal of the lesson. The next third of the lesson, focused on a slow movement that appears to pose no fundamental technical problems, is dominated almost exclusively by duo rehearsal behaviour. The remaining sixth of the lesson is focused on the *Allegretto* finale, and here it seems that duo rehearsal is not yet feasible. Performance behaviour is dominated instead by a mixture of practice and individual rehearsals, with some tension evident between the current state of play and the goal presented by Timothy's demonstrations. The only extended duo rehearsal now is one of 28 seconds that concludes performance activity in the lesson (101:48); but although this might have answered Timothy's desire, expressed in his interview, to end a lesson 'on a high', the rehearsal is cut off by a false entry from Beth (102:23). Timothy exclaims 'Ahh! That's my solo!' and Beth wails in response; 'Yeah', she adds, laughingly, perhaps pretending that the mistake had been a deliberate joke. Timothy glances at his watch, and Beth takes her right hand to her head, loosening and correcting strands of hair. It seems that this time, the peak has been missed.

Verbal Behaviour in Lesson B

In keeping with the use of space, the soundscape of Lesson B is varied; it is generally divided between two strata, coinciding with performing and verbal behaviour. The dynamic range of performing is wide, because of the contrasts within the Mendelssohn *Konzertstück*. Strong dynamics are also highlighted in the opening phase of the lesson by the attention given to the peak of the G major scale and the cadenza passage based on it: Beth's tone and pitch in this relatively extreme register are robust and ill controlled. In contrast, the verbal behaviour lies within a more limited dynamic range, generally quiet from both participants and rarely reaching *mezzo forte*. Although her nonverbal exclamations have already been noted, Beth in particular is likely to speak very quietly indeed, and on eight separate occasions her verbal remarks are entirely unclear. On three further occasions she begins to speak with a clear voice, which however trails out, as in the following example. Beth's speech is represented in italics and 'stage directions' in square brackets.

64:28	That big solo. Um, there's a lot that's good about it but can you think of other things that could be better?
64:36	*Um, these could be bigger, and smaller (unclear)* [As she steps back, she puts her right hand to her mouth – one of the reasons that her sentence becomes unclear.]
64:39	The hairpins?
64:40	*Yeah.*

(Excerpt 7.2 Lesson B)

On another occasion, the opposite effect is heard: Beth begins to verbalize almost inaudibly, and only gradually begins to speak clearly:

47:17	Um, how's this going? [Beth adjusts the hem of her blouse with her left hand, then plays a single note.]
47:19	Have you done enough practice yet?
47:21	*Mmmm*
47:22	Yeah?
47:23	[almost inaudible] *I don't know. No –*
47:23	What's that? No?
47:24	*No not really.*

(Excerpt 7.3 Lesson B)

Timothy dominates verbal behaviour, uttering 3509 of 3965 words (88 per cent) in the 60-minute lesson. To some extent, this is balanced by the fact that Beth is the larger contributor of performance behaviour, but the balance is skewed by the predominance, in performance behaviour, of duo work. The relative proportions of solo contributions to both are shown in Table 7.6.

Table 7.6   Comparison of contributions to solo performance and verbal
              behaviour in Lesson B

	Solo performance behaviour (duration)	Verbal behaviour (wordage)
Timothy	7%	88%
Beth	31%	12%

Since Timothy is the dominant partner in verbal dialogue, the discussion of findings will begin with an examination of the functions of teacher talk.

The Nature of Teacher Talk

Timothy is dominant in dialogue not only in terms of the number of words spoken but in terms of directing conversation. This is evident in quite a particular way during the overlap between the end of Andrew's lesson and the beginning of Beth's: it has already been noted in the discussion of spatial behaviour that Timothy divides his attention between the two students, conducting completely separate interactions, while the students respond to Timothy but ignore each other. This situation has its parallel in the overlap between the end of Beth's lesson and the beginning of that of a third student, Catherine. For almost two minutes Timothy and Catherine have a conversation in which Beth plays no part (103:29–105:18). The conversation begins with what seems to be a private joke: Catherine's remarks are shown here in italics:

103:29	Morning!
103:30	*Good morning.*
104:03	Thank you for the email.
104:05	*I had* <u>nothing</u> *to do with that. I didn't even know she sent it till after she sent it, that was (unclear).* [laughs]
104:12	My wife had a lot to say about that.

(Excerpt 7.4 Lesson B)

When Timothy turns his attention back to Beth and they exchange final comments about their next meeting, Catherine in turn becomes the silent bystander, except that when Beth makes a little joke, Catherine laughs aloud. In doing so she becomes the first student of the morning to acknowledge the presence of another. This little inconsistency with prevailing behaviour patterns may perhaps be linked to the fact that Catherine has not been studying with Timothy for so long as either Andrew or Beth: she is an exchange student from an American university and has been here for less than a year.

During the lesson, of course, Timothy devotes his full attention to engaging with Beth, and almost half of his verbal behaviour has the function of eliciting a response from the student. This represents 44 per cent of his total wordage. Normally elicitation involves careful attention to specific detail, as in the following example:

57:44   All the right ones down. Okay? Off we go? [Beth plays]
         Straight from the crotchets, okay? [Beth plays during this remark.]
         Crotchets? [They play together.]
         Okay? Don't let it squeak [Beth plays during this remark.]
         Just relax. Nice free, flow of air through it.

                                                              (Excerpt 7.5 Lesson B)

In this example and elsewhere Timothy often uses the intonation of a question, whether he is asking a question or not. 'Okay?' in particular seems to be rhetorical in nature: Timothy asks 'Okay?' 24 times during the lesson.

Occasionally elicitation involves an appeal to Beth's imagination, as when Timothy, having explained an issue of accentuation in context by using a metaphor concerning mountains, asks that an accent be a 'Snowdon one' rather than an Everest (65:28). Shortly afterward, having made the point that Mendelssohn wrote the *Konzertstück* for virtuoso players, he tells Beth, 'Imagine you've got your best frock on for this one. Go on' (66:59).

Only a very small proportion (1 per cent) of Timothy's verbal behaviour consists in coaching while Beth plays, presumably because so much of the playing is done in duo rehearsal. There are 19 separate remarks classified as coaching, and although these include some commands and some correction, nine of them are compliments, such as 'Yeah that's good' (50:31), 'All right' (50:50) and 'THAT'S BETTER. GO ON. THAT'S GREAT' (51:45).

The remaining teacher talk is divided almost equally between information (29 per cent) and feedback (26 per cent). Snippets of information are offered from time to time, but this is not a consistent feature of verbal behaviour, and there are eighteen episodes during the lesson when no information is offered for more than a minute. About 20 minutes into the lesson, Timothy attempts to open a more substantial, informative discussion about the background to the composition: this is quoted at some length below, in order to show how the attempt is influenced and possibly curtailed by Beth's responses:

65:53   Who were these pieces written for?
65:56   *Oh, that geezer*
65:57   That geezer called what.
66:02   *I don't know –*
66:03   Heinrich?
66:05   Baermann.
66:06   *Oh it <u>was</u> Baermann. I thought Baermann –*
66:07   And his –
66:08   *was the Weber?*
66:09   Well, he was as well, yes,
66:10   *Was that before that*
66:11   – mostly, but the Weber (unclear). But he and his son, toured around
             and Mendelssohn, wrote a sonata for Baermann and then he
             commissioned these two concert pieces, for ah, Mr and Master

Baermann to play. UM, but he was renowned and was billed as
the greatest clarinettist in the world. Can you play –
66:37   [Interrupting] *After you?*
66:40   I wasn't around then –
66:40   (Interrupting) *Oh I see.*
66:41   Cheeky! UM, [pauses and smiles] can you play it though as if you
were the greatest ...

(Excerpt 7.6 Lesson B)

Later Timothy makes another attempt to offer some reflections on the tempo
of the slow movement, in a substantial speech of more than a minute in length,
and concluding with a remark already mentioned in the discussion of nonverbal
behaviour: 'One of the big problems with a word like *andante*, it's so vague anyway.
What is "walking pace"?' Beth, who has listened almost without comment, arms
folded and with one hand to her mouth, ends the discussion with another quip,
'I've got short legs remember' (94:44).

In giving feedback, which represents about a quarter of his verbal behaviour,
Timothy employs a considerable range of valency. In places his remarks
are strongly positive, as in 'THAT WAS BRILLIANT' (83:20) or 'I was so,
flabbergasted I forgot to come in. But that was lovely. That was really good'
(88:10). Elsewhere however he is perhaps surprisingly negative, as in 'I'd rather
you tongued properly but you can get away with just going feh, feh, feh rather
than, using, your tongue like a sledgehammer' (53:01).

The relative proportions of the four functions among Timothy's verbal
behaviours are illustrated in Figure 7.5.

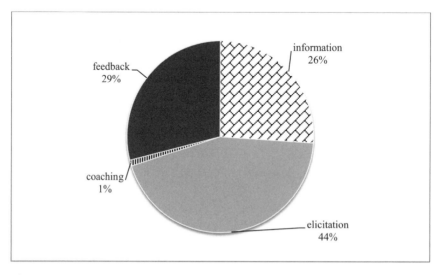

Figure 7.5   Functions of Timothy's verbal behaviour in Lesson B

Distribution of Verbal Behaviours

Although the functions of Timothy's verbal behaviour are often quite mixed, there are many short episodes during which they remain consistent. Table 7.7 lists, in order of occurrence, the ten longest of these.

Table 7.7   Episodes of consistent verbal behaviour in Lesson B

Time within the lesson	Length of lesson segment (seconds)	Type of verbal behaviour	Length of incident (wordage)
46:08–47:24	76	Elicitation	24
47:35–48:27	52	Elicitation	57
52:31–53:23	52	Feedback	84
54:19–55:07	48	Elicitation	35
55:53–57:04	71	Elicitation	39
59:26–60:23	57	Elicitation	54
80:13–81:07	54	Elicitation	28
90:20–91:17	57	Elicitation	27
93:34–94:42	68	Information	125
95:12–95:57	45	Elicitation	40
Average	*58 seconds*		51 words

In many of these episodes the density of wordage seems relaxed, in that the number of words is smaller than the length of the episode in seconds. The feedback episode (52:31) is conspicuous for being denser than most, with the wordage exceeding the length in seconds by more than 50 per cent: this is the speech in which Timothy compares Beth's tonguing to a sledgehammer. The information episode (93:34) is still more dense, and is also the most verbose: this is the speech in which the meaning of *andante* is addressed. The elicitation episodes are most numerous, and are most likely to be sparse in terms of wordage. Coaching does not appear at all in this list of sustained verbal behaviours, presumably because Timothy's participation in duo rehearsal places an obvious limit on the amount of simultaneous verbal support he is able to give.

In Figure 7.6, a fuller account of Timothy's verbal behaviour is given, with the proportions devoted to all four functions shown for each five-minute period in the lesson.

Significant features in this chart may be identified with reference to both lesson content, and the parallel chart in Figure 7.4 showing performance activity. The first two columns (45:00–54:59) roughly represent the preparatory episode

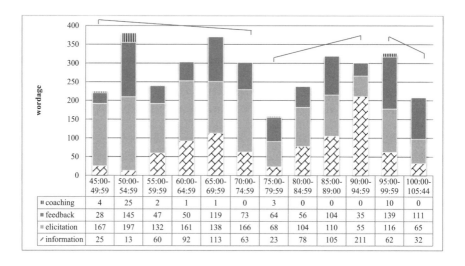

	45:00-49:59	50:00-54:59	55:00-59:59	60:00-64:59	65:00-69:59	70:00-74:59	75:00-79:59	80:00-84:59	85:00-89:00	90:00-94:59	95:00-99:59	100:00-105:44
ⵀ coaching	4	25	2	1	1	0	3	0	0	0	10	0
▪ feedback	28	145	47	50	119	73	64	56	104	35	139	111
▪ elicitation	167	197	132	161	138	166	68	104	110	55	116	65
⁄ information	25	13	60	92	113	63	23	78	105	211	62	32

Figure 7.6   Distribution of Timothy's verbal behaviour in Lesson B

of exercise and practice: in terms of both verbal and performance behaviour, activity begins gently and increases. The episode roughly represented by the next four columns (55:00–74:59) is focused on the rehearsal of the first, *Presto* movement: this episode begins with a sudden drop in verbal activity and – referring back to Figure 7.4 – a sudden rise in performance activity. This inverse relationship continues, so that although verbal activity increases, with correspondingly less performance, the episode ends with another drop in wordage alongside a rehearsal of the whole movement (74:31).

The next four columns (75:00–94:59) roughly coincide with work on the second, *Andante* movement, and as with the previous movement the work begins with less verbal and more performance activity. This is partly due to an overlap with the final rehearsal of the first movement, which does not end until 77:00. In broad terms, verbal activity once again increases as performance activity declines; but the work focused on the *Andante* ends with a fall in both (90:00–94:59). The lesson had been scheduled to end at 90:00, and although Timothy and Beth continue for a further 15 minutes, this fall might represent some decline of energy or concentration.

The last two columns (95:00–105:44) represent work on the *Allegretto* finale: now, exceptionally, both verbal and performance activity tail off. This might again suggest a loss of energy; in addition, as discussed with reference to performance behaviour, this is the movement in which Beth seems least able to proceed without systematic preparation. There is presumably no time now to include that in the lesson.

The Student's Role in Verbal Interaction

Beth contributes 138 speech acts during the lesson, and just less than half of them (55) consist of single words. The most common are 'Okay', 'Oh' and 'Yeah'; four of the single-word responses are 'Sorry'. The average wordage for Beth's speech acts is 3.0. The only speech act to exceed ten words in length is 'And then you – then you come off and I can come in on C don't I' (92:09).

Figure 7.7 represents Beth's contribution to verbal behaviour through the lesson, showing, for each five-minute period, the number of words uttered, the number of uninterrupted speech acts involved, and the average wordage of each speech act.

Once again, traces of lesson content may be detected behind the verbal activity. Beth's contribution begins modest, but then declines further during the preparatory period of exercise and practice, which ends close to the third period (55:00–59:59). Over the next four periods, largely coinciding with work on the *Presto*, there is a broad curve in wordage as Beth's contribution increases and then falls away; this reaches a trough of activity (70:00–74:59) which coincides with a similar dip in Timothy's verbal activity and a peak in performance, as the whole movement is rehearsed. In contrast, while the *Andante* is addressed, Beth's wordage forms a U-curve between 75:00 and 94:59. It will be recalled that the lesson was scheduled to end at 90:00; in what remains, Beth's contribution falls off and then rises, equally dramatically. In very general terms the number of speech acts drops between 65:00 and 94:59 while the wordage in each gently rises, so Beth speaks less often but has more to say; however, both the number of speech acts and the wordage for each rise abruptly to conclude the lesson.

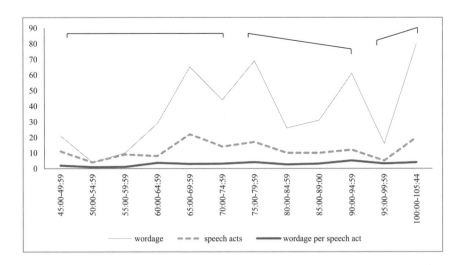

Figure 7.7   Beth's verbal behaviour in Lesson B

Back channelling does not occur consistently through the lesson. Among Beth's 138 speech acts, 39 are classified thus, as Timothy behaves in this way only once, when he says 'Right' (65:26) at the end of the lesson, while Beth is explaining why she will not be attending the next one. More than back channelling, Timothy employs questions to elicit responses from Beth. In the course of an hour, he asks no less than 115 questions. Of these, 49 are disguised instructions – commands somewhat softened by a questioning expression – such as 'Can you just do, really slowly from there' (52:22). There are 37 further questions which do not function as questions, and which Timothy seems to use to check that Beth is following or comfortable with proceedings: the most common example is 'Okay?' In all, 86 of the 115 questions (75 per cent) are rhetorical in nature.

The remaining 29 questions are interrogative, and normally straightforward in their intention. There is a relatively dense episode at the beginning of the lesson, with six such questions in just over a minute, as Timothy elicits information that he needs to proceed with the lesson. He returns to this kind of behaviour again later, in several looser episodes of approximately six minutes each, in which Timothy asks eight and then seven interrogative questions (60:08, 96:50).

Beth herself asks 15 questions during the lesson, in eight of which she is checking a detail of the information or instruction she has just been given. Twice her questions are little jokes, and when her lesson appears to be ending she utters a question – 'All right?' (103:32) – which seems rhetorical in nature. The remaining three are classified as questions because of their intonation or form, but they seem to be merely exclamations, addressed to nobody in particular: 'Uhh?' (69:41), 'Wha'?' (91:58) and 'What, that is –' (92:56). There is no evidence to suggest that any of Beth's questions have been preconceived – that she has brought any questions with her to the lesson. Beth's verbal activity, like her performance behaviour, seems generally responsive to the moment.

Verbal behaviour in Beth's lesson has been examined largely in terms of its functions. Timothy's verbal behaviour, which dominates, is itself dominated by elicitation, as he works almost constantly to exact spoken or performed responses from Beth. The student in turn does little to support spoken behaviour from her teacher. Beth engages in back channelling, which might indicate at least a formal interest in what is being said, inconsistently. This apparent lack of interest, perhaps alongside Beth's tendency to respond to information with little jokes, is arguably associated with the failure of information-based discussion to expand. Insofar as the construction of a fluent and substantive lesson dialogue is a cooperative endeavour, Timothy and Beth achieve only limited success.

Participants' Views

The main sources of data collection to be considered here are the semi-structured interviews that were conducted with individual participants, later in the same day as their lessons were filmed. Timothy's interview has already provided a sense of context for his broad approach to teaching and learning in Higher Education; interviews with Andrew and Beth serve the same function by providing some information about their own musical backgrounds, and add the further dimension of their own perceptions of what had happened in their lessons today.

All participants were asked whether the camera had had an effect on the conduct of the lessons, and there was a general agreement that there was less off-task talk than usual. Both Timothy and Beth remarked that there had been fewer jokes, and Andrew remarked that if there had been something he had wanted to discuss with Timothy, he would not have done it today. Timothy felt that he had been only 'subliminally aware' of the camera, and Andrew was similarly aware of it 'in the back of my mind'; Beth, however, added that 'it made me play worse at first because I was nervous', but 'then I got better'.

The students were asked to characterize their previous experience learning the clarinet, and had contrasting stories to tell. Andrew spent seven years in an army band, which included musical training. This 'made' him play well, and left him with disciplined habits that he appreciates, now. It also left him 'too good' at playing in time, but lessons with Timothy have supported a transformation: 'In the last three years Timothy said I have come out of my shell. It has taken three years'.

Beth's past experience is reported in more emotional terms:

> I had a really good teacher at my [school] for three years and she was brilliant and amazing and I loved her and she did miracles for me. And then I came here and it was really hard to change teachers.
>
> (Excerpt 7.7 Interview with Beth)

Pressed on this point, Beth explains that her previous teacher 'dealt with all the emotional crap that comes with it', and that 'she had this amazing way of making me feel really bad if I didn't do any practice'. Although she believes that Timothy wants her to do well, Beth feels that she needs to be 'forced to do well'.

It is interesting that Beth's narrative puts her teacher in the active position: it was the teacher who performed the miracles, and Beth's progress at that time was made 'just because she pushed me'. She seems to position Timothy too as the one responsible for her progress, now: Timothy is 'really nice, he's cool', but 'he doesn't shout at me!' Beth herself touches on issues of independence and maturity here: 'I think the difference between going to [school] and coming to university is that you are meant to be able to do everything on your own anyway but it's not that easy.'

In contrast, Andrew in his description of Timothy positions the teacher in the passive role. Asked to explain his open and enthusiastic admiration for Timothy, he says:

> Well he is just natural. For me, he brings everything out in the lesson, usually without really having to say so. It always seems to happen with him there. It is his presence really.
>
> (Excerpt 7.8 Interview with Andrew)

Andrew declares that for him, every lesson with Timothy is an ideal lesson.

Timothy's characterization of his own role helps to triangulate these perceptions in some ways. With Andrew, whose lesson content he describes in terms of fine technical detail, Timothy is currently 'trying to make him think these things before I say them now'. It is not clear how this is to be accomplished, but the remark does have resonance with a reflection made by Andrew on an interpretative point about *rubato*, discussed in the lesson. Asked whether he hadn't thought of this himself, he answers, 'Not really. It was always in the back of my mind when I listen to CDs that [professional performers] always do it but it never seems to come out!' It seems that both are referring to the need for Andrew to independently articulate and act on thoughts that are already well developed in his mind.

With Beth, Timothy seems to position his role at an earlier stage in the process of helping the student with the foundation of habits of mind, and this involves talking her through basic procedures: 'I think you will see in the lesson that we are thinking through things'. Beth's comments do not touch on her awareness of this, as she continues to cast herself in a relatively passive role: 'I had to go over bits again and again because I kept messing it up because my fingers weren't going in the right order'. Lessons are something of a testing ground:

> [Today's lesson] was nice for me because we didn't do anything I couldn't do. Sometimes I get a piece which I can't play and we spend hours on it and it just wears me down.
>
> (Excerpt 7.9 Interview with Beth)

All participants were asked whether the proximity of final examinations had affected the lessons. It has already been noted that Timothy felt that this shifted the underlying priorities: '[Obviously as] we get nearer the exams the important thing is to be able fluently to play those pieces'. The compromise with Beth's tonguing, which he now describes as resembling a 'sledgehammer to crack a nut', is an emergency measure that Timothy would not normally employ. Interestingly, both students deny the importance of the examination compared with their broader goals. Andrew almost boasts, 'that has no effect on me whatsoever – I don't mind – it is something to aim for but it is not a major accomplishment'. Beth, emphasizing that Performance is only worth a quarter of her degree, 'hadn't thought about it'; she has another exam in her other subject, before then.

Although teacher and students give accounts of their working relationships that are broadly positive, it is interesting that all three participants, without explicit prompting, also refer to lessons in terms of negative experience. Asked to describe her teacher, 'his approach, his style, his temperament', Beth remarks,

> Sometimes he would shout at me and then I would just go back, and it would have the reverse effect of what he wanted it to have, which is a bit pointless.
>
> (Excerpt 7.10 Interview with Beth)

The video evidence shows Timothy's verbal behaviour to be so carefully moderated in tone that it is difficult to imagine that he would ever shout in a lesson, though even a slight raising of his voice would probably have an impact. It will be recalled too that Beth has already complained that Timothy does not shout at her. Perhaps 'shout' is a term Beth is loosely applying, in this instance, to criticism, something that Andrew also mentions:

> I mean there are a few lessons that I have had when he has really slated me and everything, and you think 'Oh God!'
>
> (Excerpt 7.11 Interview with Andrew)

As previously noted, Timothy feels that ideally lessons should end 'on a high' with students sensing achievement; but he also asserts that this cannot be a matter of routine, and if it were, it might encourage complacency. A negative experience in a lesson can inspire better practice: 'Sometimes if you send someone out with a feeling that "Oh God I didn't play that well!" [it] means that the next lesson is fantastic'.

The notion that the impressions students take away from a lesson might feed their motivation is perhaps supported by what they recalled from the observed lessons. Andrew does not seem complacent, in that he criticizes his own tone, which was 'horrible today'. However, he does paraphrase a passing remark made by Timothy, which has clearly been important to him:

> [H]e said, 'Right, because you have got a fast tongue you can have more *rubato* at the beginning of [the scale passage] and then rush through to the top, whereas other people can't play [as] fast so they have trouble playing it at the normal speed'.
>
> (Excerpt 7.12 Interview with Andrew)

Andrew makes another comment, in accounting for the activity in his lesson, that casts light on his personal perceptions of the processes involved. As noted in the discussion of verbal behaviour, he occasionally interrupts Timothy with a question, typically supporting the subsequent answer through back channelling; in his interview, Andrew gives the impression that he thought of himself as being more active in such exchanges than the video evidence might suggest. Thus he says, '*I discussed* whether the recapitulation should be completely different' (emphasis added), and reports the conclusion that '[i]f you feel that recapitulation should be louder or should be softer then it is completely up to you'.

Beth, in accounting for the work in her lesson today, does not quote any of Timothy's compliments to her, though as previously noted, these were neither rare nor ungenerous. She does claim strength in a particular kind of technical ability, which is difficult to match with video evidence:

> There's technique as in staccato tonguing and fingers – and then there's technique as in the blowing and the coordination of the fingers which is easier for me but for some people it is harder.
>
> (Excerpt 7.13 Interview with Beth)

It seems possible that Beth might be recalling, here, a compliment from a previous lesson, perhaps slightly garbled now or perhaps imperfectly understood. It might be noted that the compliments mentioned by both students are of the kind that characterize them as performers, feeding their self-image, more than the kind that might merely refer to their specific activities today.

Motivation is addressed in broader terms, in all three interviews. Timothy and Andrew are in close agreement that Andrew wants to be, and has a good chance of becoming, a professional performer. In discussing this, too, both emphasize motivation and determination, more than specific ability. Andrew's avowed ambition is 'to become a performer, whether it be solo or orchestral', with some teaching activity necessary to support that, and he will achieve that goal by proceeding to a postgraduate degree and through the development of specialist repertoire.

For Beth, ambition seems a more complex issue. Timothy suggests that she is unlikely ever to enjoy performing, but that she might find teaching rewarding, or go into concert management. Asked whether she has any ambitions in music, Beth, curiously, replies 'No; *that's really bad!*' (emphasis added). The lack of ambition is justified in terms of both her degree structure and her career path, asthma having prevented her from joining an army band. Some of Beth's statements however are self-contradictory: for example, 'I am not going to play the clarinet for the rest of my life', but 'I just want to play music', and 'I would like to carry on playing in a band'. It is not even clear whose goals are being discussed:

> I think [Timothy] wanted me to do a lot better than I have and I wanted to do a lot better than I have [but] I can't be bothered at the end of the day.
>
> (Excerpt 7.14 Interview with Beth)

Evidence from the lessons observed, and from the attitudes and perceptions represented in participant interviews, goes some way toward suggesting the future paths of Andrew and Beth. A further signpost may be provided by their degree results. Both students graduated from SEU with a lower second degree, close to the university average, and although this cannot account entirely for their individual abilities, it does suggest that in terms of intelligence and commitment Andrew and Beth are reasonably comparable. In their final performance examinations however the distinction between the two was dramatic. Beth passed with 56 per cent, again close to the average mark, and by rising to the occasion with the support of her professional duo partner and a staff accompanist, she perhaps achieved a personal best. Andrew's mark was 88 per cent, the highest achieved by any student in the Performance Studies course that year. Soon after, he passed the Licentiate performing diploma of Trinity College of Music, and entered the Master of Music programme at SEU, where he continued to study with Timothy.

Summary

Chapters 6 and 7 have presented close accounts of Lessons A and B, which have been framed by a selection of interview data with lesson participants, and this has served to highlight a number of contextual issues that resonate with salient points among the preceding literature reviews.

From the outset of Chapter 6, the teacher, Timothy, has been quoted, giving his own perception of the broad musical culture that underlies his work in instrumental teaching and learning; his references to musical performance as a profession, and an element of competition among those seeking to enter it, is parallel in some ways to comments made by his students, when accounting for their own motivation and ambitions.

Timothy's comments on the nature of music education would seem to resonate with aspects of the epistemology of practice, insofar as the teaching of performance, like performance itself, is an experientially acquired skill; Timothy's own career development provides an illustration of this, in that he was almost thrust into a teaching career by virtue of his early success as a performer.

Timothy also refers to music in Higher Education, which has been previously presented as a frame for instrumental teaching and learning, though his discussion of this setting leans perhaps more toward the conservatoire than to the university music department. He does not expand on issues concerning the degree programme to which his students belong, though he is asked about it, and it seems that the main effect of the programme that is felt in his lessons is the proximity of performance examinations, which affects lesson behaviour. This perhaps reflects the professional isolation often experienced by instrumental teachers in Higher Education, noted in Chapter 4 and discussed by Gaunt (2008) and Purser (2005).

In discussing specific lesson strategies, Timothy touches on demonstration and imitation, features of the epistemology of skill and research focused on modelling in lessons. He also introduces an issue not previously noted, however: this is the psychological profile of the lesson, which if ideally managed, can include a refreshing break in concentration, along the way, and a positive conclusion resting on a successful, improved performance. These concern the affective aspects of learning, previously discussed in terms of mentoring relationships. The importance of such relationships is echoed in the interviews with Andrew and Beth and will be discussed further in Chapter 8.

In the analysis of lesson observations, the subunit behaviours of participants have been analyzed in terms of recurring motifs and sometimes patterns. Both lessons have been examined in terms of 'spatial' behaviours, referring to the use of space and relative proximity of both participants; the position and treatment of the music stand and the musical score; and the posture and poise – or lack of it – of individual participants, in a relatively intimate setting.

Performance behaviours have been considered in terms of the relative proportions contributed by teacher and student; the content, or nature of performance activity, classified among three chief categories of rehearsal, practice and exercise; the texture, or distribution of those kinds of activity; and the structure, interpreted in terms of measured episodes of consistent performance behaviour. Incidents of teacher demonstration have been noted, sometimes accompanied by silent fingering from the student; and – while the students tend to dominate performance behaviour – incidents of accompanying activity from the teacher, including coaching, singing and conducting.

Finally, verbal behaviours have been considered, once again in terms of the relative proportions contributed by teacher and student; the classification of activity, among the four chief functions of information, elicitation, coaching and feedback; the distribution of those kinds of activity; and episodes of consistent verbal behaviour. In addition to these, while the teacher has been seen to dominate verbal behaviour, the students have been observed in their accompanying – and varied – use of back channelling and questions. Both performance and verbal behaviours have been related to an overall lesson profile, related either to the psychological ideal mentioned by Timothy or to the repertoire in hand.

The close description of the observed lessons in Chapters 6 and 7, in the light of participants' views, has perhaps provided some vicarious experience for the reader (Stake 1995, p. 48). Stake argues that this may have the effect of 'naturalistic generalization':

> When the researcher's narrative provides opportunity for *vicarious experience,* readers extend their perceptions of happenings. Naturalistic, ethnographic case materials, at least to some extent, [are parallel to] actual experience, feeding into the most fundamental processes of awareness and understanding. (Stake 2005, p. 454; italics original)

If the lesson descriptions go some way toward illustrating the nature of lesson interactions and how they might be contextualized, the variation among participants has not yet been explicitly addressed. Chapter 8 therefore begins by making specific comparisons between the two observed lessons, before proceeding to discuss the further analysis and interpretation of the cases studied.

Chapter 8
Exploring Studio Interactions

It has been remarked that the choice of research tools is itself an interpretative act, in that the lines of inquiry are inseparable from the researcher's perspective and values. In this sense, no decisive line can be drawn between method and interpretation (Guba and Lincoln 2005, p. 205), though the reliability of both may be enhanced by, for example, making the lines of inquiry explicit, particularly in the analysis of lesson observations, and through the use of rich transcription and descriptive statistics. An element of interpretation is inevitably present to some degree, too, in the reporting of findings in Chapters 6 and 7: although an effort has been made there to present the material objectively, and in a form that perhaps allows the reader to draw some personal impressions from it, the material has of course been chosen, ordered and variously highlighted in presentation. Interpretation becomes a more explicit feature now, however, in a freer exploration of the findings.

The discussion is divided into three broad sections. The first section adheres to the three planes of lesson behaviour discussed in Chapters 6 and 7: spatial, performance and nonverbal. Specific links are drawn between findings from the two lessons, and their potential significance discussed.

In the second section a broader view is taken of lesson behaviour, and ways of understanding aspects of studio-based instrumental teaching and learning are proposed.

In the third section some reflections are offered on aspects of methodology in this study, in the context of research literature focused on instrumental teaching and learning: validity, theorizing learning and evaluating lesson interactions.

Lesson Behaviour

Spatial Behaviour

'Spatial behaviour' has been used here to refer to any nonverbal behaviour that is not more helpfully classified as musical performance. As previously remarked, the aspects of nonverbal behaviour identified and described in this study emerged from the data during analysis, as certain kinds of incident proved to be repetitive in one or both lessons, while others were conspicuous in one lesson but not the other. The selection of analytical tools is thus acknowledged to be an interpretative decision on the part of the researcher. There are obvious limits to the number and range of behaviours that can be analyzed within the scope of this case study, and in reporting the findings some are more easily described than others: incidents of laughter or of self-touching have been counted, for example, whereas behaviours such as gesture, tone of voice and facial expression are notoriously difficult to measure (Patterson and Manusov, 2006). Further, even where the observations of selected behaviours have been precise, to the point perhaps of appearing to fuss over trivial details, the interpretation of such behaviours can be highly complex and context specific, with a wide range of potential implications. The use of the score, for example, may be said to have symbolic significance in the setting of instrumental lessons. Musical anthropologists have remarked on the privileged position of the score in western classical music, with Nettl describing the *urtext* as the scriptures of the godlike composer (1995, p. 15). Kingsbury too refers to devout respect for the score, which is held to be of 'paramount importance', but he also asserts that in the lessons he observed at an American conservatory, the score was 'only a touchstone in an ongoing negotiation of relative social authority among the persons in the [studio], an authority manifested in musical and verbal performance' (1988, p. 87).

This casts an interesting light on an aspect of nonverbal behaviour in Timothy's lessons: the student owns the score, sets it up and takes it away, but for the most part, the handling of the score is the teacher's prerogative. During his lesson, Andrew makes contact with the score with his hand or his clarinet, for a total of 25 seconds; Timothy makes contact for nearly five minutes. For Beth the discrepancy is even more marked, because the teacher's contact with the score is prolonged when he leans on the music stand, in a consciously relaxed posture, and because in her lesson a pencil is used to mark the score – by Beth for 4 seconds, and by Timothy for 90 seconds.

In the light of Kingsbury's claims, this air of ownership of the score, as a central object of attention, is symbolic of Timothy's authority as teacher. It might be associated, too, with some of the questions put to Timothy by Andrew: 'What's what's the er dynamic marking – still *piano*?' (23:24); 'Is there any good reason why there's a small m and a large thick **M**?' (36:25). These do not seem to be complex issues, and Andrew could presumably deal with them himself, but here he defers to his teacher's ability to interpret and even to read the score.

The tendency for all participants to face the score during lesson time is evident in two of the four line drawings presented in Chapters 6 and 7, and reproduced in Figure 8.1.

Even here however the nonverbal behaviour of teacher and students is asymmetrical. In all four line drawings, the student squarely faces the score, even when it is not being used; it is only the teacher who steps away from it at will. In Andrew's lesson the 'default' position has Timothy slightly to the side of the score, and he does not correct that alignment even when he is demonstrating by performing an excerpt from it: his relationship with it is relatively free and assured, and while it arguably holds the students in place, the score is not *his* master.

The deference granted to Timothy and to the score might be considered analogous to the respect shown for rehearsal, in Andrew's lesson in particular. The poised preparatory moments that Andrew takes before most of his rehearsals show

Figure 8.1   Figures 6.2, 7.1, 7.2 and 7.3 compared

respect from both teacher and student, and are indicative of a serious approach to simulated concert performance. In comparison, Beth's preparation for rehearsal shows none of this ceremony: if she does take a moment before playing, it is to serve a more immediate function as she learns, with mixed success, to coordinate entries with another player.

Poise and focus are features too of the use of space in Andrew's lesson, where participants move their feet only a little and only occasionally. This relieves the prevailing air of concentration, along with the businesslike intimacy of the teacher-student dyad intent on the fine detail of the score, the instrument and the music they are crafting together. The wider, more flamboyant use of space in Beth's lesson provides a strong contrast: this dyad moves through a range of 'default' positions, and when the players are not held in position by their duo music stands, Timothy typically stands back from Beth's personal space, often signalling relaxation by leaning on the stand or the table or putting his hands in his pockets. This is a spatially expressive lesson, with moments of comedy mime: in Lesson B there are 62 incidents of smiling or laughter, where in Lesson A there are only 22; and in Lesson B there are 26 little jokes, 9 nonverbal exclamations and 8 apologies, where in Lesson A there are none.

There is a paradox here. While the focused economy of Lesson A creates an impression of relaxed concentration, the relaxation that is demonstrated in Lesson

B in – almost literally – a hundred ways, creates an impression of discord. Features of nonverbal behaviour may offer some clues to this, since they are arguably associated with the underlying attitudes of actors, which may be unconsciously expressed (Argyle 1969, p. 103; 1988, pp. 3–4). In Lesson A close proximity, appropriate touching, and even self-disclosure – as when Timothy mentions his recent dental surgery – are all among the signs of affiliation, listed by Argyle (1988, p. 88). In Lesson B, the 'relaxed postural style' of Timothy's sideways lean is held to be a typical sign of dominance in an established hierarchy (p. 97). The associated verbal behaviour, however – 'very very, relaxed, and happy' (95:06) – suggests that in this context Timothy is making an effort to put Beth at ease, having understood, whether consciously or not, that she is ill at ease. The effort is demonstrated, too, through the apparently trivial detail of putting his hands in his pockets. This relaxed postural style is adopted in the opening few minutes of each lesson, while Andrew, Beth and Catherine in turn are settling themselves. He does not adopt it otherwise, however, except for two incidents in Beth's lesson: during the most intense exercise of the problematic peak of the G major scale (54:12–55:43) and when Beth is persuaded to attempt a solo rehearsal of the finale, which apparently she has not prepared (100:36–100:49). Both of these are presumably moments of heightened tension for Beth, and Timothy's show of relaxation may well represent an effort to compensate for her anxiety.

The teacher's sensitivity toward the feelings of the student invokes the broader notion of intersubjectivity: 'how humans come to know "each other's minds"' (Bruner 1996, p. 12). For Bruner, this lies at the heart of scaffolding theory, facilitating the transition in learning from interpsychological to intrapsychological functioning. It would seem significant to the findings of this study that establishing intersubjectivity involves the creation of particular modes of communication: thus Wertsch asserts that at early stages of development, participants rely on context-bound signs more than verbal formulations and abstract definitions (1985, p. 161), while Howard, exploring interactions between singer and coach, describes 'the drama of the languages of craft and skill' (1982, p. 176):

> [A] sense of rapport between Master and Apprentice, of being on the same 'wavelength', mostly comes down to an expanding, shared understanding rooted in shared perceptions. [But] it is not just the talk but the experiences and insights that are shared. If it is clear that suggestive description (along with other forms of symbolization) plays a large part in conceptualising the perceptual flow – in directing selective attention to its aspects – it remains unclear [or] at least incomplete, how extrapolation, metaphor, and simile promote the intersubjectivity of the flow. (Howard 1982, p. 87)

The data examined in the current study do not allow direct access to the interpsychological functioning of the participants, but related evidence may be sought in their behaviour, particularly perhaps where contrasts are suggested. Broadly, the nonverbal behaviour in Lesson A is characterized by reciprocation, while in Lesson

B compensation is more in evidence. In nonverbal behaviour scholarship there are several 'affect-based theories' that attempt to explain the equilibrium struck within dyads. Affiliation is an issue central to all of them, and all similarly predict that where the level of affiliation is low, increased involvement, such as a close approach from one person, is likely to result in compensatory behaviour from the other, such as turning away; but where the level of affiliation is high, increased involvement is likely to result in reciprocal behaviour (Patterson 2006).

It cannot be asserted on the strength of the evidence in hand that Timothy and Beth do not like each other, and indeed Beth in her interview gives quite the opposite impression: 'He's really nice, he's cool'. If there is discord it is context specific, and if Beth feels a lack of affiliation with her teacher, it is apparently not a personal issue so much as one that hinges on the role the teacher takes in this context. Beth's discomfort with this situation is nowhere more evident than in her nonverbal behaviour, and self-touching gives perhaps the most dramatic illustration of this. In Lesson A, Timothy self-touches twice, and Andrew six times, while in Lesson B Timothy self-touches eight times. Beth touches her blouse five times, her skirt 18, her hair 29, and her face 58: a total of 110 gestures in the course of an hour. Most of the emotions associated with self-touching are attributable to anxiety (Argyle 1988, pp. 197–8).

Performance Behaviour

In some ways, the differences between performance behaviours in the two lessons are less obvious than the similarities between them. In each lesson, only one piece of repertoire is addressed, and although the pieces are very different, they are of comparable length: the Weber *Andante* lasts approximately six minutes, and the Mendelssohn *Konzertstück* approximately eight. These are chosen by the teacher, who indicates his choice through instructions disguised as questions: 'Let's do some Weber then shall we?' (1:00) and 'So do you want to do your, duet' (46:08). The proportion of lesson time devoted to performance activity is almost identical, with 49 per cent in Lesson A and 48 per cent in Lesson B. In both lessons, Timothy sings and conducts, and in Beth's lesson, cues duo entries. Of course, he also demonstrates, and it is in this that contrasts begin to appear.

There are 11 incidents of teacher demonstration in Lesson A, and only 7 in Lesson B, though given the large proportion of duo rehearsal in Beth's lesson, it is perhaps surprising that the difference between the two lessons is not more pronounced. Demonstration is always responsive – offered only after the student has played the same passage – except for a single incident where Timothy uses it to draw Beth's attention to his own, accompanying part.

In Andrew's lesson, demonstrated rehearsals are highly focused, and pointed verbally beforehand, afterward or both, making the demonstration an integral part of a fluent multimodal explanation. Insofar as a teacher demonstration should be pointed, and should draw the student's attention to a particular feature of performance, however (Howard 1982, ch.4), the focus of demonstration in

Beth's lesson is arguably at issue. This is because Timothy typically demonstrates at a significantly faster tempo than Beth has been using, and possibly faster than she is capable of using. In only one instance is a faster tempo the point that Timothy wants to make (79:02). In four further demonstrations (70:13, 97:20, 99:16, 86:48) a faster tempo is not the avowed aim; and yet, since the contrast in tempo is so obvious, it seems likely that the student will have noticed this more than the avowed aim, and possible that she will have noticed nothing more than her teacher's superiority of skill.

Allowing the student to be distracted from the point of a demonstration by playing at a different tempo suggests some carelessness on the part of the teacher, who has perhaps become impatient, or is perhaps feeling the pressure of time. It will be recalled that Timothy, in his interview, felt the proximity of the final performance examinations, and cites fluency as the most obvious priority now. Hence the compromise with Beth's tonguing at the peak of the problematic G major scale: in her lesson he introduces this as 'necessary, at his late stage in the term'. It should be noted however that there is no such urgency in Lesson A, where the participants have sufficient leisure to interrupt their work on the Weber duo to engage in something of a competition, with Andrew challenged to match Timothy's intonation in the extreme upper register (25:33–28:30).

This interruption would seem to represent a deliberate rest from repertoire work, a 'break in the tension' that Timothy prefers to take about half way through a lesson, just as he prefers to end on the 'high' that can come from successful rehearsal. Both the performance and the verbal activity in Lesson A may be mapped against this psychological ideal, even if all participants agreed that there were fewer smiles than usual. The structure of Lesson B however is more easily mapped against the structure of the repertoire in hand. Lesson A is pitched so that the repertoire fits neatly into the scheduled time; in Lesson B, schedule control becomes subordinate to the repertoire, which spills over into extra time, prolonging the lesson by 33 per cent.

Far from ending on a high, this extra time seems to involve some anxiety for Beth. When the lesson should be closing – as the end of the second movement of the Mendelssohn approaches – Beth shows signs of tiring, slumping her shoulders forward (89:24), slapping the keys with her right hand (89:38) and holding her clarinet over her shoulder (90:20). Timothy launches his most substantial 'information episode' now (93:34–94:42) which might reasonably conclude the proceedings, except that he rouses himself from his reflections on the meaning of *andante*, and declares 'OKAY. Let's bash on' (94:50). Perhaps sensing some tension, Timothy steps back to lean on the table, while Beth, stopping herself after several half-hearted attempts to open the third movement, makes her reluctance clear. It might be more sensitive to suspect that she has not prepared this, and that she will be embarrassed if work proceeds, but with the final examination looming, it seems that a point must be made.

The remaining portion of Lesson B exposes Beth's unreadiness for examination, and arguably her unreadiness even for a lesson on this movement.

If this is the point, however, it is demonstrated rather than spoken. As Beth remarks in her interview, Timothy does not 'shout' at her, though she would rather he did; and as Timothy remarks in his interview, 'Sometimes if you send someone out with a feeling that "Oh God I didn't play that well!" it means that the next lesson is fantastic'.

The success of this strategy – of sending a student away with a negative feeling rather than addressing such problems explicitly – cannot be evaluated here with reference to next week's lesson, which was not recorded by a research camera, and which may or may not have been fantastic. When issues are not explicitly identified and discussed, it might seem reasonable to assume that a degree-level student will reliably extrapolate from her lessons and take appropriate action in her independent work. Without longitudinal evidence, however, it is only possible to speculate on the soundness of this assumption, with reference to the opening episode of Beth's lesson, the 'preparatory ramp' of exercise and practice that leads to the first rehearsal. This procedure is effective in that it results in an obvious improvement in a short period of time. As noted in the discussion of her lesson, too, it seems clear that the procedure is familiar to Beth, and although it involves organization and perhaps some discipline, it should have been possible for her to use it in her independent work. The evidence suggests however that she has not taken that responsibility: if she had, it would not be necessary to devote the first ten minutes of her lesson to revising the whole, remedial procedure. Whether Beth should have taken responsibility, or should take it now, is not discussed.

With a premium on fluency – on meeting the most basic requirement to play in tune, on time – the performance behaviour in Beth's lesson is drawn with a broad brush. The analysis of the transcription shows swathes of consistent activity, and aside from the preparatory ramp, a dominance of rehearsal behaviour, particularly by the clarinet duo. The average length of rehearsal-dominated episodes in Lesson B is 4 minutes 13 seconds, almost double the Lesson A average of 2 minutes 25 seconds. The proportion of long rehearsals is similar: in Lesson B there are 15 that exceed 30 seconds in length, and in Lesson A, only seven.

With Beth, Timothy takes the supportive role of second clarinet, quite distinct from the role he takes in the 'competition' episode in Lesson A, where his challenge to Andrew establishes a comparable footing between two players. Andrew's willingness to match Timothy is further evident in the silent fingering that he employs during six of the seven teacher demonstrations that are offered during his lesson. In this – something that never appears in Beth's lesson – Andrew is not only rehearsing a physical aspect of the performance, but mentally engaging with the demonstration, moment by moment (Connolly and Williamon 2004, pp. 224–7).

Reciprocation and compensation are again recalled in the comparison of performance behaviours in the two lessons. Andrew's engagement in competition with the master, and his silent participation in the master's demonstrations, suggest an element of camaraderie: the student's willingness to identify with his teacher is clearly felt to be viable. Beth however is further removed from the master: the tempi of the demonstrations she is offered are typically beyond her current capability, highlighting the gap between their levels of expertise, and yet some compensation of roles is offered when the master plays second clarinet, and with mixed success, invites Beth to lead the clarinet duo. If the teaching and learning are considered in terms of apprenticeship, Andrew and Beth may have been members of the community for the same three year period, but Andrew has become the more senior apprentice.

Verbal Behaviour

As with spatial and performance behaviour, there are superficial similarities in the verbal activity found in the two lessons. Timothy is the principal speaker, responsible for 90 per cent of the wordage in Lesson A and 88 per cent in Lesson B. Among his various verbal behaviours one function dominates and comprises 44 per cent of his speech in both lessons, though in Lesson A the function is to give information and in Lesson B it is elicitation. In terms of quantity, the students' contributions also appear to be remarkably similar: they utter 137 and 138 speech acts, respectively, the average wordage for those is 2.9 and 3.0, and the range 1–18 and 1–16 words.

Once again, too, the differences are far more interesting. The average wordage of the students' speech acts, for example, conceals the variance within them: so Andrew offers 11 speech acts that exceed ten words in length, while Beth has only one; and Andrew utters 92 single-word acts while Beth has only 55. Andrew has both more, and less, to say.

One of the reasons that Andrew offers a greater number of longer speeches is that he has evidently brought some questions with him: of 11 questions that he asks during the lesson, six appear to be preconceived. These questions are relatively substantial for Andrew, in terms of wordage: four of them exceed ten words in length, and another consists of nine. Beth asks 15 questions, but all concern matters that arise in the moment. They are not substantive in nature, though one of them represents her longest speech act in the entire lesson: 'And then you – then you come off and I can come in on C don't I?' (92:09).

One of the reasons that Andrew offers a higher number of single-word speech acts is his investment in 'back channelling', the minimal response that offers support to a dominant speaker. Coates describes this as a skill requiring some sensitivity, though ironically she reports that it is used far more often by women than by men (2004, p. 87). The majority of Andrew's speech acts (77 per cent) are classified in this way, almost three times the proportion found among Beth's speech acts (28 per cent). Argyle points out that back channelling can be nonverbal as well as verbal, as the listener nods, for example, or makes eye contact. He also explains the function of this kind of feedback, which provides reinforcement for the speaker and results in an increase of the rate of production of whatever is being reinforced. If back channelling is withheld the speaker is likely to become repetitive or to stop speaking (1988, pp. 111–13).

What Andrew is reinforcing is the provision of information, and his systematic, minimal responses have the effect of supporting and encouraging his teacher in providing it. Argyle's claim that this increases the rate of production is exemplified in the statistics concerning verbal behaviour, particularly when the two lessons are compared. In Lesson A the longest episode of consistent verbal behaviour from Timothy is 190 seconds, with 263 words, consisting in information; the longest such episode in Lesson B is only 75 seconds, with 24 words, consisting in elicitation. Among the ten longest episodes of consistent verbal behaviour in each lesson, as illustrated in Tables 6.8 and 7.7, the average length in Lesson A is 53 seconds and the average wordage 99: the density of words per second is thus 1.87. In Lesson B the average length is 58 seconds, quite similar to Lesson A; but the average wordage is only 51 words, giving a density of 0.88 words per second. During these episodes Timothy says approximately twice as much in Lesson A as he does in Lesson B.

Thus, the teacher's verbal behaviour in each lesson may be clearly linked to the behaviour of the student. In Lesson A, where the student consistently demonstrates his interest through both preconceived questions and back channelling, almost half of Timothy's verbal behaviour consists in giving information. In Lesson B, the same proportion is classified as elicitation, as the teacher works hard to exact responses from a student who has brought no questions with her, and whose interest in receiving information appears to be minimal.

The emphasis on elicitation in Lesson B is further reflected in Timothy's use of questions. He asks a total of 43 questions in Lesson A; in Lesson B he asks 115, more than twice as many. In all, 86 of Timothy's questions to Beth (75 per cent) have a rhetorical function. Of these, 49 are disguised instructions, through which the teacher perhaps attempts to soften his commands. The remainder are dominated by little checks, so common and so minimal that they seem to punctuate his sentences: the most common is 'okay?' which he asks 27 times; other examples include 'yeah?' and 'all right?' With these, Timothy appears to be once again softening his delivery, as well as monitoring Beth's level of interest, understanding and possibly anxiety. With an average of more than one rhetorical question each minute, it is tempting to suggest that the dearth of back channelling from Beth leads Timothy to seek assurance, almost constantly, that he has her attention.

As with patterns of performance activity, verbal activity in Lesson A is more easily mapped against the psychological profile of what Timothy regards as the ideal lesson, while activity in Lesson B is more easily mapped against the structure of the repertoire being addressed. In very broad terms behaviour in both lessons demonstrates an inverse correlation between the amounts of performance and verbal activity. The character of the final stage of each lesson, however, offers a contrast. For Andrew, the last 15 minutes follow an 'exercise break' during which he and his teacher have entered into a gentle competition as if between two colleagues; after this refreshing episode, the remaining performance activity is dominated by rehearsal, while verbal activity accelerates with both participants, until in the final minutes Timothy delivers his most intense offering of information, serving to summarize the whole lesson.

For Beth, what should have been the last 15 minutes are similarly marked by the predominance of rehearsal, though this does not mark a significant change from previous behaviour, and an increase of verbal activity, particularly from Timothy. Now however the lesson moves into extra time: Timothy's verbal activity increases further, producing his most intense offering of information after the lesson should have ended (90:00–94:59), as he and Beth venture into the unprepared finale of the *Konzertstück*. Teacher and student alike are perhaps drained by this additional effort, and in the last five minutes of the lesson both performance and verbal activity tail off. What appears to be a last-moment flurry of activity from Beth, who suddenly utters 43 words in 18 seconds (105:21–105:39), does not serve in any way to summarize her lesson, but to arrange the next one.

Understanding Aspects of Studio-based Instrumental Learning

Learning Games

The specific differences between Lessons A and B show how aspects of instrumental teaching and learning might vary with student characteristics and behaviour. Withdrawing to another vantage point allows a broader view of participants' behaviour across 105 minutes of lesson time, a view less sensitive to individual identity. How is instrumental teaching and learning done?

The participants know how it is done, even if the knowledge of one participant is not the same as that of another, and even if the participants' knowledge cannot be entirely captured in their verbal accounts of it. These issues lie at the heart of the epistemology of skill as discussed in Chapter 2, and in the present discussion, 'skill' refers less to instrumental performance than to the collaborative accomplishment of participating in instrumental lessons. The observed lessons cannot encapsulate all aspects of instrumental teaching and learning; but – to borrow a notion from Wittgenstein – taken as examples, they can encapsulate some of the possibilities of the phenomenon.

In *Philosophical Investigations* Wittgenstein makes an extended analogy of games, demonstrating that they can be more effectively described than defined, since 'game' is better represented by a family of meanings or family resemblances than by seeking definitive features (1953, pp. 30–42). Description in this case is not an inferior substitute for a more direct kind of explanation, but a valid way of accounting for something that in a practical sense is already understood: through description, the complexity and validity of the account can be better preserved than if a definition were to be attempted. The affinity of this kind of thinking with qualitative research methodologies is obvious.

There are a number of features of studio-based instrumental teaching and learning, captured in the description of the observed lessons, that could usefully be regarded as learning games: collaborative procedures understood by the participants, with family resemblances that might include rules, roles and goals. Some of these might be regarded as 'set pieces', with formal structures defined by timing and explicit aims; others are better regarded as procedures than structures. Examples of each will be identified, described and discussed here.

Set piece 1: the preparatory ramp
Perhaps the most easily extracted set piece has already been described as the preparatory ramp at the beginning of Lesson B. A goal-oriented learning game, this is aimed at mastering the cadenza-like passage at the end of the first movement of the Mendelssohn *Konzertstück*, with phases of exercise, practice and then rehearsal, each secured and assimilated so that it can provide a platform for the next. The activity is a systematic collaboration undertaken by teacher and student together, and it seems that it is a familiar 'game' for both even if their roles are distinct, with highly instructive verbal behaviour from the teacher contrasting with promptly responsive performance behaviour from the student. The game could however be played solo: in the independent work of a more or less expert player, one person might take both roles, effectively resulting in disciplined practice. If participation in a highly instructive game can foster self-regulation, this game is potentially a model for independent work that the student might employ later.

The validity of this assertion has some support from Andrew, who in his interview claims that the discipline he experienced in the army is the basis of his approach to study, now. The close relationship between shared learning activity and the independent work that follows is highlighted in Vygotsky's explanation of skill acquisition, which suggests that in adopting a modelled procedure, the learner continues to act collaboratively; that from a psychological perspective the teacher is still, invisibly present, his 'voice' providing support (Daniels 2001, p. 65).

Is this what happens – literally – in practice? As discussed above, there is little evidence that Beth has attempted to employ the preparatory ramp prior to her lesson, and the clear progress that is made now in the 'ramp game' suggests that on the contrary, she continues to depend on her teacher to supply the discipline required to take the game through to completion. It could be argued that the value of the game as a model for independent practice has been undermined by excessive control from Timothy: Riggs warns against the authoritarian position implied when a teacher expects submission from a student, and instead recommends providing opportunities for 'creative problem solving [that] can provide freedom for individuals to discover their own connections between materials and concepts' (2006, p. 181). In this particular context, however, it could equally be argued that creativity is hardly at issue: mastery of the G major scale is attained through the acquisition of a routine use of tools, which can then be applied to other such problems.

Applying a broader lens to this particular context, however, it might be suggested that with adult participants working together to negotiate the final stages of the student's degree course, it should not be automatically assumed that it is the teacher who is controlling the game. From one perspective, the teacher's verbal behaviour, highly instructive in nature and dominated by elicitation, determines the student's performance behaviour. From the opposite perspective, the student, by declining responsibility for directing her performance activity either in the lesson or in independent practice, lays out the teacher's role for him: the student's performance behaviour determines the teacher's verbal behaviour.

Several assertions might be made here. The type of learning game represented by the preparatory ramp involves a procedure so systematic that it might be called a strategy or a tool; the type of goal to which it is applied is an essential component of skill acquisition in instrumental teaching and learning, but not necessarily a creative or negotiable one. Correspondingly, participant behaviour does not necessarily involve creative problem solving or the negotiation of roles. The strategy is learned through asymmetrical behaviour, with the teacher instructing verbally and the student responding through performance. The whole procedure can be appropriated by the student to become a component of independent practice. What the student actually appropriates however depends on more than the 'games apparatus': it varies with participants and, since this is an intrinsically collaborative enterprise, combinations of participants.

Set piece 2: task reduction

The preparatory ramp has been interpreted above as a routine, linear progression of steps, evidently preconceived as an entrée to a technically challenging passage. Much of this interaction might alternatively be interpreted as task reduction, adopted in response to a problem that has been spontaneously identified in the lesson. Task reduction is conceived here as a bull's-eye target, with concerted attention given in the first instance to the smallest possible, central point, before progressively stepping back to restore the musical and technical context.

In particular, the peak of the G major scale is targeted early in Lesson B as a problem that needs remedial work. Timothy diagnoses the problem, which hinges on unfamiliar fingering in this high register: the immediate object is to reduce it in size and difficulty, as if examining it under a microscope and in slow motion. The eye of the problem is reached when Timothy asks Beth to put her clarinet over her shoulder so that her only task is to make a visual comparison between Timothy's fingering for F sharp, and her own (48:35); this accomplished, the radius is expanded to incorporate the finger movement from F sharp to G; expanded to incorporate the playing of these notes; expanded to incorporate another note, and so on. Having initially pointed to the right keys, Timothy gradually withdraws visual aid, and gradually draws in further demands, involving the embouchure, then the stream of breath, then more notes. The request that Beth should walk around her music stand while playing the whole octave represents a further expansion of the target, in quality as well as quantity; but the beauty of this finely measured approach is that although sustained concentration is required at the level of attention – with the student always attending to the most recent request – the ongoing task never becomes significantly more difficult, never beyond the student's immediate reach.

This episode is a salient feature in Lesson B, in which – as previously remarked – verbal and performance behaviours are drawn with a broad brush. In Lesson A, incidents of task reduction and restoration seem to have become a normal, almost incidental feature of collaborative behaviour. The parenthetic use of practice, to deal with any difficulty that may have arisen in rehearsal, does not have to be initiated by Timothy, and in the example described in Chapter 6 Andrew spontaneously withdraws from rehearsal to repair a mismanaged octave leap without prompting from his teacher, whose role is now to offer feedback on the results rather than guidance on the procedure. The relative sophistication of the roles taken by teacher and student is more closely matched now, and the texture of their collaboration is marked by quick switches among various performance and verbal behaviours, creating the marbled effects illustrated in Tables 6.3 and 6.7.

Once again the nature of the engagement with this learning game depends on the participants as much as the game itself. This time the opportunity to witness the game played in two different lessons suggests how it might evolve with increasing expertise: what is still a closely guided procedure for Beth has become a normal part of Andrew's individual behaviour. Indeed, this might be regarded as a before-and-after illustration of scaffolding, where the collaborative apparatus supporting Beth is no longer evident in Andrew's lesson.

Set piece 3: demonstration

Performance and verbal behaviours are drawn together in demonstration, which might also be described as a learning game in that it evidently rests on principled procedures. It has been noted for example that demonstration has a pivotal function in being both responsive and stimulating; and that Timothy typically begins and ends his solo rehearsals without ceremony, with verbal pointing before, after or both. The close interplay between verbal and performance behaviours, and the function of demonstration in eliciting a practical response rather than merely offering information, suggest that researchers considering verbal behaviour in isolation should proceed with caution. Extracting the vocabulary from the context of goal-oriented demonstration might give the misleading impression that it lacks substance, and that it rests on what might appear to be 'hopelessly vague technical terms and metaphors enlisted more or less ad hoc as the occasion demands' (Howard 1982, p. 74).

Timothy makes some explicit remarks about his use of demonstration in lessons: it will be recalled that he says in his interview that it should not be overdone, and should follow the student's own attempt, 'not to say I am doing it perfectly but just to hear a live instrument'.

It is worth examining these remarks in some detail in the light of the observed lessons, to sketch a speculative picture of Timothy's concept of demonstration. That it should not be overdone is perhaps reflected in the relatively small proportion of performance behaviour contributed by Timothy playing alone: 12 per cent in Lesson A and 7 per cent in Lesson B. 'Overdone' however might refer to more than quantity: demonstrations are not offered until after the student has played, and when they are offered they are not intended to represent perfection, so it seems possible that Timothy is reluctant to present an exemplary model to be copied. Asking the pupil to become the exact copy of a preconceived model is the approach Greenhouse attributed to Casals (Delbanco 1985, p. 50), but from the perspective suggested by Timothy's approach, that would be overdoing it. It might not be pressing the interpretation of his remarks too far to suggest that a 'live' instrument is a variable instrument: that the model would not be a fixed one, and on the contrary, in the context of teaching and learning, it would be responsive to the student's own attempt. With each demonstration, Timothy gauges the student's current accomplishment and what might be accomplished next: the demonstration acts as a catalyst, inviting and perhaps inspiring the student to make a leap from one to the other. The relationship with the metaphor of scaffolding is clear.

At the same time, the 'live' instrument producing variable results might constitute an artistic position on musical interpretation. Evidence supporting this comes particularly from Lesson A, in which Timothy's answers to Andrew's questions sometimes indicate scope for negotiation, and can become quite expansive and reflective. The interpretation of one marking on the score for example is considered in a broader light: 'I think as an artist you've got to – think of – keeping the people's interest and expressing what you feel about it' (37:05). Timothy goes on to offer some more specific suggestions about how this might be done, including an indication of his own 'instinct', but when Andrew reports on this discussion in his interview, he indicates that there is no definitive solution: Timothy had said 'yes and no', and Andrew concludes that it is up to the performer 'at the time'.

Demonstration is potentially a highly instructive procedure, as in the example of task reduction in Beth's lesson, described above as 'Set piece 2', and in Casals' approach to interpretation in Greenhouse's lessons (Delbanco 1985). Here however its essence would seem to lie within what Schön describes as 'indeterminate zones of practice [characterized by] uncertainty, uniqueness, and value conflict' (1987, p. 6). Beth does not appear to have the same interpretative scope as Andrew, and this recalls Vygotsky's claim that the learner cannot imitate what lies beyond her current understanding: that its scope depends on the learner being able to 'use the collaborative actions (e.g., leading questions, demonstrations) of another' (Chaiklin 2003, pp. 51–2). A relatively junior apprentice, Beth's technical command of her work may not be sufficient to support a more open-ended approach to interpretation; her engagement in collaborative lesson behaviour seems less sophisticated than that displayed by Andrew; and the demonstrations she is offered seem to fall within her teacher's relatively reserved estimate of her understanding. The scope of demonstration seems to be circumscribed by both the student's evident abilities and the teacher's expectations of them.

Collaborative Procedures

It has been remarked above that participating in instrumental teaching and learning involves more than musical behaviour. From the theoretical perspective proposed by Lave and Wenger, learning consists in participation in social practice, with community members learning to talk as well as learning from talk (1991, p. 109). Several examples of this may be drawn from the findings described in Chapters 6 and 7. One may be found in the orderly verbal behaviour of teacher and students in the overlap between lessons: consistent with the power relations described by Lave and Wenger, and Cazden's explanation of the teacher's 'role-given rights' to speak (2001, p. 82), the students converse with their teacher during these overlaps but not with one another. A nonverbal example coincides with this: as one lesson ends and another begins, it is clear that the student participants have learned to reconfigure the scene quickly and efficiently, dealing with jackets, scores, music stands and clarinets. This has been routinized to the point where it is accomplished without any related verbal activity at all.

Although Lave and Wenger tend to focus their attention on everyday social practices rather than formal learning, regarding the latter as only one example of the former, learning as a product of social practice may also be identified in formal lesson activity. It is clear for instance that Andrew has learned how to simulate concert performance in his lesson rehearsals: since this is not explicitly discussed, and since Timothy himself does not simulate performance in the same way, it might also be regarded as learning that draws on participation in a wider community of practice than the lesson itself. It seems that Beth has not learned the same thing, though in her lesson today she is seen learning to cue rehearsals in the performance of a duo clarinet work.

In terms of verbal behaviour, it is clear that Andrew has learned how to interrupt his teacher, regardless of Timothy's role-given rights. Just as Timothy stops Andrew's performances with a monosyllabic interjection, Andrew asserts himself in the flow of Timothy's dominating verbal behaviour by saying, for example, 'Right' (6:27, 23:24, 35:39, 36:25), 'All right' (9:05) or 'Yeah' (13:09, 37:48). In all of these examples, too, Andrew is asserting himself in order to ask a question: he has learned how to elicit information from his teacher. This involves not just a spontaneous verbal gesture, but the formulation of questions beforehand, since the questions are so often, apparently, preconceived.

Once again it seems that Beth has not learned to do this, or if she has, it is not evident in the lesson observed. Once again however it might be useful to test the opposite perspective, to consider the possibility that Beth has learned to block information offered by her teacher. What Andrew elicits and supports through questions and back channelling, Beth effectively discourages through joking, fidgeting or silence. The teacher's role in lesson interactions might also be viewed from complementary perspectives: perhaps Timothy has learned that inducing Beth to participate in her lesson takes a closer, more constant use of elicitation than is necessary with Andrew; or, conversely, Timothy has not learned how to induce Beth's participation without constant persuasion and reassurance.

Andrew needs little persuasion, and perhaps little reassurance, though it seems that he does rely on Timothy to some extent for affirmation. Thus for example he reports in his interview that after learning a constrained approach to music-making in the army, 'In the last three years Timothy said I have come out of my shell'. The attitude that Timothy's opinion is sufficient to confirm this transformation has resonance with Kingsbury's description of talent as a social attribute, conferred by others: 'one person's talent is attributed to him or her by someone else, [and] the person making the attribution becomes an important element of the first person's very talent' (1988, p. 68). Kingsbury goes on to point out that this also makes talent a matter of social power and authority (p. 77).

A more concrete measurement of their relative talents lies in the subsequent examination marks achieved by Andrew and Beth: a difference of 32 marks gives a dramatic indication of the success of each. There are other ways however in which the accomplishments of the two students are quite different. It has already been noted that Andrew has learned how to interrupt, question and contribute in his lesson, in ways that have apparently not been grasped by Beth. More than this, the collaborative behaviour in Lesson A produces a 'marbled texture' of activity, as Andrew and Timothy together negotiate quick switches among various verbal and performance behaviours. Such behaviour constitutes a skill in itself: agile, alert and sophisticated, it exemplifies the combined expertise that has been developed by this teacher-student dyad over the three years of the degree programme.

Andrew appears to be the more accomplished student in terms of both clarinet performance and participating in lessons, and each of these skills continually informs the other. If Beth's accomplishments have fallen short in either respect, then her situation will similarly perpetuate itself. This is the dilemma described by Schön as a learning circle, which may be either virtuous or vicious: the communicative work however 'depends not only on the ability of coach and student to play their parts but on their willingness to do so. Here, feelings as well as understandings are involved, each critically bound up with the other' (1987, pp. 164–5).

Intentional Behaviour

The close relationship between feeling and understanding – the affective aspects of learning – has been illustrated most vividly by the nonverbal behaviour of lesson participants, though clear links have been noted among nonverbal, verbal and performance behaviours. Bruner discusses affective learning in terms of 'intentional states like believing, desiring, intending, [or] grasping a meaning', and argues that individual agency, hinging on such attitudes, should be taken into account in a sociocultural revision of cognitive psychology (1990, pp. 8–9). The argument would seem justified by the relatively late development of interest, among education researchers, in the affective – as distinct from the cognitive –

domain of learning (Bloom 1994, p. 2), and the emphasis on cognition has often meant that attributes such as receptivity and sensitivity have been overlooked (Furst 1994, p. 33). In more recent years the importance of affective learning in Higher Education has been given more attention. Thus for example Kember et al. (2008) have drawn links between anxiety-provoking assessment systems and a surface approach to learning; Smith et al. (2002) have argued that a student whose self-efficacy is poor is likely to suffer a loss of intrinsic motivation when faced with examination (p. 184); in the context of music education, Brändström has reported that students given more freedom in their instrumental tuition may react with anxiety, even in settings of Higher Education (Jørgensen 2000, p. 71). Clearly this is a complex and significant aspect of learning that warrants further attention.

In this study the intentional states of lesson participants have been represented in their interviews as well as their lesson behaviour. Beliefs and desires are reflected in Andrew's focused motivation to learn, and to succeed in a performing career; they are equally reflected in the rather apologetic way in which Beth accounts for her failure to embrace the same kind of ambition. The intentions of each student, too, cast light on aspects of their lesson behaviour, and add a further dimension to the analysis of their verbal, nonverbal and performance activity. It seems highly significant that what might have appeared a short and simple question from Andrew, regarding the interpretation of a symbol on the score, was in his own view an issue that he raised and 'discussed' with his teacher: in his own perception he gives himself a far more active and influential role in the interaction than the mere examination of the lesson script would suggest.

Beth's perceptions of her own lesson are also valuable in indicating what she has taken away from it. It has been remarked, on the basis of lesson behaviour, that she appears at times to lack interest in what her teacher has to offer, and even suggested that she effectively blocks the flow of information through her own apparent passivity. In her interview, however, Beth recalls aspects of her lesson clearly, referring for example to the preparatory ramp in lucid terms, and to the historical background of the Mendelssohn *Konzertstück*: the very information that she had appeared to block. Beth's tone remains slightly flippant, but this might be an ongoing symptom of the anxiety detected in her lesson behaviour. It may be possible, then, that Beth is more interested than she seems in receiving information, and is alert to the function of the learning games in her lesson: perhaps a genuine desire to engage with the subject has been thwarted by her inability to express her interest, on one hand, and to appropriate the learning games for her independent work, on the other. It may be that in this environment, Beth has been unable to operationalize her interest.

Given that all participants – including Timothy – bring individual agency to the setting, it is perhaps unhelpful to examine the interactions between teacher and student from the individual perspective of either: taken together, they might suggest something of a tug-of-war between participants, as they either elicit or block behaviours from each other, and effectively negotiate the procedure and product of the learning game. Even this analogy however has a weakness in the assumption that the forces at work lie along a single line of tension. Aspects of the biographies of individual participants, lesson behaviour, the institutional setting, musical culture and – possibly not least – the presence of the research camera, all serve to complicate the situation.

One way of accounting for situated differences among individuals is to extend Piaget's developmental psychology to include phases of adult life. Keegan, considering the 'vast discrepancies in basic coping capacities found in people within the same life phase', proposes three distinct stages of adult development, which however are not successfully navigated by all (McGowan, Stone and Keegan 2007). According to this theory, the late adolescent or young adult tends to define herself in terms of relationships, feeling that she is controlled by them instead of authoring them herself. Individuals at this stage 'often experience difficulty separating out the self from the relationship or in establishing relational boundaries' and they 'will likely expect a career mentor to be an authority in his or her field, providing instruction, definitions of reality, performance assessment, and expert guidance' (McGowan et al. 2007). This might well be an apt description of Beth, who discusses her learning history in terms of the personal roles taken by her current and previous teachers. In applying this constructivist-developmental theory to mentoring relationships, McGowan et al. recommend that such students be encouraged to self-author their own beliefs, so that they can 'accept responsibility for internal feelings, decision making, and behaviour'.

Variance among individual participants might also be explained in terms of Lave and Wenger's concept of legitimate peripheral participation (1991), particularly in depicting them as more or less full members of a community of practice. It has been argued that Andrew is better able than Beth to manage some of the 'learning games' in lessons, and to match aspects of Timothy's lesson behaviour, and this suggests that he has gained more seniority in the apprenticeship setting. It would also suggest that Beth's case represents, in some ways, what Lave describes as 'the sociocultural production of failure to learn' (1993, p. 10). Yet the evidence from single lesson observations for each of these students, taken together, would not seem to indicate that Andrew is merely further than Beth along the path toward full membership of the community – as if all roads led to Rome, all steps to Parnassus – but that they are travelling different paths altogether.

Wenger, reflecting on situated learning within formal educational settings, asserts that a student's ability to identify with the goals laid out before her may have a significant effect on the quality of learning:

> [F]or many students, school presents a choice between a meaningful identity and learning – a choice that creates a conflict between their social and personal lives and their intellectual engagement in school. What appears to be a lack of interest in learning may therefore not reflect a resistance to learning or an inability to learn. On the contrary, it may reflect a genuine thirst for learning of a kind that engages one's identity on a meaningful trajectory and affords some ownership of meaning. To an institution focused on instruction in terms of reified subject

matters sequestered from actual practice, this attitude will simply appear as failure to learn. (Wenger 1998, p. 270)

From this perspective, Beth's apparent failure to operationalize her interest might be driven by a lack of affinity with, or confidence in, the perceived goals of her lessons. In terms of the curriculum and its assessment, the dramatic difference between the examination marks awarded to Andrew and Beth certainly gives the impression that one has succeeded and the other failed. The impression is reinforced by Timothy's suggestion, in his interview, that while Andrew might be able to build a career for himself as a performer, Beth might perhaps go into management; and by Beth's own apparent confusion about whether she would like to continue to play the clarinet at all, once her formal studies have been completed. Ironically, however, although it falls short of Andrew's outstanding result, Beth's mark is close to the average, and represents a personal best for her.

Such a result could only be considered a failure if the real yardstick were professional concert performance. This notion would seem to be supported by Timothy's interview discussion of the Performance Studies course, particularly in the light of the broader musical profession: he speaks of '[South England] versus the rest of the world', in a competitive environment that allows for few legitimate successes. Even Timothy himself might be regarded as evidence for this argument: insofar as the teacher embodies both the state and the history of the art, it may be – in Andrew's words – 'his presence really' that symbolizes the implicit goal of instrumental teaching and learning. This is not a view formally espoused by the university, which publishes far broader aims and learning outcomes for its degree programmes, but is arguably an assumption derived from the musical, professional and artistic culture from which the subject is drawn. Thus Jørgensen asserts that 'we (sometimes) have a tendency to be too narrow-minded and focussed on one and only one outcome: The performer of high quality', in spite of a formal commitment to producing graduates 'who deliver high quality work in whatever musical profession they enter' (2009, p. 179). Lesson interactions and behaviour, the intentions and identities of participants, and the specific outcomes of the Performance Studies course, are all enmeshed in a complex and dynamic sociocultural framework.

Methodological Reflections

Validity

The meaning of validity is given a straightforward account in a gloss from Maxwell: 'How might you be wrong?' (2005, p. 103). The concept is not always taken to be so self-evident, and indeed it has been hotly contested, particularly in the light of paradigm differences in research methodologies (Guba and Lincoln 2005, p. 205). In Euclidian geometry propositions were traditionally held to be true because of their demonstrable logic, providing rules 'which had never been "proved" but which *everyone knew* had validity' (Lincoln and Guba 1985, p. 33; emphasis added). It is no longer always assumed that everyone shares self-evident truths, however, and in qualitative research, validity depends on local particulars, 'including the particular investigator-respondent (or object) interaction, the contextual factors involved, the local mutually shaping factors influencing one another, and the local (as well as investigator) values' (p. 42).

Maxwell supposes that validity is an issue concerning results and conclusions (2005, p. 4) but if no decisive line can be drawn between method and interpretation, validity becomes a matter of quality craftsmanship, at all phases of research (Kvale 1996, ch.13). Kvale further suggests that in practical terms, validity in qualitative research 'is ascertained by examining the sources of invalidity' (p. 241).

Perhaps the most obvious potential threat to validity in this particular study is the effect of the researcher on the researched. This is represented in one way by the presence of the research camera, though to some extent this has been contained by asking the participants to comment on its effect, and by considering the video evidence in the light of their comments so that the effects that they noticed themselves are made noticeable to the reader. The presence of the researcher as symbolized by the camera, is a less tangible consideration; Becker argues however that in natural settings, 'an observer is generally much less of an influence on participants' behavior than is the setting itself' (Maxwell 2005, p. 109). The video camera might constrain some aspects of participant behaviour – such as the smiles or jokes that were reported missing today – and exaggerate others – such as Beth's apparent anxiety in this situation – but it seems probable that the behaviour would be driven less by the presence of the camera than by the routine of the lessons.

The researcher's presence is of course tangible and active in obtaining interview data, which has been used to enhance validity by triangulating findings from the analysis of lesson observations, adding a further dimension to the data in hand. The interview data itself is subject to questions of validity in the sense that interviews are collaboratively constructed by the interviewer and the individual respondents (Kvale 1996, p. 14). It is interesting to note however that in this case, the use of an interview schedule does not prevent all three respondents from taking initiatives in their interviews, with little detours from the main topics or themes of the schedule. Timothy for example begins to discuss demonstration and imitation, highlighting their importance in instrumental teaching and learning, without having been asked about them. He also answers some questions so expansively that he provides a powerful sense of context for the subjects discussed; this is perhaps accidentally expanded further when he apparently mishears a question about the Performance Studies course, and answers in terms of performance in general. In spite of the misunderstanding, the fluency and substance of the digression might suggest that Timothy tends to focus more on performance culture than on the course itself; a notion supported by the fact that in a busy portfolio career, his teaching at SEU normally occupies only one or two days each week.

If initiatives taken in interviews hint at the personal priorities of the participants, it might also be significant that all three respondents refer to affective issues when discussing their work, without being specifically asked to do so. Their independent references to negative experiences in lessons have already been noted; in addition to this, the students refer to their experience with teachers in terms of emotion. Thus Beth reports that her previous teacher 'was brilliant and amazing and I loved her', while Andrew remarks that Timothy's very presence is enough to make things happen: 'I absolutely adore his style'. Thus the students themselves introduce to the conversation the affective aspects of learning, which have been described previously as an important but rarely noted aspect of apprenticeship.

In discussing the findings an important validity check is to seek alternative interpretations of the data. This has been attempted, for example, in the account of the collaborative verbal behaviour in Lesson B: the reasons underlying the nature of that interaction might be considered from either the student or the teacher perspective. The exercise of alternating perspectives however does not serve to ascertain which is correct, but – perhaps more usefully – suggests that the observed activity incorporates multifaceted realities.

On this premise, the validity of findings, or the interpretation of them, will depend at least partly on the research questions and tools employed. Verbal and performance behaviours have been analyzed according to functions that have been identified within this study, through the analysis of data: those functions might have been defined in a different way, perhaps with different points of focus, and certainly with different kinds of results. An illustration of this point may be drawn from a comparison between this study and, for example, previous work with the same data pool, in which verbal behaviour was viewed through the lenses of subject matter and teaching strategies (Young et al. 2003), distribution among participants (Burwell et al. 2003), questions (Burwell 2005) and vocabulary (Burwell 2006). All of these interrogate the data in ways that are quite different to the functions – information, elicitation, coaching and feedback – sought in the current study, and all therefore examine different faces of the reality represented in the observed lessons.

For this project, verbal and performance behaviours are explored and described more thoroughly, too, through a far smaller case study, in an effort to engage with what Parlett and Hamilton describe as the most powerful check on the validity for qualitative research: 'Does the study present a "recognizable reality" to those who read it?' (Entwistle 2005, p. 15). The addition of another layer of exploration in the form of nonverbal activity is at once a way of bringing the lessons descriptions to life, through everyday and easily recognizable features of behaviour, and of accessing the intentional states of the observed participants. McCroskey, Richmond and McCroskey (2006) explain a significant difference between verbal and nonverbal behaviours in the context of education:

> [V]erbal messages stimulate primarily cognitive meanings in receivers (what the students learn about the subject matter), whereas the nonverbal messages stimulate affective meanings in receivers (i.e., the feelings and attitudes toward

the content as well as feelings and attitudes toward the teacher). (McCroskey, Richmond and McCroskey 2006)

The same authors claim that 'nonverbal communication has its largest impact on affective learning', which in turn 'has its primary impact on long-term, not short-term, cognitive learning' (McCroskey et al. 2006). The intentional states suggested by nonverbal behaviour may, then, be crucial in the lifelong learning envisaged for its students in the university's strategic plan.

Validity in the interpretation of nonverbal behaviour depends on the context, and in this light the meaning of self-touching, in some ways one of the most striking features observed in Lesson B, might be debated. In some contexts self-touching is taken to be a sign of 'preening' or courtship display, through gestures such as 'hair stroking' (Scheflen and Scheflen, in Argyle 1988, p. 199). While it cannot be decisively proved that Beth is not flirting with Timothy in self-touching so often, however, the triangulation of verbal and nonverbal data, and of the interview evidence all point toward the more common conclusion that anxiety is the emotion associated with this behaviour (Argyle 1988, pp. 197–8). Perhaps once again it should be acknowledged that both interpretations might have some validity in a multifaceted reality, even if one has been given more weight and credence, in this context, than the other.

Theorizing Learning

A salient feature of early studies in instrumental teaching and learning, mentioned repeatedly in Chapter 3, is that theoretical premises are typically drawn from classroom research. Entwistle (2005) argues that for the sake ecological validity, '[psychological] theories must be derived from the settings to which they are to be applied' (p. 11); but researchers must start somewhere, and so long as theories are not transplanted uncritically or untested from one context to another, ideas from classroom research and psychology might be regarded as providing a point of departure for the gradual development of ecological validity in theories about instrumental teaching and learning.

Examples of theoretical constructs that have been imported from the classroom into research on studio-based instrumental teaching and learning include the 'correct teaching cycles' sought by Yarbrough and Price (1989), and the use of teacher approvals and disapprovals (again, Yarbrough and Price 1989; Colprit 2000; Henniger, Flowers and Councill 2006; Zhukov 2008). They also include the set of teaching strategies sought in the observation of individual lessons at SEU, ultimately derived from sports science literature (Young et al. 2003). Related to these strategies, which range along a continuum from student- to teacher-led, are discovery and expository approaches to teaching (Marchand 1975) and self- and learner-oriented climates (Verrastro 1975).

As previously noted, however, Kennell (1992) warns against framing research questions to suit the evaluative tools in hand: hence his own adaptations of scaffolding theory to suit the natural setting observed in individual instrumental lessons (Kennell 1992; 1997; 2002), and the more inductive approach to scaffolding strategies in this new context, taken by Gholson (1998). Gholson is able to take an inductive approach by focusing on the case of a single teacher, and what is lost in generalizing power is arguably balanced by the enhancement of authenticity.

The current case study of course also observes a single teacher, focusing on the description of lesson interactions. Contextualization is sought through reference to the biographies of participants, and links to the sociocultural framework of their lessons; the use of multiple lenses, too, allows one kind of behaviour to be contextualized by others, and the participants' behaviour to be contextualized by one another. No participant functions entirely independently in instrumental lessons, and if one appears to be dominant in verbal, performance or spatial behaviour, the other is always implicated in the asymmetry. Perhaps more than in classroom situations, the authoritative teacher in the studio has a student seeking and helping to maintain his authority; the performing student has a teacher guiding, supporting and directing the performance; the dominating speaker has the support and encouragement – or lack of these – of a back-channelling listener; and each teacher-student dyad negotiates collaborative spatial behaviour that may ˙ be reciprocal or compensatory in nature.

It is in the nature of instrumental teaching and learning, or of some aspects of it, that a commanding approach may be required: the nature of clarinet performance, for example, is not entirely a matter of creativity and decision-making, but also involves a range of routine procedures developed through instruction and drill, as befitting the acquisition of a complex skill. If lesson interactions in studio-based instrumental teaching and learning do not meet the expectations drawn from classroom behaviour, perhaps research questions that concern student activity and independence should be reframed, to better suit the nature of the subject being studied. In Chapter 4 a pyramid representation of the student's performance work was cited (Burwell et al. 2004), showing that the instrumental lesson functions as a significant but limited proportion of the whole: far more concentrated is the performance goal, and far more expansive is the student's independent practice. The student in the instrumental lesson may appear to be relatively passive, particularly if behaviours such as listening, reading, silent fingering, back channelling and thinking are not sought by researchers; but the same student has presumably spent many more hours preparing for the lesson, both during the week preceding the lesson and during the years preceding entry to the university.

This is hardly a picture of a passive recipient of knowledge, though the perception of the student's activity or inactivity will depend on the perspective taken. Aside from the large proportion of activity being undertaken outside the lesson, independently, the perspective adopted by Froelich (2002) compares music education to teacher training, and suggests that the skill-based nature of their subject, and their involvement in performances, gives music students the greater sense of participation and active learning. The music student's independence may not always be in evidence in the instrumental lesson, but in order to pursue a course of lessons, and to sustain the activity, a good deal of independent work is implied. Indeed, the evidence presented by Kemp (1996) suggests that musicians' personalities exhibit traits of both dependence and independence, and although research findings to date attribute each of these to a different stage of development, it does not seem unreasonable to suppose that aspects of either might be engaged, as appropriate, in the lesson, on the concert platform and in the practice studio.

The extent to which music students in Higher Education rely on their teacher's approval is another complex issue that must be affected by the perspective adopted. If instrumental lessons are regarded as constituting an apprenticeship, then the legitimacy conferred or withheld by the master will influence the student's career in practical terms, as well as her evolving sense of identity as a member of the community. There are affective implications in the teacher's approval, too, perhaps highlighted by the emotional investment made in musical performance, and the importance of the interpersonal relationship between teacher and student. Researchers seeking 'teacher approvals' in instrumental lessons are often disappointed, but Duke and Henniger (1998) argue that verbal approval is only one way of signalling success, and that that can also be provided, in the lesson, through the student's own performance:

> Instructional settings in music performance provide numerous opportunities for students to receive feedback about their progress and accomplishment. This feedback emanates not from the teacher directly, but from students' perceptions of their own accomplishment of proximal performance goals. This is not a trivial point. (Duke and Henniger 1998, p. 484)

The authors go on to assert that excellent teachers are able to control the student's performance success in lessons, in a manner that resembles scaffolding theory. Findings from the current study suggest that the teacher cannot entirely control such things, since the student's preparation is presumably variable, and affective states ranging from confidence to anxiety may influence the success of the student's participation. At the same time, however, the intention of providing performance success for the student is made explicit in Timothy's interview, when he describes the 'high' at the end of an ideal lesson:

> Quite often I will deliver the pace so that they play through a whole section at the end to finish with so it gives a sort [of] feeling of going out on a high because they have achieved something complete.
>
> (Excerpt 8.1 Interview with Timothy)

That Timothy is able to 'deliver the pace' in this way is demonstrated in the profile of Lesson A, drawn through both verbal and performance behaviour; it is arguably demonstrated again in the first half of Lesson B, in which success is approached through what have been described as learning games, brought to fruition in the full rehearsal of the Mendelssohn *Presto* (74:31). That the delivery of pace is not entirely the teacher's prerogative, however, is demonstrated in the overall profile of Lesson B, shaped as it is by the need to achieve fluency in a performance that has been unevenly and perhaps minimally prepared, but which is shortly to be formally examined.

Evaluating Lesson Interactions

All of these considerations – these lines of tension within and among participant behaviours and lesson frameworks – suggest that the evaluation of instrumental lessons should be approached with caution. Context once again is crucial, and there is evidence to suggest that the criteria for success are often altered, for example, with learners of different ages. It will be recalled that Mills and Smith (2003), reporting on the perceptions of teachers, and Davidson et al. (1998), on the perceptions of pupils, emphasize the importance of the teacher's personal attributes for children, but professional attributes for adult learners. The perceptions of participants should not be dismissed lightly, even when they seem to contradict the expectations and observations of researchers: the contradictions are too numerous for researchers simply to suppose that we know better. Thus, for example, Duke and Henniger (2002) report with some surprise that undergraduate music students were not swayed, in evaluating instrumental lessons, by the teacher's use of positive or negative feedback. Koopman et al. (2007) report that students accounting for their lesson and practice activity gave themselves credit for taking more initiative than observers had been able to discern: a finding that would seem to be endorsed in the current study by Andrew's account of his own participation in lesson dialogue. As suggested in the study of doctor-patient dyads, an individual's satisfaction with a working relationship might not be fully in evidence in the observation of a single consultation, being perhaps multidimensional and historical in nature (Koss and Rosenthal 1997).

Drawing criteria for success from other settings brings particular problems to evaluators of instrumental teaching and learning, even when those settings are broadly conceived. The concepts of situated learning (Lave and Wenger 1991) and of learning through participation in a community of practice (Wenger 1998) for example, would seem to imply that the student will learn to talk through talk, and that successful learning will therefore be demonstrated in the student's verbal activity in lessons. This assumption would appear to be challenged however by Remedios, Clarke and Hawthorne (2008) in their study of 'the silent participant' in collaborative learning contexts: where perhaps traditionally they were allowed to 'privately construct understandings, students are now obliged to publicly display their construction of knowledge before their peers' (p. 202). Silent participants, often but not always overseas-educated, tend to utter short speech acts and ask few questions: a description that recalls Beth's behaviour in her clarinet lesson. Although the applicability of their study of group settings is clearly limited with respect to individual lessons, it seems pertinent that Remedios et al. ask whether such students choose to be silent, or are silenced by the sociocultural context (p. 203). In addition, although the benefits of making learning explicit are widely accepted, there is perhaps a risk that the demonstration of learning might become an object in itself:

> Students are not only required to learn but to demonstrate to others that they are learning. The risk is that the preoccupation for students and staff becomes verbal input. Tutors may come to perceive their jobs as facilitating student speaking rather than as facilitating their learning. The insistence that verbal expression is seen as the only reflection of active engagement in learning is problematic. (Remedios, Clarke and Hawthorne 2008, p. 212)

It has already been mentioned that in previous research at SEU, higher achieving students, identified either through their performance examination results or their final degree classes, tended to talk more in their lessons (Burwell 2003a, p. 11). In the current case study however Andrew, a remarkably high achiever in terms of clarinet performance, speaks less than Beth, whose examination marks are nearer the average. The difference between their proportional contributions to verbal dialogue is narrow, but this exceptional case of a relatively quiet achiever serves to emphasize the possibility of individual differences in lesson behaviour.

In addition to this, of course, music students demonstrate learning in individual lessons through performance activity. Indeed, the performance activity might be regarded as a source of almost constant feedback for the student which the teacher's guidance and coaching support and frame. This might help to explain the observation of positive student attitudes and high levels of attentiveness (Kostka 1984, p. 120) even when the teacher's verbal feedback is deliberately focused on negative correction (Duke and Henniger 1998, pp. 483–4).

Performance should also be considered, too, as a salient criterion for success in instrumental teaching and learning. That the participants in the current case study consider excellent performance the sign of success seems clear in the interview data. Timothy discusses performance in terms of professional concert careers, and the musical future of his students in terms of whether they might be able to have such as career or not. Andrew rather dismisses the performance examination as a goal, in that it is 'not a major accomplishment' – though he is evidently confident enough to assume that it will be an accomplishment – but promptly states when asked that his ambition is 'to become a performer, whether it be solo or orchestral'. Beth's answer to the same question is that she has no ambitions in music: and she promptly apologizes for this – 'That's really bad!' – as if it is self-evident that she should be ambitious in this context.

While it may be less explicit, excellent performance as the underlying goal of lessons may be evident too in the lesson observations undertaken. Andrew's self-declared ambition to become a performer would seem to be illustrated in the preparatory moments he takes before simulated performances in his lessons; although his teacher rarely makes the same kind of gesture before playing, these moments are never disturbed or interrupted, and this would seem to signify a shared understanding of their broader significance. The expectation that this implies – that a future in professional performing is felt by both to be viable for Andrew – is quite distinct from that underlying Beth's lesson. Here, the closely observed details of lesson behaviour, noting the awkward cues, and some indecision about whether Beth should be preparing her rehearsals in this way at all, might offer some insight into the shared vision for her future, as expressed in interviews: Beth is not regarded as a potential concert artist, and while she and her teacher persist in rehearsing a flamboyant concert piece, they seem to be aiming at the more modest goal of examination survival, even if this means making technical compromises.

It has been claimed that the Performance studies modules at SEU 'neither labour under nor aspire to the ideal of the solo concert artist as a goal for their students', but although performance students are asked to document their studies through critical self-evaluation, the major assessment task each year is the final performance examination. This must signal to students what is expected of them, at least as much as the formal aims and learning outcomes listed for their modules. Perhaps more importantly, too, it seems abundantly clear that the attitudes and perceptions of lesson participants are not entirely moulded by the undergraduate curriculum. A range of musical cultures is in evidence in the practices undertaken within the Performance studies course, and taken together, musical culture – in terms of both the history and the state of the art – extends far beyond the institution itself.

Chapter 9
Conclusions

Research Questions

The method, findings and interpretation for each of the three research questions posed in this study are summarized here.

1. How is instrumental teaching and learning undertaken?

This question has been investigated chiefly through the micro-analysis of two clarinet lessons undertaken by an expert teacher working with undergraduate students. Drawing on video observation, rich data has been derived from these lessons through the close description of three distinct kinds of behaviour: spatial, performance and verbal. Of these, spatial behaviour has been, to date, the least explored in the research literature on instrumental teaching and learning. Here, it has helped to bring the lesson descriptions to life through the observation of everyday details of activity; it has cast some light on the interpretation of the behaviour of lesson participants, since nonverbal behaviour may be unconscious as well as conscious; and it has suggested a certain balance, either reciprocal or compensatory in nature, in the patterns of behaviour established within each teacher-student dyad. Arguably, too, the observation of nonverbal behaviour has provided some access to the affective states of participants, supported by the semi-structured interviews in which each offered their own perceptions of the lessons observed.

Performance behaviour has been timed, and classified according to the strength of its resemblance to full concert performance. This classification has been taken to correspond in some ways to intensity, and the distribution of performance behaviours has been used to map the profile of lesson activity. On a local scale, it has also helped to identify incidents of what have been described as 'learning games', variously conceived as a preparatory ramp engineered to approach specific problems, a bull's-eye target focused on task reduction and then restoration, and the use of demonstration and imitation as a collaborative activity.

Verbal behaviour too has been classified according to its function, with the teacher's behaviour divided among information, elicitation, coaching and feedback, and the students' behaviour chiefly divided among information, elicitation and back channelling. In terms of wordage the teacher's dominance is consistent across the two lessons, but his speech should not be considered a solo accomplishment. Coaching and feedback in particular have been found to be closely related to the students' performance activity, to the point where it might be highly artificial to analyze them without considering that relationship. Parallel to this, information and elicitation, comprising most of the teacher's talk, have been found to be closely related to the student's verbal activity, to the point where the student's talk considered in isolation might give quite a misleading impression of their role in lesson interactions.

It has not been suggested, in the close description of lesson activity, that any of the participants are inactive. If the quantity of performance activity is dominated by students, the teacher nevertheless appears to guide it; if the quantity of verbal activity is dominated by the teacher, the students are able to influence its flow through minimal but significant contributions.

Lesson activity is multidimensional and collaborative, constructed by teacher and student together. Although distinct aspects of it, or of individual behaviour, may be described as separate components of the whole, their functions have been considered in an interactive context in order to understand how instrumental teaching and learning is undertaken.

2. How does the conduct of instrumental teaching and learning vary with participants?

Although the two students observed in this study differ in their abilities, as demonstrated by their performance examination results, the intention in this study has not been to compare lessons in order to identify the components of outstanding student success. Instead, the investigation of two lessons has provided what has been called a 'stereo effect' that might bring a further dimension to the observed interactions. Thus the physical composure and relaxed focus observed in one interaction has been highlighted by the uncomfortable busyness of the other; reciprocal behaviour by compensatory behaviour. Features like silent fingering, joking and apologizing seem all the more noticeable, and perhaps more significant, because of their absence from one lesson or the other.

Given that lesson behaviour is collaborative, differences in student behaviour are reflected and perhaps even amplified in differences within the teacher's behaviour, and this effect is particularly marked in verbal activity. The flow of information delivered in Lesson A provides a clear contrast with the consistent use of elicitation in Lesson B, implying that the teacher has the opportunity to give what he has to offer in one, while in the other, the effort to engage the student becomes more imperative. The student's role in this is indicated by the use of questions – preconceived and asserted in Lesson A, superficial reflexes in Lesson B – and in a different way by back channelling, through which one speaker supports and encourages the verbal activity of another. Thus the students' employment of questions and back channelling may be seen to regulate the teacher's verbal activity.

The contrasting performance behaviour in the two lessons seems to offer a further opportunity, to understand 'learning games' which begin as collaborative endeavours but which may be appropriated for solo use. Thus in Lesson B, for example, the teacher takes what might be considered scaffolding roles in identifying a problem and a strategy for dealing with it, and then providing the discipline required to guide and monitor the student through the solution; in Lesson A, in contrast, a similar procedure is recognizable when the student spontaneously withdraws from the flow of lesson activity to undertake the same procedure alone. No verbal comment is made on this by participants, either during their lessons or in the interviews following, and it perhaps offers an example of a tacit appropriation of skill that might escape the notice of an observer who is focusing her attention on verbal behaviour alone.

These little windows on lesson interactions show some of the complexity involved in the problem of identifying who is doing the work in the lesson, or to borrow a notion from Jørgensen (2000), who is taking responsibility for the learning. In terms of performance behaviour, the development of a student's practice skills and progress might depend on the ability to tacitly appropriate skills that are employed collaboratively in the lesson, particularly if those skills are not made verbally explicit in lesson dialogue. In terms of verbal behaviour, too, a student who is unwilling or possibly unable to display an interest in what the teacher has to offer may be trapped in a 'vicious circle' where an apparent lack of personal investment reinforces a lack of achievement. Without implying linear causality, then, the contrast between the two lessons suggests circular relationships between procedure and product, and between lesson behaviour and student learning, with one always implicated in the other.

3. How is the interaction between teacher and student contextualized?

In the background of this study, a sense of context for the lesson interactions is evoked through the cross-referencing of participant interviews with lesson observations, to take participants' perceptions of their own activity into account. The interview data has also provided some explicit discussion of the participants' biographies, and their perceptions of the personal and sociocultural contexts of their lessons together.

One of the most striking features of the participants' sense of context is the reference to musical culture that extends beyond the Music Department. For all of the participants, the formal Performance Studies course is apparently only one phase in what may well be a lifetime's engagement with music. Prior to these lesson observations, Timothy had become a mature professional artist, and both Andrew and Beth had been studying clarinet since childhood; alongside the observations, Timothy was engaged in a portfolio career, in which teaching at South England was by no means the dominant component, while the students' attendance will have represented only single sessions in a busy week of study activity. All participants demonstrate a sense, too, of the students' musical future: Timothy speculates on his students' prospects in terms of professional concert performance, and Andrew is assertive with his own ambitions in this regard, while Beth apologizes for a lack of them.

Musical values are evidently not dictated by the Performance Studies course, and although the course prescribes a formal set of aims and learning outcomes, it seems that the aims of these participating students and their teacher are in some ways more closely related to professional concert performance as the measure of success. Ironically, this, according to Timothy, may not be a realistic aim even for the best students; ironically, too, the motivation of both of the observed students seems tied to an emotional investment with the subject matter. On these terms, the prospect of success seems unlikely and the prospect of failure, potentially, emotionally damaging.

This tacit aim of instrumental teaching and learning, apparently embedded in the broader musical culture, is approached in different ways by individual students, whose behaviour may be variously contextualized by personality theory (Kemp 1996), for example, or constructive developmentalism (McGowan et al. 2007). Between the contextual pillars represented by individuals and by the broad culture, however, various conceptual frames might usefully be placed. Apprenticeship is one of these, since so many of its features – including experiential knowledge, demonstration and imitation, and a significant relationship between master and apprentice – resonate with the conduct of instrumental teaching and learning. The institution too provides an active framework, including elements of tradition associated with teacher training, university and conservatoire. Although in this study the institution has remained in the background of lesson activity, it makes direct links with teachers through staff development, increasingly informed by research; and makes direct links with students through their seminar courses, which cultivate the academic background to musical performance and to teaching and learning. Through all of these links, the institution seeks to encourage reflective practice.

Higher Education itself, which provides a broad framework for the instrumental teaching and learning investigated in this case study, may be conceptualized as an interactive system combining the environment, subject matter and participant characteristics (Entwistle 2007, p. 1). In implicating history as well as the contemporary setting, all of these have horizontal and vertical dimensions. The complexity of the context suggests that the nature of research findings will depend very much on the specific frames and lenses adopted.

Implications

A social constructionist view of knowledge 'encourages us to be suspicious of our assumptions about how the world appears to be'; it is historically and culturally specific, regards knowledge as negotiated and sustained through interaction, and holds that knowledge and social action are inseparable (Burr 2003, pp. 2–5). For researchers this poses a perpetual dilemma of identifying appropriate units for analysis. For the sake of ecological validity, those units must lie somewhere between the isolated individual at one extreme and the infinite context at the other, since neither can be grasped without some reference to the other. If meaning is constantly, collaboratively constructed, too, rather than being fixed and definite, researchers must be prepared to regard all findings as conditional. The characterization of an historically rooted practice implies embracing the ambiguity that allows for the ongoing negotiation of meaning among practitioners (Wenger 1998, p. 83); eschewing definition of a kind of knowledge that is always in flux; and respecting practitioners and the practice while we deepen our understanding of both.

To respect practitioners is not merely to allow for their personal idiosyncrasies, but for their personal cultures: although teachers and students are members of the Music Department as a community of practice, they are also members of others, and in many ways their identities are likely to be drawn either from elsewhere or from social contexts broader than the institution itself. If for example students are inspired by the figure of the solo concert artist, and even if the desire to achieve such standing in the musical community may seem unrealistic – if 'they know that they will not become a Rubinstein but it is still Rubinstein who drives them on' (Nielsen 1999, p. 113) – their motivation represents a resource for teaching and learning that should not be set aside lightly.

Indeed, the Music Department, drawing as it does on a range of musical and educational traditions, would do well to maintain the richness and ambiguity among them, and to support the development of individuality among student musicians, as appropriate to the nature of their subject matter. Module designers and leaders may be seen as policymakers, but they are in no position to change the culture by decree: culturally endowed traits are not personal properties that can be simply laid down by either teachers or students. This is not to suggest that the institution is or should be inert. The university has responsibilities that extend beyond those that characterize traditional apprenticeship settings, as Wenger argues:

> [Education, in its deepest sense] concerns the opening of identities – exploring new ways of being that lie beyond our current state. Whereas training aims to create an inbound trajectory targeted at competence in a specific practice, education must strive to open new dimensions for the negotiation of the self. It places students on an outbound trajectory toward a broad field of possible identities. Education is not merely formative – it is transformative. (Wenger 1998, p. 263)

This perspective applied to the context of the current case study might suggest that it is in the nature of the traditional music studio to regard excellence in instrumental performance as the central goal for trainees; but it further suggests that the educational institution embracing the studio, and others that may be more or less like it, can and should be providing other possible trajectories, other possible sources of identity, for its students.

Until musical communities of practice have developed and agreed on a better approach to the teaching and learning of performance skill, the studio should remain intact, its practice respected by the institution. The collaborative behaviour demonstrated by all participants in the current case study seems uniquely adapted to their subject matter, with responsive individual attention given to each student by a highly expert practitioner who has shown himself to be a sophisticated, adaptable and caring teacher. What the institution might usefully contemplate is opening the studio door. The one-to-one mode of passing on the art and craft of performance may remain unsurpassed in many ways, but it has an inbuilt constraint in terms of education: it is designed to cultivate the learning of performance skill, but not the skill of teaching performance. Having entered a studio during childhood as an apprentice player, the learner gradually develops performance skill, does a certain amount of performing and typically begins to do a certain amount of teaching. Timothy has described his own experience in this sense as being 'thrown in at the deep end'.

Although there are now a number of formal courses available in instrumental teaching, the performer's teaching skill is still more commonly developed in relative isolation, presumably with reference to the small handful of individual teachers that each has known well, but relying chiefly on personal reflections and accumulating experience. The educational institution is perhaps uniquely positioned to facilitate the development and sharing of teachers' reflections, ideas, stories, problems and approaches to practice. At SEU this has been addressed in part through the research undertaken within the department, fed back to participant teachers in staff development events; without attempting to demonstrate or define a model of good practice, this has hinged on identifying issues that seem to be significant in supporting student learning. Responding to research evidence drawn from a context of obvious relevance to them, and yet presented in objective and depersonalized terms, tutors have taken a particular interest in sharing their reflections on the student's contribution to verbal dialogue in lessons, for example, and on students' approaches to their personal practice. It should be acknowledged that although such points have served to start conversations among practitioners, they have more often served as a point of departure than as self-contained problems to be resolved.

The door of the studio may be opened, at SEU, in another sense: through the student. Performance students often choose to study modules based on instrumental teaching and learning, to complement their principal study work, and one of the strategies employed in these modules is to send students as observers into the studios of other teachers as well as their own. It is hoped that this will give them more scope for reflection on the approaches available in instrumental lessons, than perhaps their own teachers were able to enjoy at a similar stage of development.

Assessment tools are another resource that may be adapted by the institution in an effort to broaden learning and its potential outcomes. Once, the annual examination recital at South England represented the only assessment task for performance students; this emphasis on the performance product was somewhat softened by the introduction of the additional assessment of process, made by the teacher in response to the student's work in and around lessons (1996–2001); and finally the responsibility for accounting for the student's independent work, in a series of assessed written exercises, was shifted to the student herself (2002–present). One of the most recent developments in the formal cultivation of student independence (2006) has been the introduction of an assessment project during the final year of study, in which performance students must identify, prepare and perform a piece of suitable repertoire without the assistance of their instrumental tutor. Making the 'lifelong learning' agenda explicit, the students, as participants in a university degree programme who are expected to develop the ability to 'articulate, discuss and write about' their learning experiences, also submit a reflective written commentary on their engagement with the project.

Heightening teachers' awareness of what the institution asks of students is an essential corollary to these developments, and this remains a work in progress, subject to obvious constraints. Work in the Music Department typically represents one role among many in the portfolio careers of instrumental and vocal tutors, and although participation in staff development events is encouraged and funded, it is not yet a formal expectation. When tutors are able to participate their attitudes are typically open and interested, as they welcome the opportunity to discuss their work with one another as much as with module leaders; but even identifying times and spaces to bring a significant number of tutors together can be a challenging task. Managing such exercises effectively amounts to an attempt to influence established and dynamic cultures, in which performance tutors are themselves valuable human resources; it is important that the roles of researcher and module leader are, and are seen to be, respectful of students and teachers, junior through to senior members of a complex community of practice.

Research: Limitations and Prospects

The limitations of the current research are perhaps most obvious in the boundaries of the case study. The research has been bounded by two single lesson observations, represented by 105 minutes of video evidence, and single interviews with the three lesson participants. These are mere snap-shots in the musical lives of individual musicians, and in the complex cross-current of musical cultures, social practices and institutions of education, merely a drop in the ocean. It is suggested however that the lesson interactions described here represent authentic possibilities in the practice of instrumental teaching and learning, explored for their intrinsic interest and perhaps allowing extrapolation to other settings and circumstances. The more convincing case study descriptions and interpretations are, the more likely that other researchers and practitioners are to regard them as contributions to understanding.

Of course, description is selective, and although the use of quantitative strategies to account for subunit lesson behaviours might enhance the rigour of the study, numbers are themselves adjectives, and the use of statistics in this study, also descriptive. If description, analysis and interpretation can contribute to the development of reflective practice, among lesson participants, policymakers and researchers, it does not represent, and in this study is not intended to represent, either proof or definition of the current state of affairs. The dynamic nature of the complex skills involved in instrumental teaching and learning, and the multidimensional nature of the apprenticeship setting, are arguably better represented by the rich description of behaviour in authentic settings, even if the results are necessarily tentative and conditional. Thus Bowman asserts that research, as much as music and education, must be 'inherently fluid, ever under construction' (2005, p. 163). The attitude again recalls Wittgenstein's suggestion that sometimes an indistinct picture is 'exactly what we need'. His argument is couched in terms of 'language games', but the parallel example of lesson procedures, proposed in Chapter 8, would seem to be well supported by it:

> And this is just how one might explain to someone what a game is. One gives examples and intends them to be taken in a particular way. – I do not, however, mean by this that he is supposed to see in those examples that common thing which I – for some reason – was unable to express; but that he is now to *employ* those examples in a particular way. Here giving examples is not an *indirect* means of explaining – in default of a better. For any general definition can be misunderstood too. The point is that *this* is how we play the game. (Wittgenstein 1953, p. 34; italics original)

This is not to say that instrumental teaching and learning cannot be the subject of useful reflection, and indeed one of the more compelling tasks for the future is to theorize music education and its research (Bowman 2005). It has often proved fruitful to import theoretical premises from other areas of study, including classroom teaching and learning, rehearsal and ensemble behaviour, and social psychology; it will be recalled however that the development of research specific to studio-based instrumental teaching and learning has largely consisted in identifying, testing and then adapting assumptions taken from those areas. At the same time, the theories implicit in current practice may be explored, including the epistemology of practice and the apprenticeship setting. In this study, once again, these have been examined not for the sake of defining them but to see what they might be worth, in developing the shared understanding of what instrumental teaching and learning is. Bowman argues that theory and philosophy should be an intrinsic part of empirical research:

> [The] trouble with conceiving of philosophy simply as one 'method' of research among others is the temptation (apparently considerable) to opt out, on grounds 'it's not what I do'. ... What this creates, in effect, is a philosophical ghetto where those with such (unfortunate?) propensities can pursue them without troubling the rest of the profession. (Bowman 2005, p. 155)

The same author goes on to recommend the development of 'theory or philosophy ... concerned not so much with dispensing answers as exploring vital questions and issues' (p. 155). The current study would seem to suggest that the issues which need further exploration, theoretically and empirically, include the interactive nature of lesson behaviour, and the role taken by demonstration and imitation in the teaching and learning of complex musical skills. In this study, aspects of lesson behaviour have been foregrounded, with contextual frameworks forming the background to the researched cases; it will continue to be important that such studies are complemented by work that alters or reverses those perspectives, so that a more textured and fluid understanding of the subject may be developed.

The importance of context is no doubt what inspires Jørgensen (2009), in an overview of research 'from a quality improvement perspective', to emphasize the need for more relational studies, seeking links for example between the acts of teaching and performing (p. 62); between the students' perceptions of themselves and the institution, and achievement (p. 76); and between students' personal stages of development and their varied approaches to learning (p. 80). An ongoing theme for Jørgensen is the call for research focused on the institution's role as an implicit and influential feature in instrumental teaching and learning (2000; 2002, p. 117; 2009), and certainly the development of reflexive practice on the part of the institution, researchers, teachers and students, would seem to be essential as embedded educational practices are continually supported and renewed. The formal aims of university programmes have become broader over the last generation, to embrace notions of widening participation and lifelong learning; the student's development as an independent and reflective practitioner is widely accepted as a more appropriate goal than the traditional but narrower focus on excellence in musical performance. Having laid out such goals for teachers and students, however, the institution must actively support the apprehension and practical pursuit of them. Questions about what happens in individual instrumental lessons, what is best learned in that setting, and how learning is undertaken, within and beyond the studio, may in turn be framed among questions concerning the newly adapted aims and learning outcomes in formal educational programmes, and the institution's responsibility in supporting the practitioners who are to operationalize them.

References

Aldrich, R. (1999) 'The Apprentice in History', in Ainley, P. and Rainbird, H. (Eds) *Apprenticeship: Towards a New Paradigm of Learning*, pp. 14–24. London: Kogan Page.

Argyle, M. (1969) *Social Interaction*. London: Methuen.

Argyle, M. (1988) *Bodily Communication*, 2nd edn. London: Routledge.

Baillie, H. (1956) 'A London Gild of Musicians, 1460–1530', *Proceedings of the Royal Musical Association*, 83rd Session, pp. 15–28. Oxford: Oxford University Press on behalf of the Royal Musical Association.

Barrett, J.R. (2007) 'The Researcher as Instrument: Learning to Conduct Qualitative Research through Analyzing and Interpreting a Choral Rehearsal', *Music Education Research*, 9:3, pp. 417–33.

Barten, S.S. (1998) 'Speaking of Music: The Use of Motor-affective Metaphors in Music Instruction', *Journal of Aesthetic Education*, 32:2, pp. 89–97.

Benson, C. and Fung, C.V. (2005) 'Comparisons of Teacher and Student Behaviors in Private Piano Lessons in China and the United States', *International Journal of Music Education*, 23:1, pp. 63–72.

Bloom, B.S. (1994) 'Reflections on the Development and Use of the Taxonomy', in Anderson, L.W. and Sosniak, L.A. (Eds) *Bloom's Taxonomy: A Forty-year Retrospective*, pp. 1–8. Chicago: University of Chicago Press.

Bowman, W. (2005) 'More Inquiring Minds, More Cogent Questions: The Need to Theorize Music Education – and its Research', *Music Education Research*, 7:2, pp. 153–68.

Bronfenbrenner, U. (1979) *The Ecology of Human Development: Experiments By Nature and Design*. Cambridge, MA and London: Harvard University Press.

Bruner, J. (1990) *Acts of Meaning*. Cambridge, MA and London: Harvard University Press.

Bruner, J.S. (1996) *The Culture of Education*. Cambridge, MA and London: Harvard University Press.

Bunn, S. (1999) 'The Nomad's Apprentice: Different Kinds of "Apprenticeship" among Kyrgyz Nomads in Central Asia', in Ainley, P. and Rainbird, H. (Eds) *Apprenticeship: Towards a New Paradigm of Learning*, pp. 74–85. London: Kogan Page.

Burland, K. and Davidson, J.W. (2002) 'Training the Talented', *Music Education Research*, 4:1, pp. 121–40.

Burr, V. (2003) *Social Constructionism*, 2nd edn. London and New York: Routledge.

Burwell, K., Young, V. and Pickup, D. (2003) 'Taking the Lead: The Development of Student as Reflective Practitioner in Instrumental Lessons at HE level'. Paper presented to the *Research in Music Education* conference, 9 April, University of Exeter.

Burwell, K. (2003a) 'The Meaning of Interpretation: An Investigation of an Area of Study in Instrumental Lessons in Higher Education'. Paper presented to the PALATINE conference on *Instrumental and Vocal Teaching*, Canterbury Christ Church University College.

Burwell, K. (2003b) 'Speaking of Instrumental Teaching and Learning: An Investigation of Dialogue in Instrumental and Vocal Lessons, in Higher Education'. Paper presented to the *Conference for Instrumental and Vocal Teachers*, Royal Northern College of Music.

Burwell K., Young, V. and Pickup D. (2004) 'The Dynamics of the Instrumental Tutorial', in Hunter, D. (Ed.) *How am I Doing? Valuing and Rewarding Learning in Musical Performance in Higher Education*, pp. 22–33. Ulster: University of Ulster.

Burwell, K. (2005) 'A Degree of Independence: Teachers' Approaches to Instrumental Tuition in a University College', *British Journal of Music Education*, 22:3, pp. 199–215.

Burwell, K. (2006) 'On Musicians and Singers: An Investigation of Different Approaches Taken by Vocal and Instrumental Teachers in Higher Education', *Music Education Research*, 8:3, pp. 331–47.

Burwell, K. (2009) 'A University Degree in Music', in *Handbook for Instrumental and Vocal Teachers* [unpublished: South England University].

Burwell, K. and Shipton, M. (2011) 'Performance Studies in Practice: An Investigation of Students' Approaches to Practice in a University Music Department', *Music Education Research*, 13:3, pp. 255–71.

Burwell, K. (2012) 'Rich Transcription: Exploring Lesson Interactions in Higher Education Music', *Scientia Pedagogica Experimentalis* (in press).

Callaghan, J. (1998) 'Singing Teachers and Voice Science: An Evaluation of Voice Teaching in Australian Tertiary Institutions', *Research Studies in Music Education*, 10, pp. 25–41.

Cazden, C.B. (1996) 'Selective Traditions: Readings of Vygotsky in Writing Pedagogy', in Hicks, D. (Ed.) *Discourse, Learning, and Schooling*, pp. 165–85. Cambridge: Cambridge University Press.

Cazden, C.B. (2001) *Classroom Discourse: The Language of Teaching and Learning*, 2nd edn. Portsmouth: Heinemann.

Chaiklin, S. (2003) 'The Zone of Proximal Development in Vygotsky's Analysis of Learning and Instruction', in Kozulin, A., Gindis, B., Ageyev, V.S. and Miller, S.M. (Eds) *Vygotsky's Educational Theory in Cultural Context*, pp. 39–64. Cambridge: Cambridge University Press.

Coates, J. (2004) *Women, Men and Language: A Sociolinguistic Account of Gender Differences in Language*, 3rd edn. Harlow: Pearson Longman.

Colprit, E.J. (2000) 'Observation and Analysis of Suzuki String Teaching', *Journal of Research in Music Education*, 48:3, pp. 206–21.

Connolly, C. and Williamon, A. (2004) 'Mental Skills Training', in Williamon, A. (Ed.) *Musical Excellence: Strategies and Techniques to Enhance Performance*, pp. 221–45. Oxford: Oxford University Press.

Cope, P. (2002) 'Informal Learning of Musical Instruments: The Importance of Social Context', *Music Education Research*, 4:1, pp. 93–104.

Creech, A., Papageorgi, I., Duffy, C., Morton, F., Hadden, E., Potter, J., De Bezenac, C., Whyton, T., Himonides, E. and Welch, G. (2008) 'Investigating Musical Performance: Commonality and Diversity Among Classical and Non-Classical Musicians', *Music Education Research*, 10:2, pp. 215–34.

Daniel, R. (2004) 'Innovations in Piano Teaching: A Small-Group Model for the Tertiary Level', *Music Education Research*, 6:1, pp. 23–43.

Daniels, H. (2001) *Vygotsky and Pedagogy*. Abingdon: Routledge Falmer.

Davidson, J.W. (2007) 'Qualitative Insights into the use of Expressive Body Movement in Solo Piano Performance: A Case Study Approach', *Psychology of Music*, 35:3, pp. 381–401.

Davidson, J.W., Moore, D.G., Sloboda, J.A. and Howe, M.J.A. (1998) 'Characteristics of Music Teachers and the Progress of Young Instrumentalists', *Journal of Research in Music Education*, 46:1, pp. 141–60.

Davidson, J.W. and Correia, J.S. (2002) 'Body Movement', in Parncutt, R. and McPherson, G. (Eds) *The Science and Psychology of Music Performance*, pp. 237–50. New York: Oxford University Press.

Davidson, L. (1989) 'Observing a Yang Ch'in Lesson: Learning by Modeling and Metaphor', *Journal of Aesthetic Education*, 23:1, pp. 85–99.

Delamont, S. and Hamilton, D. (1986) 'Revisiting Classroom Research: A Continuing Cautionary Tale', in Hammersley, M. (Ed.) *Controversies in Classroom Research: A Reader*, pp. 25–43. Milton Keynes: Open University Press.

Delbanco, N. (1985) *The Beaux Arts Trio*. New York: William Morrow.

Denzin, N.K. and Lincoln, Y.S. (2005) 'Introduction: The Discipline and Practice of Qualitative Research', in Denzin, N.K. and Lincoln, Y.S. (Eds) *The Sage Handbook of Qualitative Research*, 3rd edn, pp. 1–32. Thousand Oaks, CA, London and New Delhi: Sage.

Dewey, J. (1916) *Democracy and Education: An Introduction to the Philosophy of Education*. New York: Macmillan.

Dewey, J. (1922) *Human Nature and Conduct: An Introduction to Social Psychology*. London: George Allen and Unwin.

Dewey, J. (1933) *How We Think. A Restatement of the Relation of Reflective Thinking to the Educative Process*. Boston: Heath.

Dewey, J. (1938) *Experience and Education*. New York: Touchstone.

Dibben, N. (2006) 'The Socio-Cultural and Learning Experiences of Music Students in a British University', *British Journal of Music Education*, 23:1, pp. 91–116.

Dickey, M.R. (1991) 'A Comparison of Verbal Instruction and Nonverbal Teacher-Student Modelling in Instrumental Ensembles', *Journal of Research in Music Education*, 39:2, pp. 132–42.

Dickey, M.R. (1992) 'A Review of Research and Modelling in Music Teaching and Learning', *Bulletin of the Council for Research in Music Education*, 113, pp. 27–40.

DirectGov: Supporting gifted and talented children. http://www.direct.gov.uk/en/Parents/Schoolslearninganddevelopment/ExamsTestsAndTheCurriculum/DG_10037625.

Duke, R.A. and Prickett, C.A. (1987) 'The Effect of Differentially Focused Observation on Evaluation of Instruction', *Journal of Research in Music Education*, 35:1, pp. 27–37.

Duke, R.A. and Henniger, J.C. (1998) 'Effects of Verbal Corrections on Student Attitude and Performance', *Journal of Research in Music Education*, 46:4, pp. 482–95.

Duke, R.A. and Henniger, J.C. (2002) 'Teachers' Verbal Corrections and Observers' Perceptions of Teaching and Learning', *Journal of Research in Music Education*, 50: 1, pp. 75–87.

Duke, R.A., Simmons, A.L. and Cash, C.D. (2009) 'It's Not How Much; It's How: Characteristics of Practice Behavior and Retention of Performance Skills', *Journal of Research in Music Education*, 56:4, 310–321.

Egan, K. and Gajdamaschko, N. (2003) 'Some Cognitive Tools of Literacy', in Kozulin, A., Gindis, B., Ageyev, V.S. and Miller, S.M. (Eds) *Vygotsky's Educational Theory in Cultural Context*, pp. 83–98. Cambridge: Cambridge University Press.

Elliot, D.J. (1991) 'Music as Knowledge', *Journal of Aesthetic Education*, 25:3, pp. 21–40.

Entwistle, N. (1988) *Styles in Learning and Teaching: An Integrated Outline of Educational Psychology for Students, Teachers and Lecturers*. London: David Fulton.

Entwistle, N.J. (2005) 'Contrasting Perspectives on Learning', in Marton, F., Hounsell, D.J. and Entwistle N.J. (Eds) *The Experience of Learning: Implications for Teaching and Studying in Higher Education*, 3rd (Internet) edn, pp. 3–22. Edinburgh: University of Edinburgh, Centre for Teaching, Learning and Assessment.

Entwistle, N. (2007) 'Research into Student Learning and University Teaching', in Entwistle, N. and Tomlinson, D. (Eds) *Student Learning and University Teaching*, pp. 1–18. Leicester: The British Psychological Society.

Ericsson, K.A., Krampe, R.T. and Tesch-Romer, C. (1993) 'The Role of Deliberate Practice in the Acquisition of Expert Performance', *Psychological Review*, 100:3, pp. 363–406.

Folkestad, G. (2005) 'Here, There and Everywhere: Music Education Research in a Globalised World', *Music Education Research*, 7:3, pp. 279–87.

Folkestad, G. (2006) 'Formal and Informal Learning Situations or Practices vs Formal and Informal Ways of Learning', *British Journal of Music Education*, 23:2, pp. 135–45.

Frederickson, J. and Rooney, J.F. (1990) 'How the Music Occupation Failed to become a Profession', *International Review of the Aesthetics and Sociology of Music*, 21:2, pp. 189–206.

Froelich, H. (2002) 'Thoughts on Schools of Music and Colleges of Education as Places of "Rites and Rituals": Consequences for Research on Practicing', in Hanken, I.M, Nielsen, S.G. and Nerland, M. (Eds) *Research in and for Higher Education*, pp. 149–65. Oslo: Norges musikkhøgskole.

Furst, E.J. (1994) 'Bloom's Taxonomy: Philosophical and Educational Issues', in Anderson, L.W. and Sosniak, L.A. (Eds) *Bloom's Taxonomy: A Forty-year Retrospective*, pp. 28–40. Chicago: University of Chicago Press.

Gamble, J. (2001) 'Modelling the Invisible: The Pedagogy of Craft Apprenticeship', *Studies in Continuing Education*, 23:2, pp. 185–200.

Gardner, H. (1983) *Frames of Mind: The Theory of Multiple Intelligences*, 2nd edn. London: Fontana.

Gaunt, H. (2008) 'One-to-one Tuition in a Conservatoire: The Perceptions of Instrumental and Vocal Teachers', *Psychology of Music*, 36:2, pp. 215–45.

Gaunt, H. (2009) 'One-to-one Tuition in a Conservatoire: The Perceptions of Instrumental and Vocal Students', *Psychology of Music*, 38:2, pp. 178–208.

Gholson, S.A. (1998) 'Proximal Positioning: A Strategy of Practice in Violin Pedagogy', *Journal of Research in Music Education*, 46:4, pp. 535–45.

Guba, E.G. and Lincoln, Y.S. (2005) 'Paradigmatic Controversies, Contradictions, and Emerging Confluences', in Denzin, N.K. and Lincoln, Y.S. (Eds) *The Sage Handbook of Qualitative Research*, 3rd edn, pp. 191–215. Thousand Oaks, CA, London and New Delhi: Sage.

Haddon, E. (2009) 'Instrumental and Vocal Teaching: How do Music Students Learn to Teach?', *British Journal of Music Education*, 26, pp. 57–70.

Hallam, S. (1997) 'What do we Know about Practising? Towards a Model Synthesising the Research Literature', in Jørgensen, H. and Lehmann, A.C. (Eds) *Does Practice Make Perfect? Current Theory and Research on Instrumental Music Practice*, pp. 179–231. Oslo: Norges musikkhøle.

Hallam, S. (2001) 'The Development of Expertise in Young Musicians: Strategy Use, Knowledge Acquisition and Individual Diversity', *Music Education Research*, 3:1, pp. 7–23.

Hamann, D.L., Lineburgh, N. and Paul, S. (1998) 'Teaching Effectiveness and Social Skill Development', *Journal of Research in Music Education*, 46:1, pp. 87–101.

Hays, T., Minichiello, V. and Wright, P. (2000) 'Mentorship: The Meaning of the Relationship for Musicians', *Research Studies in Music Education*, 15, pp. 3–14.

Heath, C. (1997) 'The Analysis of Activities in Face to Face Interaction using Video', in Silverman, D. (Ed.) *Qualitative Research: Theory, Method and Practice*, pp. 183–200. Thousand Oaks, CA, London and New Delhi: Sage.

Henley, P.T. (2001) 'Effects of Modeling and Tempo Patterns as Practice Techniques on the Performance of High School Instrumentalists', *Journal of Research in Music Education*, 49:2, pp. 169–80.

Henniger, J.C., Flowers, P.J. and Councill, K.H. (2006) 'Pedagogical Techniques and Student Outcomes in Applied Instrumental Lessons taught by Experienced and Pre-Service American Music Teachers', *International Journal Of Music Education*, 24:1, pp. 71–84.

Heritage, J. (1997) 'Conversation Analysis and Institutional Talk. Analysing Data', in Silverman, D. (Ed.) *Qualitative Research: Theory, Method and Practice*, pp. 161–82. Thousand Oaks, CA, London and New Delhi: Sage.

Hewitt, A. (2004) 'Students' Attributions of Sources of Influence on Self-Perception in Solo Performance in Music', *Research Studies in Music Education*, 22, pp. 42–58.

Hewitt, M.P. (2001) 'The Effects of Modeling, Self-Evaluation, and Self-Listening on Junior High Instrumentalists' Music Performance and Practice Attitude', *Journal of Research in Music Education*, 49:4, pp. 307–22.

Hewitt, M.P. (2002) 'Self-evaluation Tendencies of Junior High Instrumentalists', *Journal of Research in Music Education*, 50:3, pp. 215–26.

Highben, Z. and Palmer, C. (2004) 'Effects of Auditory and Motor Mental Practice in Memorized Piano Performance', *Bulletin of the Council for Research in Music Education*, 159, pp. 58–65.

Holstein, J.A. and Gubrium, J.F. (2005) 'Interpretive Practice and Social Action', in Denzin, N.K. and Lincoln, Y.S. (Eds) *The Sage Handbook of Qualitative Research*, 3rd edn, pp. 483–505. Thousand Oaks, CA, London and New Delhi: Sage.

Howard, V.A. (1982) *Artistry: The Work of Artists*. Indianapolis: Hackett.

Howard, V.A. (1992) *Learning by All Means: Lessons from the Arts. A Study in the Philosophy of Education*. New York: Peter Lang.

Howard, V.A. (2008) *Charm and Speed: Virtuosity in the Performing Arts*. New York: Peter Lang.

Hultberg, C. (2000) *The Printed Score as a Mediator of Musical Meaning: Approaches to Music Notation in Western Tonal Tradition*. Malmö: Lund University.

Hultberg, C. (2002) 'Approaches to Music Notation: The Printed Score as a Mediator of Meaning in Western Tonal Tradition', *Music Education Research*, 4:2, pp. 185–97.

Hultberg, C. (2005) 'Practitioners and Researchers in Cooperation – Method Development for Qualitative Practice-Related Studies', *Music Education Research*, 7:2, pp. 211–24.

Jorgensen, E. (1997) *In Search of Music Education*. Urbana and Chicago: University of Illinois Press.

Jorgensen, E.R. (2006) '"This-with-that": A Dialectical Approach to Teaching for Musical Imagination', *Journal of Aesthetic Education*, 40:4, pp. 1–20.

Jørgensen, H. (2000) 'Student Learning in Higher Instrumental Education: Who is Responsible?', *British Journal of Music Education*, 17:1, pp. 67–77.

Jørgensen, H. (2002) 'Instrumental Performance Expertise and Amount of Practice among Instrumental Students in a Conservatoire', *Music Education Research*, 4:1, pp. 105–19.

Jørgensen, H. (2009) *Research into Higher Music Education: An Overview from a Quality Improvement Perspective*. Oslo: Novus.

Juchniewicz, J. (2008) 'The Influence of Physical Movement on the Perception of Musical Performance', *Psychology of Music*, 36, pp. 417–27.

Kamin, S., Richards, H. and Collins, D. (2007) 'Influences on the Talent Development Process of Non-Classical Musicians: Psychological, Social and Environmental Influences', *Music Education Research*, 9:3, pp. 449–68.

Karlsson, J. and Juslin, P.N. (2008) 'Musical Expression: An Observational Study of Instrumental Teaching', *Psychology of Music*, 36:3, pp. 309–34.

Karpov, Y.V. (2003) 'Vygotsky's Doctrine of Scientific Concepts: Its Role for Contemporary Education', in Kozulin, A., Gindis, B., Ageyev, V.S. and Miller, S.M. (Eds) *Vygotsky's Educational Theory in Cultural Context*, pp. 65–82. Cambridge: Cambridge University Press.

Kember, D., Leung, D.Y.P. and McNaught, C. (2008) A workshop activity to demonstrate that approaches to learning are influenced by the teaching and learning environment, *Active Learning in Higher Education*, 9, pp. 43–56.

Kember, D., Wong, A. and Leung, D.Y.P. (1999) 'Reconsidering the Dimensions of Approaches to Learning', *British Journal of Educational Practice*, 69, pp. 323–43.

Kemp, A. (1996) *The Musical Temperament: Psychology and Personality of Musicians*. Oxford, New York, Tokyo: Oxford University Press.

Kendall, M.J. (1988) 'Two Instructional Approaches to the Development of Aural and Instrumental Performance Skills', *Journal of Research in Music Education*, 36:4, pp. 205–19.

Kennell, R. (1992) 'Toward a Theory of Applied Music Instruction', *Quarterly Journal of Music Teaching and Learning*, 3:2, pp. 5–16.

Kennell, R. (1997) 'Teaching Music One-On-One: A Case Study', *Dialogue in Instrumental Music Education*, 21:1, pp. 69–81.

Kennell, R. (2002) 'Systematic Research in Studio Instruction in Music', in Colwell, R. and Richardson, C. (Eds) *The New Handbook of Research on Music Teaching and Learning*, pp. 243–56. New York: Oxford University Press.

Kingsbury, H. (1988) *Music, Talent, and Performance: A Conservatory Cultural System*. Philadelphia: Temple University Press.

Koopman, C., Smit, N., de Vugt, A., Deneer, P. and den Ouden, J. (2007) 'Focus on Practice-Relationships Between Lessons on the Primary Instrument and Individual Practice in Conservatoire Education', *Music Education Research*, 9:3, pp. 373–97.

Koss, T. and Rosenthal, R. (1997) 'Interactional Synchrony, Positivity, and Patient Satisfaction in the Physician-Patient Relationship', *Medical Care*, 35:11, pp. 1158–63.

Kostka, M.J. (1984) 'An Investigation of Reinforcements, Time Use, and Student Attentiveness in Piano Lessons', *Journal of Research in Music Education*, 32:2, pp. 113–22.

Kurkul, W.W. (2007) 'Nonverbal Communication in One-to-one Music Performance Instruction', *Psychology of Music*, 35:2, pp. 327–62.

Kvale, S. (1996) *Inter Views: An Introduction to Qualitative Research Interviewing*. Thousand Oaks, CA, London and New Delhi: Sage.

Laukka, P. (2004) 'Instrumental Teachers' Views on Expressivity: A Report from Music Conservatoires', *Music Education Research*, 6:1, pp. 46–56.

Lave, J. and Wenger, E. (1991) *Situated Learning: Legitimate Peripheral Participation*. Cambridge: Cambridge University Press.

Lave, J. (1993) 'The Practice of Learning', in Chaiklin, S. and Lave, J. (Eds) *Understanding Practice: Perspectives on Activity and Context*, pp. 3–32. Cambridge: Cambridge University Press.

Lebler, D. (2007) 'Student-as-master? Reflections on a Learning Innovation in Popular Music Pedagogy', *International Journal of Music Education*, 25:3, pp. 205–21.

Lehmann, A.C. and Gruber, H. (2006) 'Music', in Ericsson, K.A. (Ed.) *The Cambridge Handbook of Expertise and Expert Performance*, pp. 457–70. New York: Cambridge University Press.

Lincoln, Y.S. and Guba, E.G. (1985) *Naturalistic Inquiry*. Thousand Oaks, CA, London and New Delhi: Sage.

Lindström, E., Juslin, P.N., Bresin, R. and Williamon, A. (2003) '"Expressivity Comes From Within Your Soul": A Questionnaire Study of Music Students' Perspectives on Expressivity', *Research Studies in Music Education*, 20, pp. 23–47.

Lisboa, T., Williamon, A., Zicari, M. and Eiholzer, H. (2005) 'Mastery Through Imitation: A Preliminary Study', *Musicae Scientiae*, 19:1, pp. 75–110.

Madsen, C.K., Standley, J.M. and Cassidy, J.W. (1989) 'Demonstration and Recognition of High and Low Contrasts in Teacher Intensity', *Journal of Research in Music Education*, 37:2, pp. 85–92.

MANA (1995) *Instrumental Teaching and Learning in Context*. Bath: Music Advisers National Association.

Manturzewska, M. (1990) 'A Biographical Study of the Life Span Development of Professional Musicians', *Psychology of Music*, 18:2, pp. 112–39.

Marchand, D.J. (1975) 'A Study of Two Approaches to Developing Expressive Performance', *Journal of Research in Music Education*, 23:1, pp. 14–22.

Matusov, E. (2007) 'In Search of "The Appropriate" Unit of Analysis for Sociocultural Research', *Culture and Psychology*, 13, pp. 307–33.

Maxwell, J.A. (2005) *Qualitative Research Design: An Interactive Approach*, 2nd edn. Thousand Oaks, CA, London and New Delhi: Sage.

May, L.F. (2003) 'Factors and Abilities Influencing Achievement in Instrumental Jazz Improvisation', *Journal of Research in Music Education*, 51:3, pp. 245–58.

McCroskey, J.C., Richmond, V.P. and McCroskey, L.L. (2006) 'Nonverbal Communication in Instructional Contexts', *The Sage Handbook of Nonverbal Communication*. Accessed 2 September 2009. http://sge-ereference.com/ hdbk_nonverbalcomm/Article_n22.html.

McGinn, M. (1997) *Routledge Philosophy Guidebook to Wittgenstein and the Philosophical Investigations*. London, New York: Routledge.

McGowan, E.M., Stone, E.M. and Kegan, R. (2007) 'A Constructive-Developmental Approach to Mentoring Relationships', *The Handbook of Mentoring at Work*. Sage Publications. Accessed 2 September 2009. http:// sage-ereference.com/hdbk_workmentor/Article_n16.html.

McIntyre, D. and MacLeod, G. (1986) 'The Characteristics and Uses of Systematic Classroom Observation', in Hammersley, M. (Ed.) *Controversies in Classroom Research: A Reader*, pp. 10–24. Milton Keynes and Philadelphia: Open University Press.

Mills, J. (2003) *Teaching Performance*. Federation of British Conservatoires Good Management Practice, Project 41. London: Royal College of Music.

Mills, J. (2007) *Instrumental Teaching*. Oxford: Oxford University Press.

Mills, J. and Smith, J. (2003) 'Teachers' Beliefs about Effective Instrumental Teaching in Schools and Higher Education', *British Journal of Music Education*, 20:1, pp. 5–27.

Mosston, M. (1972) *Teaching: From Command to Discovery*. Belmont, CA: Wadsworth.

Mosston, M. and Ashworth, A. (1994) *Teaching Physical Education*, 4th edn. New York: Macmillan.

Nerland, M. (2001) 'Discourses and Practices of Instrumental Teaching'. Paper presented to the *Research in Music Education* conference, 3–7 April, University of Exeter.

Nerland, M. and Hanken, I.M. (2002) 'Academies of Music as Arenas for Education: Some Reflections on the Institutional Construction of Teacher-Student Relationships', in Hanken, I.M., Nielsen, S.G. and Nerland, M. (Eds) *Research in and for Higher Education*, pp. 167–86. Oslo: Norges musikkhøgskole.

Nerland, M. and Hanken, I.M. (2004) 'Apprenticeship in Late Modernity: Trust as a Critical but Challenged Dimension in Teacher–Student Relationships'. Paper presented to the *Professionalism, Trust and Competence* conference, Oslo University College, Centre for the Study of Professions, 17–19 June.

Nerland, M. (2006) 'Instrumental Teaching as Discursive Practice: The Construction of One-to-one Teaching at an Academy of Music'. Paper presented to the *Reflective Conservatoire* conference, 18 February, Guildhall School of Music and Drama.

Nerland, M. (2007) 'One-to-one Teaching as Cultural Practice: Two Case Studies from an Academy of Music', *Music Education Research*, 9:3, pp. 399–416.

Nettl, B. (1995) *Heartland Excursions: Ethnomusicological Reflections on Schools of Music*. Urbana and Chicago: University of Illinois.

Nicholl, C. (2004) *Leonardo da Vinci. The Flights of the Mind*. London: Penguin.

Nielsen, K.N. (1999) *Learning at the Academy of Music as Socially Situated*. Risskov: Psykologisk Intitut, Aarhus Universitet.

Nielsen, K. (2006) 'Apprenticeship at the Academy of Music', *International Journal of Education and the Arts*, 7:4. Accessed 30 November 2006. http://ijea.asu.edu/v7n4.

Parsonage, C., Fadnes, P.F. and Taylor, J. (2007) 'Integrating Theory and Practice in Conservatoires: Formulating Holistic Models for Teaching and Learning Improvisation', *British Journal of Music Education*, 24:3, pp. 295–312.

Patterson, M. (2006) 'The Evolution of Theories of Interactive Behaviour', *The Sage Handbook of Nonverbal Communication*, accessed 2 September 2009. http://sage-ereference.com/hdbk_nonverbalcomm/Article_n2.html.

Patterson, M.L. and Manusov, V. (2006) 'Nonverbal Communication: Basic Issues and Future Prospects', *The Sage Handbook of Nonverbal Communication*. Accessed 2 September 2009. http://sage-reference.com/hdbk_nonverbalcomm/Article_n27.html.

Peräkylä, A. (1997) 'Reliability and Validity in Research Based on Tapes and Transcripts', in Silverman, D. (Ed.) *Qualitative Research: Theory, Method and Practice*, pp. 201–20. Thousand Oaks, CA, London and New Delhi: Sage.

Persson, R.S. (2000) 'Survival of the Fittest or the Most Talented?', *Journal of Secondary Gifted Education*, 12:1, pp. 25–39.

Petters, R. (1976) 'Student Participation in Decision-making Processes Concerning Musical Performance', *Journal of Research in Music Education*, 24:4, pp. 177–86.

Pickup, D. and Young, V. (2010) Email communications, 29 and 31 January.

Pitts, S. (2001) 'Investigating the Transition between School and University Music Education'. Paper presented to the *Research in Music Education* conference, 3–7 April, University of Exeter.

Pitts, S. (2003) 'What do Students Learn when we Teach Music? An Investigation of the 'Hidden' Curriculum in a University Music Department', *Arts and Humanities in Higher Education*, 2:3, pp. 281–92.

Polanyi, M. (1958) *Personal Knowledge: Towards a Post-critical Philosophy*. London: Routledge and Kegan Paul.

Polanyi, M. (1983) *The Tacit Dimension*. Gloucester, MA: Peter Smith.

Potter, J. (1998) *Vocal Authority: Singing Style and Ideology*. Cambridge: Cambridge University Press.

Presland, C. (2005) 'Conservatoire Student and Instrumental Professor: The Student Perspective on a Complex Relationship', *British Journal of Music Education*, 22:3, pp. 237–48.

Pring, R. (2000) *Philosophy of Educational Research*, 2nd edn. London and New York: Continuum.

Pugh, A. and Pugh, L. (1998) *Music in the Early Years*. London: Routledge.

Purser, D. (2005) 'Performers as Teachers: Exploring the Teaching Approaches of Instrumental Teachers in Conservatoires', *British Journal of Music Education*, 22:3, pp. 287–98.

Reid, A. (2001) 'Variation in the Ways that Instrumental and Vocal Students Experience Learning through Music', *Music Education Research*, 3:1, pp. 25–40.

Reimer, B. (2004) 'Once More with Feeling: Reconciling Discrepant Accounts of Musical Affect', *Philosophy of Music Education Review*, 12:1, pp. 4–16.

Remedios, L., Clarke, D. and Hawthorne, L. (2008) 'The Silent Participant in Small Group Collaborative Learning Contexts', *Active Learning in Higher Education*, 9:3, pp. 201–16.

Riggio, R.E. and Feldman, R.S. (2005) 'Introduction to Applications of Nonverbal Communication', in Riggio, R.E. and Feldman, R.S. (Eds) *Applications of Nonverbal Communication*, pp. xi–xv. Mahwah, NJ: Lawrence Erlbaum Associates.

Riggs, K. (2006) 'Foundations for Flow: A Philosophical Model for Studio Instruction', *Philosophy of Music Education Review*, 14:2, pp. 175–91.

Rogoff, B. (1995) 'Observing Sociocultural Activity on Three Planes: Participatory Appropriation, Guided Participation, and Apprenticeship', in Wertsch, J.V., del Rio, P. and Alvarez, A. (Eds) *Sociocultural Studies of Mind*, pp. 139–64. Cambridge: Cambridge University Press.

Rosenthal, R.K. (1984) 'The Relative Effects of Guided Model, Model Only, Guide Only, and Practice Only Treatments on the Accuracy of Advanced Instrumentalists' Musical Performance', *Journal of Research in Music Education*, 32: 4, pp. 265–73.

Rostvall, A. and West, T. (2003) 'Analysis of Interaction and Learning in Instrumental Teaching', *Music Education Research*, 5:3, pp. 213–26.

Ryle, G. (1949) *The Concept of Mind*. London: Penguin.

Säljö, R. (1997) *Learning and Discourse: A Sociocultural Perspective*. The British Psychological Society.

Scheffler, I. (1965) *The Conditions of Knowledge: Introduction to Epistemology and Education*. Chicago: Chicago University Press.

Scheffler, I. (1991) *In Praise of the Cognitive Emotions, and Other Essays in the Philosophy of Education*. New York, London: Routledge.

Schmidt, C.P. (1989) 'Applied Music Teaching Behavior as a Function of Selected Personality Variables', *Journal of Research in Music Education*, 37:4, pp. 258–71.

Schön, D.A. (1983) *The Reflective Practitioner: How Professionals Think in Action*. New York: Basic Books.

Schön, D.A. (1987) *Educating the Reflective Practitioner: Toward a New Design for Teaching and Learning in the Professions*. San Francisco and London: Jossey-Bass.

Siebenaler, D.J. (1997) 'Analysis of Teacher–Student Interactions in the Piano Lessons of Adults and Children', *Journal of Research in Music Education*, 45:1, pp. 6–20.

Sloboda, J. (2005) *Exploring the Musical Mind: Cognition, Emotion, Ability, Function*. Oxford: Oxford University Press.

Smith, M., Duda, J., Allen, J. and Hall, H. (2002) 'Contemporary Measures of Approach and Avoidance Goal Orientations: Similarities and Differences', *British Journal of Educational Psychology*, 72, pp. 155–90.

Sosniak, L.A. (1985a) 'Learning to be a Concert Pianist', in Bloom, B.S. (Ed.) *Developing Talent in Young People*, pp. 19–67. New York and Toronto: Ballantine.

Sosniak, L.A. (1985b) 'The Phases of Learning', in Bloom, B.S. (Ed.) *Developing Talent in Young People*, pp. 409–38. New York and Toronto: Ballantine.

Speer, D.R. (1994) 'An Analysis of Sequential Patterns of Instruction in Piano Lessons', *Journal of Research in Music Education*, 42:1, pp. 14–26.

Stake, R.E. (1995) *The Art of Case Study Research*. Thousand Oaks, London, New Delhi: Sage.

Stake, R.E. (2005) 'Qualitative Case Studies', in Denzin, N.K. and Lincoln, Y.S. (Eds) *The Sage Handbook of Qualitative Research*, 3rd edn, pp. 443–66. Thousand Oaks, CA, London and New Delhi: Sage.

Tait, M. and Haack, P. (1984) *Principles and Processes of Music Education: New Perspectives*. New York and London: Teachers College Press, Columbia University.

Triantafyllaki, A. (2005) 'A Call for More Instrumental Music Teaching Research', *Music Education Research*, 7:3, pp. 383–87.

Triantafyllaki, A. (2010) '"Workplace landscapes" and the Construction of Performance Teachers' Identity: The Case of Advanced Music Training Institutions in Greece', *British Journal of Music Education*, 27:2, pp. 185–201.

Uszler, M. (1992) 'Research on the Teaching of Keyboard Music', in Colwell, R. (Ed.) *Handbook of Research on Music Teaching and Learning*, pp. 584–93. New York: Schirmer Books.

Verrastro, R.E. (1975) 'Verbal Behavior Analysis as a Supervisory Technique with Student Teachers of Music', *Journal of Research in Music Education*, 23:3, pp. 171–85.

Walker, R. (1986) 'The Conduct of Educational Case Studies: Ethics, Theory and Procedures', in Hammersley, M. (Ed.) *Controversies in Classroom Research. A Reader*, pp. 187–219. Milton Keynes and Philadelphia: Open University Press.

Webb, E. (1999) 'Making Meaning: Language for Learning', in Ainley, P. and Rainbird, H. (Eds) *Apprenticeship. Towards a New Paradigm of Learning*, pp. 100–110. London: Kogan Page.

Weber, W. (n.d.) Conservatories. I. 'The Rise of the Conservatory', *Grove Music Online* (Ed.) Macy, L. Accessed 9 April 2008. http://www.grovemusic.com.

Welch, G. (2007) 'Addressing the Multifaceted Nature of Music Education: An Activity Theory Research Perspective', *Research Studies in Music Education*, 28, pp. 23–37.

Wenger, E. (1998) *Communities of Practice: Learning, Meaning, and Identity*. Cambridge: Cambridge University Press.

Wertsch, J.V. (1985) *Vygotsky and the Social Formation of Mind*. Cambridge, MA and London: Harvard University Press.

Wertsch, J.V. (1991) *Voices of the Mind*. Cambridge, MA and London: Harvard University Press.

Williams, E.A., Butt, G.W., Gray, C., Leach, S., Marr, A. and Soares, A. (1998) 'Mentors' Use of Dialogue within a Secondary Initial Teacher Education Partnership', *Educational Review*, 50:3, pp. 225–39.

Wittgenstein, L. (1953/1972) (Tr. Anscombe, G.E.M.) *Philosophical Investigations*. Oxford: Basil Blackwell.

Wood, D., Bruner, J.S. and Ross, G. (1976) 'The Role of Tutoring in Problem Solving', *Journal of Child Psychology*, 17, pp. 89–100.

Woody, R.H. (1999) 'The Relationship Between Explicit Planning and Expressive Performance of Dynamic Variations in an Aural Modelling Task', *Journal of Research in Music Education*, 47:4, pp. 331–42.

Woody, R.H. (2000) 'Learning Expressivity in Music Performance: An Exploratory Study', *Research Studies in Music Education*, 14, pp. 14–23.

Woody, R.H. (2002) 'Emotion, Imagery and Metaphor in the Acquisition of Musical Performance Skill', *Music Education Research*, 4:2, pp. 213–24.

Woody, R.H. (2003) 'Explaining Expressive Performance: Component Cognitive Skills in an Aural Modeling Task', *Journal of Research in Music Education*, 51:1, pp. 51–63.

Woody, R.H. (2006a) 'The Effect of Various Instructional Conditions on Expressive Music Performance', *Journal of Research in Music Education*, 54:1, pp. 21–36.

Woody, R.H. (2006b) 'Musicians' Cognitive Processing of Imagery-Based Instructions for Expressive Performance', *Journal of Research in Music Education*, 54:2, pp. 125–37.

Wooffitt, R. (2005) *Conversation Analysis and Discourse Analysis. A Comparative and Critical Introduction*. Thousand Oaks, CA, London and New Delhi: Sage.

Yarbrough, C. and Price, H.E. (1989) 'Sequential Patterns of Instruction in Music', *Journal of Research in Music Education*, 37:3, pp. 179–87.

Yin, R.K. (1998) 'The Abridged Version of Case Study Research: Design and Method', in Bickman, L. and Rog, D.J. (Eds) *Handbook of Applied Social Research Methods*, pp. 229–59. Thousand Oaks, CA, London and New Delhi: Sage.

Young, V., Burwell, K. and Pickup, D. (2003) 'Areas of Study and Teaching Strategies in Instrumental Teaching: A Case Study Research Project', *Music Education Research*, 5:2, pp. 139–55.

Zhukov, K. (2008) 'Exploratory Study of Approvals and Disapprovals in Australian Instrumental Education', *International Journal of Music Education*, 26:4, pp. 302–14.

Index